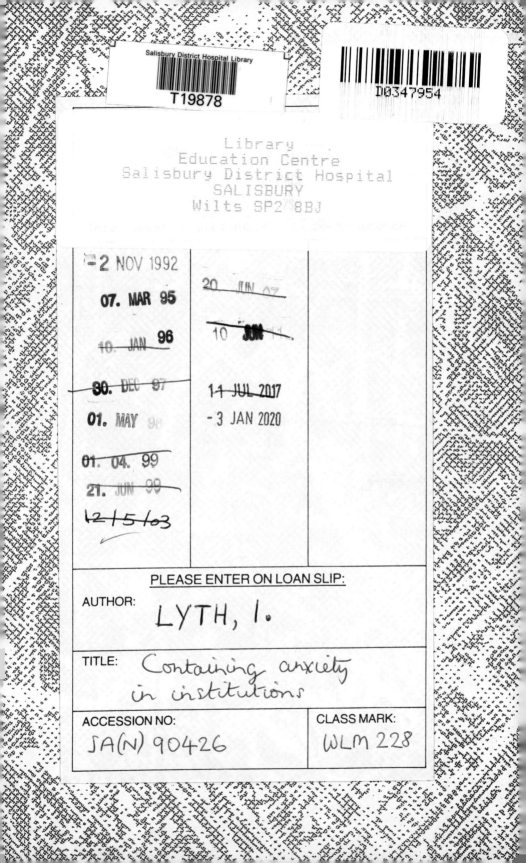

2 NOV 1992

07. MAR 95

10. JAN 96

30. DEC 97

01. MAY 98

01. 04. 99

21. JUN 99

12/5/03

20 JUN 07

10 JUN

1 1 JUL 2017

- 3 JAN 2020

PLEASE ENTER ON LOAN SLIP:

AUTHOR: LYTH, I.

TITLE: Containing anxiety in institutions

ACCESSION NO: SA(N) 90426

CLASS MARK: WLM 228

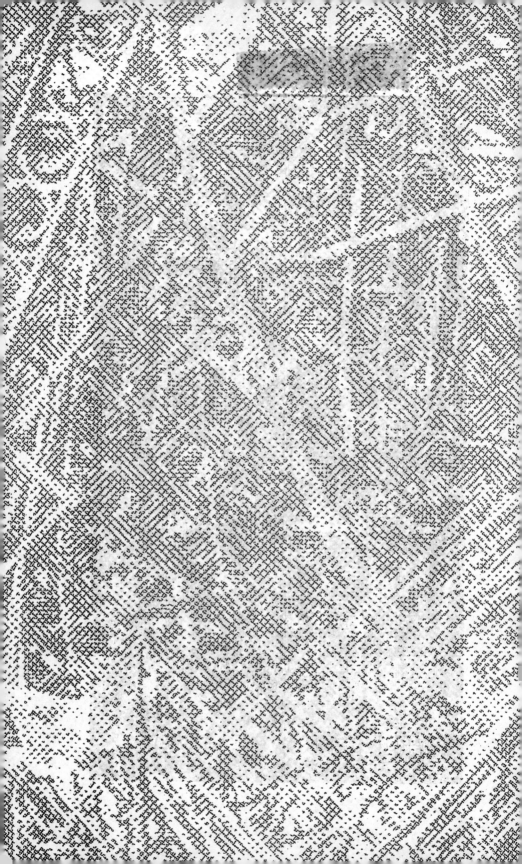

CONTAINING ANXIETY IN INSTITUTIONS

Isabel Menzies Lyth has formulated a way of thinking about social structures as forms of defence – as ways of avoiding experiences of anxiety, guilt, doubt and uncertainty – that is as challenging as it is persuasive. She believes that the individual is engaged in a lifelong struggle against primitive anxiety.

A psychoanalyst writing in the tradition of Klein and Bion, her writings span more than thirty years of research in applied psychoanalysis and are here collected in the first of two volumes.

In her classic paper on nursing, she writes: 'By the nature of her profession the nurse is at considerable risk of being flooded by intense and unmanageable anxiety.' The organization and bureaucracy of the nursing profession have failed to contain the high levels of anxiety and stress that nurses experience, attempting instead to take practical steps to enhance recruitment and stem job wastage. The 'real nature' of the problem remains untouched.

This is a controversial collection, which makes available to a wider public an important part of the research tradition of the Tavistock Institute of Human Relations. The author extends her analytic range to cover themes of children in long-stay hospitals and day-care institutions, and the maternal role today. All the essays combine her two main professional interests: the dynamics of the individual in his or her own right and the psychodynamics of the social world.

Isabel Menzies Lyth came into psychoanalysis from a background of economics and experimental psychology. She has combined part-time private practice as a psychoanalyst with consultancy work and many research projects. A second volume of her essays, *The Dynamics of the Social*, is also published by Free Association Books.

Containing Anxiety in Institutions

Selected Essays

Volume I

By Isabel Menzies Lyth

'an association in which the free development of each is the condition of the free development of all'

Free Association Books / London / 1988

First published in Great Britain 1988 by
Free Association Books
26 Freegrove Road
London N7 9RQ

British Library Cataloguing in Publication Data

Menzies Lyth, Isabel
  Containing anxiety in institutions.
  Vol. 1
  1. Man. Neuroses. Anxiety
  I. Title
  616.85'223

ISBN 1–85343–000–5 Hbk
     1–85343–001–3 Pbk

Typeset by Input Typesetting Ltd , London

Printed and bound in Great Britain by
Bookcraft Ltd, Midsomer Norton, Avon

Contents

Preface and acknowledgements

It would not, I think, have occurred to me that my papers were worth collecting, although the initial reception and continued demand for a few of them might have suggested there was something worthwhile in them. I am grateful, therefore, to Robert Young of Free Association Books for suggesting that a selection of my writings over the years should be published. It was something of a surprise to me that there were so many papers that they should be selected and not merely collected, and the selection was not easy. There was a very large number of papers of varying quality and interest. Important in the selection was the degree of excitement reviewing each paper aroused in me, the enjoyment and sense of discovery in the original work, and the extent to which the paper seemed to contain a novel view of a familiar situation. However, many of the papers were basically the same paper given in different contexts, so we have tried not to be boringly repetitive. Minor changes have been made in some papers to reduce such repetition but this could not always be avoided in those papers dealing with the same subject matter but addressed to a different readership. Some papers have been published before; others have been seen previously only by the people for whom they were written, bodies which funded research (notably the Department of Health and Social Security), or clients for whom I acted as a consultant.

Collecting and selecting the papers has made me review my work over some forty years and has re-evoked some of the excitement colleagues and I shared when we did the work originally. I was surprised to find the enormous variety of the situations in which I have worked: from the London Fire Brigade to community children's homes, the Royal National Orthopaedic Hospital in Stanmore, Middlesex, day nurseries, mental hospitals, road safety, consumer research, group-relations conferences. All this has given me a rich and varied view of how ordinary people feel and behave in their ordinary work and personal lives and has broadened and deepened my view of life.

For this I am above all grateful to the Tavistock Institute of Human Relations, particularly its founder members who invited me to join them and shared with me their fellowship and their concerns. This enabled me to bring together in my practice two main professional interests, the individual as a person in his or her own right – psychoanalysis – and the individual in a multi-plicity of interpersonal, group and community relationships – social science – or, to state the matter somewhat differently, to relate the internal world of object relationships with the external world of society. The Tavistock Institute was, at that time, a unique place in combining these two approaches and directing them towards practice, research and training.

I have all my life had an aversion to writing. I have written only when someone or something put pressure on me to write: two theses for my MA, a paper to become a Member of the British Psycho-Analytical Society, countless papers and reports at the Tavistock Institute. I can honestly claim that I have never spontaneously written a paper in my life. I was the more pleased, therefore, that this book could go ahead without my anticipating too much writing or rewriting. Papers already published mainly appear in their original form; reports to clients have usually been revised to some extent to make them more suitable for the general reader. Lest this sounds too negative, I sometimes do enjoy writing once I have started and am even grateful to the people who have put on the pressure.

This aversion may partly explain why I have done much less writing on purely psychoanalytic topics, although my head often buzzes with interesting ideas that patients or students have evoked and what I have made of them. So far the beneficiaries of these ideas have largely been patients and students. Psychoanalytic colleagues may be less aware of what is brewing in one's mind, since psychoanalysis can be a rather isolated and isolating profession. One is less likely, therefore, to experience pressure from colleagues to publish than when one is working in a close group or in a project team. Patients do not usually press one to publish. I have some regrets about having yielded to my aversion, since my published works reflect my professional interests and thinking in a rather unbalanced way.

This volume includes what is now often referred to as my 'classic paper' on work in a general teaching hospital, 'The functioning of social systems as a defence against anxiety', and papers about similar work in a variety of other institutions, generically known as 'humane' or caring. The second volume includes a range of topics more widely spread in society, although I hope the common thread in the thinking will still be clear.

Finally, I come to the difficult question of acknowledgements to so many people in so many different contexts. In nearly fifty years of professional study and practice, so many people have taught, encouraged, supported and sometimes inspired me that I find mentioning individuals almost impossible. Some individuals are mentioned in the conversation which forms Chapter 1. First, I must express my gratitude to my colleagues – professional, administrative and secretarial– at the Tavistock Institute and Clinic. The Tavistock Institute was an exciting place to work. It was also 'nice to come home to' when one had perhaps been a bit battered in the field. My colleagues contributed a great deal to the insights I developed. Secondly, there are my mentors and colleagues in the British Psycho-Analytical Society who helped me develop and maintain my psychoanalytic skills and insights. And last, but certainly not least, there have been thousands of people who have collaborated in various projects. Many were respondents in research studies who gave short-term help for which I am grateful. But I am very particularly grateful to the staff and clients in institutions where I worked as a consultant, over months or years sometimes, in work that was often hard and stressful for them, as well as for us.

I am grateful to a number of people who have helped in producing this volume: to my editor, Ann Scott of Free Association Books, who has generously supported and encouraged me, has been ready with creative suggestions and has done a great deal of the work herself; to Margaret Walker, Librarian of the Tavistock Joint Library, and Jill Duncan, Librarian of the Institute of Psycho-Analysis, London, who have taken a great deal of trouble to provide and check information; and to Rita Friend of the Tavistock Institute, who has dug out from the archives – and reproduced copies of – old Tavistock manuscripts when we needed them.

Acknowledgement is due also to the following publishers for permission to reprint papers: *Journal of Child Psychotherapy* for 'Thoughts on the maternal role in contemporary society' and 'The development of the self in children in institutions'; Tavistock Publications for 'The functioning of social systems as a defence against anxiety' and for 'Some methodological notes on a hospital study'; *Nursing Times* for 'Defence mechanisms in nursing: a review', subsequent correspondence, and 'Nurses under stress'; Routledge & Kegan Paul for 'Task and anti-task in adolescent institutions'; and the Tavistock Institute of Human Relations for 'Action research in a long-stay hospital'.

Note

'The functioning of social systems as a defence against anxiety: a report on a study of the nursing service of a general hospital' appeared first in 1959 in the journal *Human Relations*, was reprinted in 1961 by Tavistock Publications, and then again in 1970 as part of the Tavistock Institute of Human Relations pamphlet series. Within this volume the paper is cited variously as Menzies, 1959, 1961b and 1970, but readers should note that the paper itself remained the same.

Reflections on my work

Isabel Menzies Lyth in conversation with Ann Scott and Robert M. Young

Robert Young (*RY*): We wanted to achieve two purposes in talking to you. One of them was by way of introduction to the book and the other was to put you and it in a broader context – that is, to ask questions about how you got into these things and how you see them now. The first question I wanted to approach was: which came first, your interest in institutional aspects or analytic work itself, and how you've seen them evolve over time.

Isabel Menzies Lyth (*IML*): I'll tell you about my first experience of this kind. I did my first experiment at the age of sixteen, I suppose. Looking back on it, it seems a kind of portent of what was coming. I went to a new school at fifteen, into the fifth form. I had been there a month when the headmaster called me out of class and said he was going to make me a house captain. I remember thinking: 'He must be crazy! There are girls here who have been in this school for four or five years and he's jumped me over all of them to make me a house captain. They must resent this.' But perhaps he was not crazy. I did what had been done at my last school, which I must have valued but no one at my new school did. I ran the house through a committee of one elected representative from every form and all three fifth-form girls. The other houses were run from the top. The enthusiasm was tremendous, and whereas the house had been bottom of the house competition when I started, in two years it was at the top. I must already have been on the way to believing in the efficacy of worker participation and self-government.

RY: Where did this happen? Where did you grow up?

IML: That happened in St Andrews. I grew up in another part of Fife, and I went to school there, but changed schools when I was in the fifth form to a state school called Madras College in St Andrews. Then I started out to read medicine, actually with a view to being a psychiatrist – I was already in that field – and in my usual way put off trying to get a university place. So when I went to apply to medical school I was too late, so I said: 'Well, I'm not waiting a year,' (which it would have meant) 'I'll do psychology instead.'

Then I had to find another subject to go along with psychology and I chose economics. But it was the choice of psychology that brought about one of the most fortunate things that ever happened to me professionally – ultimately what took me to the Tavi [Tavistock Institute of Human Relations]. I met Eric Trist. He was acting head of the Psychology Department during my final honours year when the head, Oscar Oeser, was on a sabbatical. Eric was remarkable in his breadth of vision and in his respect and encouragement for me, his only student, as it happened. Such was the position of psychology in St Andrews then. It was an odd year, since Eric had then no great sense of time or place, and I spent a fair amount of time just looking for him. But it was always immensely worthwhile when I found him. He was one of several geniuses or near-geniuses I have been fortunate enough to work with.

RY: It's a kind of research, I suppose.

IML: Yes. He was just inspiring, and in particular he already had an interest in anthropology by then and was very interested in dynamic psychology. He hadn't started his own analysis or anything by then, but he was into it intellectually. Then there was research going on in Dundee which was run by Oeser, Trist and Babington Smith.[1]

So that was all going on. I finished my degree in 1939 and then the war started. I made a pact with my father that I had until Christmas, and if I hadn't got a job by Christmas I could join the ATS [Auxiliary Territorial Service], which I really wanted to do. I had a job by October – I was offered a lectureship at St Andrews because the university staff were being taken out and going to government departments and other war work. The lectureship was in economics. It suited my social life to go back to St Andrews for a few more years, so I did.

RY: You taught economics?

IML: I did. For six years, during which I was a member of the staff of the Nuffield College Social Reconstruction Survey run by G. D. H. Cole.[2] I worked in the Dundee area. My first publication came from that research and was in *Chambers' Encyclopaedia* and was about the jute industry. I don't think it's worthwhile telling you about that one. And from 1940 I was in a reserved occupation so I couldn't – or thought I couldn't – move. But I got fed up with university teaching and economics after a while, so in 1945 I decided to resign and see what happened.

I resigned and nothing happened. I had in the meantime done a number of vacation jobs in various kinds of war work, and I had spent two summer vacation months at No. 25 WOSB. Does that ring any bells? This was the research and training centre of War Office Selection Boards. Trist was there and that was how I got there. He had found me sitting in a basement in the War Office and organized my transfer. Trist was there, and Bowlby and Jock Sutherland[3] and various other people who had been or later become involved with the Tavistock. So I spent two months there, and then in 1945 when I resigned from St Andrews I got in touch with Eric Trist again and said: 'I need a job', and he offered me one very soon, and I went to Civil Resettlement. This was another Tavi predecessor. Its function was to receive and resettle British prisoners of war coming back from the army – not the air force or navy – from Europe first and then from the Far East. I was a psychologist again.

RY: So the social perspective came well ahead of the psychodynamic field for you?

IML: Well, yes and no. The psychology I studied had a lot of psychodynamic stuff in it, and I would never have been interested in a more orthodox academic approach and all that statistical stuff. And I always had a 'therapeutic' urge.

RY: I was thinking that you actually had a very social perspective well established before you went into strictly analytic work.

IML: Oh yes, certainly. We had a very nice six months or

thereabouts in Hatfield House [in Hertfordshire], the home of the Marquis of Salisbury. That was the headquarters unit of Civil Resettlement. We had twenty units throughout the country with prisoners of war coming and spending up to three months in various kinds of resettlement activities. There were social workers and what we called vocational officers, who helped with resettlement into work. The units were linked up with local industry and so on to help the men get back into the community. HQ finished up on an anti-aircraft gun site in Richmond Park [in Surrey] which wasn't quite so nice as Hatfield House. And then we began to return to civilian life. There were a lot of Tavistock people in Civil Resettlement. There was Tommy Wilson and Eric Trist, Harold Bridger, John Harvard-Watts,[4] so that again there was a coming together of a lot of people who already intended to move to the Tavistock. Gradually in 1945/46, as we were demobbed, we all collected at the Tavistock where the psychodynamic stuff came more to the fore, and everybody more or less at that time began an analysis.

RY: Was there then this cheek-by-jowl situation, where you had an institute and a clinic?

IML: No, not at first. In 1946 it was all one institution. It was only when we looked forward, with some alarm, to the setting up of the National Health Service that there was a legal split and we became a kind of Siamese twins, still very closely linked.

RY: What was the source of the alarm?

IML: We felt the Minister of Health wouldn't probably regard what we were doing as medicine or psychiatry. We regarded ourselves as being in preventive mental health but we didn't think that the Minister of Health would see it that way, and we thought we wouldn't have the freedom to explore and do the sorts of things we wanted to do as part of the Health Service.

Ann Scott (AS): If I may come in here – I'm surprised, because one of the remarks John Bowlby made at the recent launch of The Child Psychotherapy Trust[5] was that it was the work done with evacuated and other children during the Second World War which was then enshrined in government legislation, so that a discipline like child psychotherapy, pioneered at the Tavi, became accepted as a statutory service.

IML: That's the Clinic. Yes, but that's different from the kind of things that we in the Institute had intended, like going out to work in industry and institutions.

AS: So there was always that division.

RY: It seems more like industrial psychology in the academic division.

IML: That's right, or social psychology. It would not have been seen as preventive health by most people. The child psychotherapy development in the Clinic was a therapeutic service and acceptable in a different way. In the early days, many of us worked in both places, though. There wasn't much division between the two bodies, and everyone attended the staff meetings. It was a very small staff, and everyone more or less did a bit of everything. It was only after a few years that we differentiated out, and there was more distinction between Clinic and Institute, with separate heads and separate staffs. The Institute was legally incorporated as a charitable organization with its own Council.

RY: What premises were there?

IML: We were then in Beaumont Street in central London, next to the King Edward VII's Hospital for Officers.

RY: Was there Rockefeller Foundation support?

IML: Yes. Very generous Rockefeller support with no strings, just to help set up the Institute. It was very good. It really gave us time just to think and get to know each other and all the rest of it, and get in touch with potential clients, of course. We had to earn our living, which has always been an important thing at TIHR [Tavistock Institute of Human Relations]. You had to be self-financing through clients.

RY: It's always been on a customer-contract basis?

IML: Well, yes, there's always been a heavy element of that plus, of course, a lot of research money, but as you know that takes time to get, so we needed time also to make connections with government funds as well as other sources of research money. There's always been the two strings – client-based and research.

RY: What was the political flavour of the place in those days?

IML: Left-wing, definitely. We had several ex-Communists. I think most of us would have been socialist or unofficial left-wing liberal.

RY: I ask because I have met Eric Miller.[6] I asked him this question and he said he thinks of himself as rather Liberal/SDP.

IML: He wasn't there then. He was one of the later ones, you know!

RY: You say Trist to me and I think of Miller, because of their mutual interest in what I take to be ways of palliating class conflict.

IML: No, Trist had been a Communist, but not by the time he was at the Tavi. I don't remember when Eric Miller came but it was quite a bit later, and he came through Ken Rice,[7] who wasn't there at the beginning either, although he was closely associated. He was in those days at the Industrial Welfare Society[8] and he came into the Tavi from there. Bion was around then, very much so; and John Rickman[9] was around a lot at that time, and Michael Balint. There were a lot of people like them, sort of on the edge between the two institutions.

RY: If you look at the Tavi now, by which I mean the Clinic side, it's very much having to learn again to think about society, having spent a time (as I've experienced it) rather blinkered.

IML: That's right, but with exceptions like Pierre Turquet[10] and, later, Alexis Brook,[11] Anton Obholzer,[12] and others.

RY: So it is curious to have this evolution, isn't it?

IML: Yeah. Well, I think the Clinic had to get down to establishing itself in the Health Service. I mean, there was not too much freedom for manoeuvre, and the Health Service could make difficulties if the Clinic wasn't doing enough ordinary service operations and that kind of thing. They've always had to be very careful to keep a big enough case-load to satisfy the Department. The Department of Health was trying to keep the service going. The Clinic was having quite a lot of difficulty, for example, in doing as much teaching as it wanted to do because the teaching it did was not necessarily 'orthodox' by the Department of Health's standards. So there has always been that pressure – I don't know if Anton Obholzer taking over from Alexis Brook will make a difference to that, but it might.

RY: I think Alexis certainly thought about the community, but I think Anton is more of an entrepreneur and thinks more about society and the public relations (in both senses) of the place.

IML: I think so, yes.

RY: So I think it would be more outgoing. They've started a number of new things, haven't they?

AS: Well, that was what was coming to mind. I'm thinking of the recent spate of public gatherings. Initially the conference on surviving a disaster, organized in the wake of Zeebrugge.[13] The international conference to celebrate John Bowlby's eightieth birthday[14] was in a slightly different area, because although the media were invited, the media presence wasn't nearly so strong and the feel of the event was of something internal to a field of work. The Child Psychotherapy Trust launch, on the other hand, was targeted quite carefully and co-operatively at the media. All this gives the impression of a much greater awareness of the need for psychoanalysis to project some sense of itself as having a specific contribution to make towards the understanding of public events.

IML: Yes, but I am not sure if it is psychoanalysis *per se*; rather some of its derivatives.

You know the Institute of Psycho-Analysis is doing a set of lectures and seminars in 1988, which should be very interesting. They're having a series of distinguished lecturers, each with a psychoanalyst as commentator on what they are lecturing about. Eric Miller is doing one with me. There is quite a mixed bag of speakers. I think it's the same kind of thing, Ann. The Institute of Psycho-Analysis is at last getting a little more outgoing as well. I think there will be about eight or ten of these.

RY: That's progress.

IML: Yes, it is. And I hope they go well, because it could be very interesting.

RY: One of the reasons I was pursuing the line I was is because the application of Kleinian ideas to larger-scale social phenomena has a very small literature. I've been recommending your hospital study [Menzies, 1961b; see below, pp. 43–85] to people for years, literally pressing Xeroxes into their hands, but if I was asked to produce ten more papers of that ilk – by which I mean intense and intimate psychoanalysis connected to larger-scale structures – I don't think I could come up with five.

IML: No. This is partly what is preoccupying Elizabeth Spillius[15] in her forthcoming book. She's trying to sort out why it is that Bion's work on groups has caught on as it has, and the similar or parallel work in institutions such as hospitals has not.

RY: Do you have a view?

IML: She and I have been talking about it. Yes, I think partly institutional work is much more difficult . . .

RY: I give you that.

IML: . . . and I personally don't think that you can do the institutional work unless you are also a social scientist. An analyst who goes out, just working with sensitivity, as it were . . .

RY: . . . has too narrow a perspective.

IML: Much too narrow a perspective, and they get into difficult situations; it's money for old rope to make people more sensitive, actually, because they usually want to be anyway. But then you send them back to where they came from, and they're back in the old situation which does not allow them to deploy more sensitivity. All that happens is that they slip back, or they get very disgruntled and discontented, or they leave, or something. This is why I think it's the combination of skills that is important. I mean, you get it from either direction – you can get it from analysts who are social scientists, or you can get it from social scientists who have had a serious analysis themselves and do a lot of reading. The Tavi had a mixture of both.

RY: But I wouldn't be able to name five people associated with you who had done much in this area.

IML: Oh, I could. When I think of Eric Trist . . .

RY: Perhaps five, perhaps *just* five!

IML: Ken Rice, Eric Miller, John Hill,[16] Harold Bridger, Elliott Jaques,[17] Eric Trist, Alastair Bain.[18] Are you familiar with Alastair Bain?

RY: No, I'm not. I've seen his work cited in yours, but I don't know it.

IML: Well, now, his paper on the Baric experiment[19] is bang into this one – right in the middle – and I think it is very good. He really formulated the psychoanalytic-type consultancy very neatly in that paper, although I don't think it was wholly original. But take Eric Trist – I haven't been really awfully closely in touch with where he's been for the last five years, but have been again lately, and find it very exciting to see what's been happening round him. I think a lot has been happening in America. In this field now there's a chap called Jim Krantz. He spent a year or two at the Tavi, and he's gone back. He thought of becoming an analyst, but I think he may have given that up. But I'm sure he's analytically orientated and he's into this work as well, and other people in America are too. There is now an international society with a name something like 'Application of Psychoanalysis to Institutions'. They are very active round this area of work. Eric Trist was in Philadelphia as a professor for a long time. He's now retired and gone to live in Florida, but he obviously collected a very influential and inspired group of people. He still inspires many people, as he did me in St Andrews.

RY: One of the things that I feel about your work is – and it's almost a contradiction – that you use the phrase 'social change' a lot at the same time as you describe factors that seem so intractable I don't know how you manage to go on hoping. I cite this in the context (Ann and I were talking about this earlier today) of your nursing studies. As far as I can tell, bugger all has changed.

IML: Not there. But there has been change in other places.

RY: But it's very striking that here it is, laid bare for all to see, yet what were you [Ann] saying to me today? The statistics are roughly the same, you say?

IML: Oh, yes.

AS: Yes, I was looking into the statistics on the dropout rate from nurse training now. There is now a new initiative by the UK Central Council for Nursing and Midwifery – Project 2000 – attempting once more to professionalize the training of nurses, by tying the training more closely to the higher education system. Of course one of the things we wanted to talk to you about, anyway, was your response to that; and then I noticed that the wastage rate is still 30 per cent – as it was when you did your first work in hospitals in 1959. The dropout rate is high; the feeling of inadequate job satisfaction is still there.

Now one of the things that interested me very much in your initial nursing paper was the distinction you draw between the 'presenting symptoms' and the 'real nature' of the difficulties. I was particularly struck by the similarity between the description of the presenting symptom in your original study and the sketch given by the UKCC of what *purports* to be the 'real nature' of the problems in the 1980s – that is, a problem of wastage, and so on. I can't help wondering how you see the situation in nurse training at the moment, more than twenty-five years on from the paper on social defence systems.

IML: Well, actually, that last paper I gave, at University College last year . . .

RY: Yes, this is what I've just opened, yes.

IML: Now that one has got some of the explanation in it [Menzies Lyth, 1986; see vol. 2]. I think that it may be too hard for workers to focus on the basic problem, and they pick on the ambience of the job as a means of expressing something of their discontent. This was what Bain found when he went into Baric and heard the usual sort of complaints: we need more venti-lation, we need more cups of tea, we need higher wages, we need better holidays. He didn't believe this was the basic problem any more than I do when I get that sort of complaint. He worked through with the operatives on the computers to a much deeper understanding of what the real problems were: depersonaliz-ation, alienation, being turned into automata.

RY: You're just quoting the passage I opened.

IML: That's right. Well, that's it.

RY: Literally those words.

IML: I made a remark about having heard the general secretary of a professional association on the radio that morning more or less as I wrote the paper. It was nursing, and it was the same recipe as before: more status, more prestige, let us be trained like university students – and it's not the point! I don't believe these things would do much to help. I think the trouble lies in the difference between making blueprints, and *building* a model. I think this is an essential difference between the way the Tavistock-type consultants work and other kinds of consultants.

This is what's happened, I don't know how often, in the Health Service, and it's happened again with nurses. They get some kind of experts in who have a look at the situation and draw up a blueprint of what needs to be done, and then they go home. That's in fact what they do. Whereas what we did in the Tavi was to go in and work with one institution to *build* a model out of which you can extract principles – but not blueprints. You see, the blueprints don't usually take, because they don't allow for the other side. The blueprint deals with structure and role but it doesn't do the change in attitudes and cultures, and so on, without which you get this one-sided thing happening.

AS: Yes. You see, a remark in one of your papers from the early sixties [Menzies, 1961b; see below, p. 74] rather haunted me. You say – and I hope I'm remembering you rightly – that in your view the social defence system is substantially immutable, and yet you . . .

IML: No, one can get into it! Substantially, but not absolutely immutable.

AS: Well, yes, that was what I was wanting to get into.

RY: Yes, it's a question of hope.

AS: Going by the research you did which gave rise to the original nursing paper, and from your description of the work with hospitalized children at the Royal National Orthopaedic Hospital at Stanmore [see below, pp. 130–207], it's clear that in that context of action research, and by making suggestions for a radical restructuring of the work and a way of thinking about the mutual interactions between junior and senior nursing staff, you can create a basis for a different kind of psychic relationship to the task. But I can't help wondering whether you feel institutions can't *spontaneously* generate that kind of change.

IML: Oh, no, they can. They can. But you've got to have people with flair.

AS: That's why I wanted to talk to you about this, because for me it raised the issue of just what enables change to take place.

IML: Institutions are not immutable; they are just hard to change, and you can get consultants who can work by interpretation and that kind of thing, and the institution changes.

RY: Facilitators, in effect?

IML: To facilitate changes in the defence system and work through the anxieties as they come up and set up better adaptations. Sometimes, fortunately, you also get people who spontaneously in themselves have got flair and, without necessarily using the same language or anything, will do this. It's like me with my schoolgirl experiment. I just knew, in my heart of hearts, this was the thing to do. I couldn't have told you why, and I would never have used that language, but it was a dead cert for success. Alastair Bain's work in Baric was just a bigger, more professional example of what I did in my school.

RY: I want to press you a bit more on this, because of what you say in the original version of the [University College] paper: 'Just as in Baric it [the problem] lies in the core of professional work and training, alienation, depersonalization, devaluation of the worker, and so on. It needs more basic action aimed at the heart of the matter' [Menzies Lyth, 1986, p. 4; for revised version of this paper, see vol. 2]. But then you say, in the conclusion: 'Unfortunately, I have come to a depressing conclusion, that institutions have a natural tendency to become bad models for identification and the bigger the institution the more likely this is. I have already discussed the reasons why this should be so' [1986, p. 14]. I agree that that is rather depressed.

IML: Yes, it is. Now Eric Trist has got into the next stage of our industrial – post-industrial – society. He's away beyond me, and he thinks something is going to happen, hopefully, which may make my view out of date. Not untrue, as of the moment, but out of date. You see, both my paper on the development of the self – which was written about children, but is true for adults just as much as children [see below, pp. 236–58] – and Alastair Bain's paper on Baric show little models of how institutions can be changed, and you also get people who do it spontaneously. They know, for example, that if you delegate downwards and stretch people, they are stretchable and they like it, and they work better and their level of personal development rises.

Now you could do that with nurses, but – just coming back to your question, Ann, about the proposals for them – it won't make a significant difference. They're doing something like it in Australia, and from what I hear it is not going well. The new courses are finding it hard to get off the ground. The directors of nursing in the hospitals were furious because they had lost their schools. The student nurses were based in colleges and they were sent out to hospitals where they did not always seem welcome, and as supernumeraries they were not actually getting good practical experience. They're not getting into what student nurses get into when they actually work in wards as junior staff. I know that's got problems of its own, but it is a more relevant experience because they have responsibility, and they are in the maelstrom of anxiety and all that.

AS: This makes me think about the distinction that in your writing you've tried to draw between the avoidance of anxiety (itself pathological as a social defence) and the working through of anxiety, which you advocate. Would you say that you have seen changes in the way in which some hospitals are managing with that? After all, it's one of the key problems that you try to address.

IML: I've seen changes in hospitals I've been working in. I've come from one this afternoon where I've been working for a couple of years only for an hour and a half every Friday afternoon. That's changed quite a lot and is quite different from what it was like two years ago. It's more lively, and the patients feel like people as the staff talk about them. There is far more open talk about violence and the problems they have to manage. That has certainly changed in a couple of years of hard work for everybody. The Orthopaedic Hospital certainly changed a lot.

RY: So you're telling me that change occurs in local ways with the right kind of catalyst?

IML: That's right. But, you see, if you can get properly into the training schools then you can do a lot more. The trouble is you get kind of pushed out. We tried. Tim Dartington[20] and I tried to get into the training of nursery nurses at one point after the Orthopaedic Hospital study, and we simply didn't make it. I think we raised so much anxiety in the people who were teaching the courses that they couldn't bear it. Alastair Bain and Lynn Barnett[21] did a very nice piece of work in a day nursery where, among other things, they reduced labour turnover from 438 per cent per annum – imagine – to under 100 per cent, which was still high. But can you imagine? Four times a year the entire staff of that nursery changed, and that is just exactly what children don't need.

RY: Same is true with McDonald's Hamburgers.

IML: And Alastair and Lynn, they actually got a lot of attitude change and change in defences in that nursery. But my guess is that this didn't go any further with other nurseries. No, that's not quite true. Lynn Barnett then helped set up another better nursery-care system in Devon, where she works [Barnett, 1987], but that was Lynn again. I don't know. I think this is partly the answer to Elizabeth Spillius's question as to why institutional work has not caught on very well. Moving out from the model into the whole of the field – I don't think we've solved that problem.

RY: I want to ask a question, but I have to sketch the reasons I'm asking it first. A lot of us – including a lot of people who work in Free Association Books and on *Free Associations* – came through the libertarian politics of the sixties at a time when people were really being very critical of institutions, believing that a lot of change could occur. Depending on whether you want to tell the story politically or psychologically, they were poleaxed by forces they did not comprehend at all. The reason I first started reading your work (it must be ten or twelve years ago) was that I was in a discussion group, saying: 'Well, you know, this is so bewildering and so depressing, and we don't know what is happening. People say let's work in small groups, let's not have hierarchical structures, let's do this that and the other.' We found that we made very little headway, which is how some of us got into analysis and ended up doing therapy. When we looked at that literature we had two feelings. One of them was – and this is especially true of your nursing study – 'Aha, now we begin to see how stuff from individual psychoanalysis can be interpreted', and Bion was of course the other obvious source.

The other feeling we had – and this is why I'm asking the question – was evoked when we began to read some of the work on the use of psychology in industry, by which I mean Taylorism, the Hawthorne experiment, etc.[22] That trajectory is from a manipulative tradition. When you then begin to look at the work of people like Trist and Rice and Miller, and some of the work of the Institute, and some of the motivations of the Rockefeller charities,[23] it's very easy to see in it a kind of 'This is what the bastards are up to: they're palliating labour unrest; they're getting coal miners to be less militant.' I have a genuine and deep ambivalence about our post-sixties bewilderment and the relevance of the Tavi work to it, on the one hand, and the conservative tendencies of much of that work, on the other. I now wish to lay this problem at your feet.

IML: Sure.

RY: The problem lies between what people who care about social change need from these studies and some of the uses to which they have been put. How do you relate to this question?

IML: I would have a similar anxiety. I would be anxious about some of my colleagues, and I wouldn't always trust myself, I think, to be genuinely orientated to – well, to the benefit of the client, by which I don't mean the boss man who makes the profits but everyone who works in the place. I think I do genuinely believe that if you delegate downwards and give people maximum scope to run their own lives and so on, that it actually does benefit them. They get more satisfaction and they are healthier. You may also be increasing profits. You probably are, but that really doesn't matter, that's not the issue.

Coming back to the liberal thing, I too grew up in a Liberal kind of background, and then I became Labour when there wasn't much Liberalism going and then I moved back again. I don't go along with some of the ideas that the Liberals and the

SDP have about workers' partnerships in industry, because I don't think sitting on the board with a few shares to your name is what we're on about. The real place where the workers benefit from sharing is in their everyday setting, and having more control over that and over their own experiences. This is the Baric model again, where the workers actually got more control over the running of their own section [of the company]. What tends to happen is that you find there are fewer supervisors; they are not necessary any more. This to me is a far more important kind of liberal tradition, in fact, than having workers sitting up there on the board – a few workers who, because they are up there, may not represent the others anyway. What gives people self-respect and a feeling of status and reward and so on is actually having control in the small part in which they are closely involved.

RY: Have you continued to work with the Leicester and Mini-Leicester Conferences?[24]

IML: Not for a few years. I do them in Australia, but not here.

RY: One of my ambivalences about them (and I'm about to do one next year) is that if most of the people who come along are management it's one thing, but if they're agitators or worker priests or something else it's quite another, because it's actually enhancing one's ability, if I understand it correctly, to have a better conception of unconscious forces and therefore to be able – to some extent, at least – to control them. That's a powerful weapon. It's not easy to guarantee that it will be used for good.

IML: No, you simply can't guarantee that. The trouble about Leicester Conferences, in a way, is that however powerful they are they are terribly short.

RY: From what I've heard, if they got any longer more people wouldn't manage. You're talking about the proper residential Leicester Conferences?

IML: Yes.

RY: It's a tough thing to take two solid weeks out of your life if you're busy with clinical or other serious commitments.

IML: It is. Because you're taking more than a fortnight. It takes people a long time sometimes to settle down again afterwards. Anyway you can repeat the experience. I think I distrust the Americans more than the British, if I had to make a distinction on this matter, having seen some of them. They are more likely to take up gimmicks.

RY: There is a whole tradition of industrial psychology there that really is fundamentally biased. How much of your time have you spent doing strictly psychoanalytic work as opposed to what we've been talking about?

IML: Well, roughly half-time since I qualified in psychoanalysis in 1954, and a bit more since I moved to Oxford in 1976.

RY: What's changed the balance?

IML: A number of things. One was that when I moved to Oxford it became more difficult to work from the Tavistock, and secondly the Tavistock is not really what it was anyway.

RY: In what way has it changed?

IML: Well, it went through a very bad patch, you know, when everybody had cuts. The Tavistock had cuts, too, and it became increasingly difficult to keep the work going; that's one thing. There were several important deaths, like Rice and Turquet. Eric Trist had gone to America. The psychoanalytic component was less central.

RY: Because the atmosphere wasn't congenial?

IML: Partly. Not wholly. And there was a kind of takeover bid, I suppose, by the more orthodox social scientists. We had this terrible period when we split up into small units around personal and methodological differences. In the end there were only two units which carried on the psychoanalytic connection. The others did a different kind of consultancy and were more interested in pure and programmed research. Very few people now carry the psychoanalytic tradition – mainly Harold Bridger, Lisl Klein,[25] Eric Miller, and Tim Dartington, who left to work elsewhere.

RY: Where?

IML: He's now with the National Council of Voluntary Organizations, as Head of the National Organization Management Unit. I'm sure he will continue the Tavi tradition. He'd been freelance for some time and working with the Tavi a bit until recently.

RY: I wonder if there is any way of getting a broader and more social perspective into training, because the trainings seem very narrow from this point of view.

IML: The analytic trainings, do you mean?

RY: Yes. Well, it begs the question for the training to be only an analytic training, unless we broaden the range of issues considered psychoanalytically. Social, cultural and political forces have their own efficacy, even though we can view them analytically, and most trainees are woefully ignorant, and some are blinkered.

IML: Yes, it's the basic training for psychoanalysts at the Institute. They decided that resources are very limited and on the whole they should be invested in the best possible training for analysts. But the question of other training is an open one.

RY: But what happens is that they become analysts who only treat individuals and only think in those terms, on the whole.

IML: Well, I'm not sure that's strictly true. You'd be amazed. Certainly it's not true if you mean they sit in their own consulting rooms and see patients five times a week.

RY: Oh no, many work in the NHS and so on. I'm not saying they have no social conscience, but they don't think socially. They don't think about society, or group dynamics as opposed to . . .

IML: I think that's a fair comment, but with exceptions.

RY: And one of the things we're trying to do at Free Association Books is bring both perspectives to bear, and it's not easy.

IML: It would be worth talking to Elizabeth Spillius about this, you know, as she is into this question, and as I said she is very interested in why the institutional side of the Tavi hasn't grown and flowered like the group-relations side and the group-therapy side.

RY: I must say she communicated brilliantly on the Channel Four television series on psychoanalysis [*Voices*, 1987].

IML: She's good, yes, a marvellous brain. She is very much in this area of thinking. She worked at the Tavi for a time and wrote some lovely papers there, afterwards bringing together an anthropological and a psychoanalytic approach, one on the Kava ceremony in Tonga and one on Napsbury Hospital.[26] And you know her book, no doubt.

RY: I don't, no.

IML: *Family and Social Network* [Bott (later Spillius), 1957]. That was when she was at the Tavi before she went to Tonga and came back to finish her psychoanalytic training. She doesn't work in this tradition any longer, but she certainly thinks in it still. She's very much interested by it, and her book (the book that she's writing now) will have a lot of the social approach in it.

RY: It sounds as though this tradition isn't carrying on.

IML: I was very sad today, actually. I had a phone call from one of the senior social workers in a London borough, who asked me to go in there and work with the top managers' group to consider the management, and I had to say no. I think if it had been Oxford Social Services I wouldn't have been able to say no. The nature of the work would have been too important and too tempting. But I couldn't cope with coming up to London, so I referred them on to the Tavi, to Eric Miller.

RY: I think you've earned the right, but the question is where is the next generation of people doing it?

IML: Alastair Bain is reasonably young, and there is a group in Australia called the Australian Institute of Social Administration which has got several analysts in it as well as social scientists.

AS: I was wanting to raise another of the social aspects – the social implications of your writing. It links with the remarks Bob made earlier about the cultural-political tradition, as it were, of people like us, because it relates to what you say in your paper on the maternal role [1975; see below, pp. 208–21]. What interested me about it was that in comparison with many of your other papers, where you write with great intricacy about the complexity of interactions between family members . . . I'm sure you can tell what I'm about to get on to!

IML: We've had this conversation before! Go on.

AS: You give a description of the context in which what you think of as the best kind of infant care can be provided. For me it suddenly had the feeling of an idealization of conventional family life and family structure. You talk about the devotion that the mother feels for her husband, and the devotion that the ordinary good mother feels for her infant. I wouldn't for a moment want to deny that those kinds of families exist, but it's very hard not to have what may seem like the clichéd response that it *is* a guilt-inducing description – of an abstract, somewhat idealized form of family life. At the moment people are either choosing to bring up – or simply are bringing up – children in a variety of contexts, and what are they to make of what you say? Going on from that, one of the issues that particularly interested me was related to what felt like a misdescription of what some feminists have tried to say about mothering and work outside the home. I would be very interested to know how you're thinking about those issues now. I remember your mentioning in conversation that when you gave that paper, I believe at the Tavi . . .

IML: No, it was at a conference of English-speaking European psychoanalysts.

AS: . . . it stimulated a great deal of anxiety on the part of some of your audience. It seemed to me that there are a lot of issues around the way in which that kind of psychoanalytic language can seem to produce a very normative account . . .

RY: . . . which very few women are *able* to live up to, for other reasons.

AS: . . . of a kind which perhaps not that many people are able to live up to.

IML: I think you want to look at this in context again. What may not have come across as clearly as I wanted it to in that paper was the failure of society – or the comparative failure of society – to provide the context within which there would be more of what Winnicott calls the 'good ordinary family'. It's not an idealized family, it's a good ordinary family; goodness knows it has plenty of problems. So that's one thing. How the core family gets support to maintain its existence – it can be absolutely ghastly being a mother in some parts of London; there's no question about that. You know: the mother is stuck in a great big block of flats.

RY: It's not so wonderful in some parts of South Africa, either!

IML: No, that's right, but you know what I mean. When we were doing a lot of work on infant care at the Tavi, it was heartbreaking when one discovered these girls. They could be totally isolated up in a block of flats. They didn't know the neighbours. They'd moved in from the north or somewhere, and they had just got their babies. Their husbands were at work from eight in the morning until seven or eight at night and were absolutely no help at all during those hours. It's no good talking about a mother like that being so happily involved with her baby, because she is quite likely to have a depression or a paranoid state and be quite desperate. The husband may get phone calls all day long because she can't cope with no adults to talk to.

That's partly what I mean about a societal *context* within which mothering and the family can be supported and become more enjoyable and less of a hassle. The other side of this one, Ann, is when you have worked, as I have, for years in children's institutions, you are absolutely shattered by the damage that may be done to children in institutions. Now I wouldn't be so fussy about the good ordinary family if we had good ordinary day nurseries, or even good ordinary childminders. There are more of these than there were when we did the original work on day care for the under-fives [1971; see vol. 2]; I think that's true. You see, part of the difficulty is that not only mothers go out to work, but so do grandmothers. The grandmothers are not taking over the children as they used to do. It's the isolation of the nuclear family which is the problem and it's awfully easy to think in idealized terms about extended families, but you know they're extended all over the world, many of them, and unless you live in a neighbourhood where you've got neighbours who can to some extent take over that role it can't be denied that a mother becomes very isolated, and it's no good. Some mothers like being at home with children and some don't, that's all. I'm sorry if my view sounded harsh and idealized; it really wasn't meant to.

RY: Bowlby had the same problem, of course.

AS: I think what stood out about it was that the feel of the *writing* was so different from the feel of your descriptions of other kinds of networks of people.

IML: Yeah. I don't think I ever wanted to write that paper.

AS: That *is* interesting, in the light of one of the Chair's opening remarks to the Bowlby eightieth birthday conference: that there had in recent years been a *rapprochement* between Bowlby's views and those of women's liberation, especially those feminists working clinically. Your paper was published in the seventies; the Bowlby conference took place in the late eighties.

RY: Changes on both sides, I would think. That is, a lot of women who wanted twenty-four hour crèches so that they could just get shot of the thing actually discovered needs in themselves that they were denying.

IML: Well, that's marvellous when they do. I've watched some of my younger colleagues in Oxford go through this exercise, with various results, and some of them are aware – so aware – of what they're doing to themselves as well as to their children. The Robertsons' hospital work,[27] so sensitive about the effect of hospitalization on the child, paid rather less attention to the effect on the mother of being separated from her child [Robertson, James, 1958a]. The mother misses her child dreadfully, and if this goes on too long attachment to him may weaken, or if he is very small, may never really form. She may become less confident in her mothering. Several of these young colleagues have said they could not go back to work full-time, because *they* could not stand being away from the baby all that time. I well remember a student who came to see me for the first time after her baby was born. She got very restive, so much so that I shortened the supervision, saying she seemed to be working on 'baby time' herself and had been here too long. These young mothers are making a compromise between their careers and their own and their baby's need to be together, which can work quite well.

RY: But the career niches are only slowly allowing for this.

IML: Yes, that's true, absolutely.

AS: In the last four or five years I've come across feminist reconsiderations of that early demand for twenty-four-hour nurseries. They've acknowledged that the demand was not just misconceived but that its wording gave the impression that to be a feminist meant believing that children had no *specific* emotional relationship to their parents.

RY: It was a product of alienation.

AS: A product of alienation, yes. The irony is that these first feminist writings on child care, in the early seventies, took as their starting point the view that a dissatisfied, home-bound mother would pass her distress and frustration on to her child. Consciously, the demand for nursery care was designed to create a space for women to find satisfaction in work outside the home, the better to enjoy their relationship with their child, and so help the child's development. When one looks at the generation that preceded it – for instance, my mother was someone who responded to the view that women 'ought' to have children, but it wasn't, fundamentally, what she wanted to do – I think one sees that in the previous generation the pressure to have children, whether or not you felt it was how you really wanted to be fulfilled, was as great as the pressure for women to go out to work of which you speak now. I see the early-seventies women's movement approach to child care – however mistaken it might now seem, with hindsight – very much as a response to this earlier set of constraints. I can't help wondering how one brings a lot of these conflicting needs and impulses (as well as the sense of the past bearing down on the present) together.

RY: That's funny. My mother never went out, and I wish she had!

AS, laughing: Yes, I wish my mother had! I feel if my mother had gone out to work she might have been able to combine the two, work and home.

IML: Well, my mother was a part-time unpaid assistant to my father, so she did work, actually, a lot. Yes, I think the whole issue is very complex and I do think that what one really needs is tailor-making to the individual mother/wife and husband, or partner, and family.

RY: Which the structure of the job market wouldn't begin to think about.

IML: I've seen some of these young colleagues manage to talk their way into four or five [hospital] sessions a week.

RY: But it's not getting better for working-class women looking for work.

IML: I think it is, actually; I think it is.

RY: Things are getting tough.

IML: A lot of people now do part-time jobs or job share. At the Orthopaedic Hospital, when I worked there, a patient's mother and aunt had a job between them. One worked mornings and the other worked afternoons, and one looked after all the children in the morning and the other looked after all the children in the afternoon.

RY: Several people here work part-time and have child-care sharing, but it's a very unusual place, and it's inconvenient for production. There's no denying it.

AS: And the fact that some of us are in analysis is inconvenient for production as well.

RY: That's true.

IML: I don't know what we can do about the day nurseries – I got the figures all wrong last Saturday morning at the Disaster meeting [revised version, Menzies Lyth, 1987; see vol. 2], but there are over 30,000 children in this country in day nurseries. Many day nurseries have been shown to be damaging to children. It's made worse by the fact that the children who go there are often damaged already. The evidence is that they get worse, not better, and that is shocking.

RY: That connects to something I was talking about earlier that I don't feel comfortable about. Where is the tradition that is bringing these issues and this perspective on these issues into the universities, and into the places where teachers are taught? I have a sense of a broken tradition that isn't actually feeding in as much as it needs to. Maybe the publication of this book will transform everything . . .

IML: I do hope . . .

RY: I *do* hope, of course, for several reasons! For example, I taught in Cambridge for many years, and Ann studied there. None of this stuff was on our agenda at all.

IML: 'None of this stuff', you mean . . . ?

RY: None of the social appropriation of psychoanalysis in a subtle way; it just wasn't on the agenda at all. I say of the present that any kind of psychoanalysis – not to mention psychoanalysis applied to institutions – is making very little headway.

IML: Sure, and Oxford is worse than Cambridge.

RY: Yes, it is; that's right. As far as I know they don't have any lectures on this.

IML: The last time I visited St Andrews they were doing something about cats in the Psychology Department. Changed days!

RY: In Cambridge they had lectures on it. I used to give some of them. The Professor of Psychology set the serious or core curriculum, and psychoanalysis was a sort of ornament. It wasn't at the heart of it.

IML: That's the trouble. I feel I am an ornament on the face of a hospital in Oxford where I do just a tiny bit of psychotherapy teaching. There is a lot of lip service.

RY: People who were either in or around tertiary education in the late sixties and early seventies have discovered, to our own distress, that these are important questions. Yet they have little purchase on the institutions. It's very slow.

IML: I was wondering, though, Bob, about how little seems to be going on here, but listening to Eric Trist I get the impression that there is a good deal going on around his particular set in America. He was saying something very interesting which I hadn't thought of and which makes some of my comments not quite relevant: that not everybody who's now working in this field has got the combination of social sciences and analysis.

RY: I would think it's very rare.

IML: Listen to this, though. He says, nevertheless, they work the way we do, and he says there is something going on for which he said the best word he could think of was osmosis. Something is happening to certain people – it must again be people who have a natural feel for it – who, without necessarily going through the analytic process, are working in this kind of way. Now these are people like the Philadelphia group. We're going to have to wait until his book comes out, I'm afraid, to see a bit more of what he means by this, but I found meeting with him recently very exciting, actually.

RY: When's it coming and what's it called?

IML: Well, he's only just started. I don't think he's got a title. He's only just collecting the relevant Tavi and other papers and he's over here for a month to see his authors to begin this.

RY: This is the three-volume one you mentioned.

IML: And there is a little patch going on in Australia: Alastair Bain and others in AISA [Australian Institute of Social Administration], and Harold Bridger works there too. I don't quite know what he does out there but he spends quite a bit of time in Australia. I don't know, maybe there will be more of the osmosis.

AS: If one thinks in local terms, one sees certain changes. When I think back to my own undergraduate years at Cambridge in the early seventies (I also began as a medical student and gave it up) I remember then there was no support at all for students – psychological support – in dealing with the anxiety of the training. A few years later I heard that one of the newly qualified doctors had formed some kind of self-help group where junior doctors and, I think, clinical students could address and share together the problems and the stresses induced by their work.

RY: There was no place for *students* to go, in psychological distress, but I'm glad to say that some of us helped to get a student counselling service set up, and there are now quite a few psychotherapists at work in Cambridge. The therapy situation has changed, though the curriculum hasn't very much.

AS: It may be that it's through a self-help network that these things begin to spring up, and that formal change comes later. Then of course there is the wider movement, in terms of hospice care and self-help patients' groups for cancer patients and their relatives, which I follow a little. Even if it's not been taken up in a hospital-institutional way, it's clearly a change of direction in the way that cancer as an illness is thought about.

RY to *IML*: Have you done any work on that? I say that because I would have thought that there's one kind of nursing that contradicts your worst conclusions. Hospice nurses really do focus; they really do relate to the whole person.

IML: Absolutely.

RY: And they really do bear the distress.

IML: Yes, the hospice movement, but don't generalize too much as it hasn't really hit the hospitals as a whole. Staff still find illness and death, anxiety and distress terribly difficult to listen to and talk about with patients and relations.

RY: I'm sorry – I *only* meant hospices.

IML: Yes, that's tremendous.

AS: And that might support what you were saying: 'There can be change, but it calls for individuals with flair.'

IML: Like Cicely Saunders.[28] Yes, and there is a hospice in Oxford as well, you see, where they've got a psychiatrist called Averil Stedeford as a consultant. She's a Jungian, and a very sensitive person who can stand a lot of stress and strain. There is also Helen House for dying children in Oxford. I'm not quite sure where that one has got to but they did have a child psychiatrist, Gillian Forest, working there as a consultant to the staff.

RY: A bit like rape crisis – who deals with the counsellors at a Rape Crisis Centre?

IML: Yes, but of course the Scots are always ahead, you understand. You know when I was a student in St Andrews . . .

RY: My middle name is Maxwell, by the way!

IML: Robert Maxwell?

RY: I was born to it. He picked it out of an ash can.

IML: He did, didn't he . . . We had a system at St Andrews, it has been there for hundreds of years, and I'm happy to say it still is. Senior students – i.e., third- or fourth-year students – each 'adopted' a first-year student of the same sex. But this was more than a one-to-one relation, since the seniors were likely themselves to be in a fairly stable friendship group. This helped the first-years to form their own group. It was actually an amazingly effective informal social system, which greatly smoothed the introduction of new students and was extremely

27

supportive when anyone was in trouble. One felt very contained. It has survived so long, I am sure, not just for the sake of tradition, but because it is so useful.

RY: You reminded me of my earliest experience as a medical student because, looking back on it, you start out in anatomy with somebody who has been dead for some time, and then you do pathology, and they are just cold. You don't really meet a live one until your third year!

IML: I know!

RY: And by that time your humanity has gone through quite a lot of astringency.

IML: I know. Tommy Wilson used to have a lot to say on that at the Tavi.

RY: Do you think there is any hope that the Tavi will regenerate this tradition, because I'm very struck by . . .

IML: I think if it continues and becomes stronger it will be from one of the offshoots. Eric Trist has a list of places, actually . . .

RY: I wouldn't mind seeing that.

IML: I'll try to remember to send you a copy – of other institutes or groups who are working in this kind of way that he is in touch with.

RY: You should be giving lectures regularly.

IML: Who, Trist?

RY: No, you.

IML: Me! I hate writing things. I'm always happy with seminars or talks, but I'm never happy with lectures.

RY: I don't know if you suffer from false modesty or not, but that kind of integration is very, very rare.

IML: I never did think I was of much importance.

RY: What are you going to be doing henceforward? You're not allowed to retire.

IML: Oh, I am retiring in the next few years. I've taken my last new patient.

RY: Oh, really?

IML: Yes. Well, I think it's omnipotent to think your mind goes on being as good as it was. I've watched colleagues really deteriorate, and of course they don't realize it because their mind's not functioning well. I've watched them go on seeing patients and teaching students and distressing them in consequence. Like Herbert Rosenfeld,[29] who had a massive stroke just before a seminar with the students already there.

And that, you know, as I just said, I do not want to happen to me. I had a colleague in Oxford and we had a pact that we would tell each other if we were going gaga, but she's left so there's no one to tell me now!

AS laughing: You'll have to find another one!

IML: So I've told myself. Probably by a year's time I will have finished with patients, and I will probably go on doing supervision for a little bit longer.

RY: Do people come up from London or are they mostly from Oxford?

IML: They are mostly Oxford people and professionally much more varied than in London. I'll continue my architecture course.

RY: You're studying architecture?

IML: The history of architecture. It's fascinating, actually.

RY: We'll probably have some buildings from you based on these principles!

IML: There's something interesting in that.

AS: You know, I can remember in the last few years reading about a project somewhere in the States, again in relation to cancer care, for a rethinking of hospital building. Rooms could be set aside for nurses and patients – either mixed or on their own – because the stress of being with a terminally ill patient is so great; and soundproofed, so that people could give full vent to their feelings.

RY: Yes – I could use one of those.

AS: It struck me as very welcome – if something like that were to happen it would really signal a change in hospital practice.

IML: I can remember when my husband was dying that I was on the edge of tears, patently, and the sister came up, was very kind, and said: 'Come into my office', and I thought, 'God, it can't be true, she's going to take me in her office.' She took me into her office and gave me a cup of tea. I thought for a moment she was going to stay and talk to me, but she disappeared. I had hoped for more I suppose, but she could not face my anxiety and grief. She was a good and kind sister, but just did not know how to cope with bereavement. She didn't want me crying on her ward so she took me off it and, well . . .

AS: One of the experiences that has given me my lasting interest in hospital practice is from when my mother was dying of cancer. This was in a crack London hospital. I was visiting her one day, and while I was at my mother's bedside her doctor asked me to step into her office. In a concerned, but without-more-ado kind of way, she said: 'Well, we're keeping her in now. It's a matter of days, or at most a month.' I had a few moments to compose myself – I'd already gathered that my mother was on a Brompton Cocktail – and went back to my mother's bedside. My mother said: 'What did the doctor want to tell you?'

When you have an experience like that you just know you will always be interested in the way nurses and doctors respond to and defend themselves both against the anxiety induced by such illnesses, and their feelings for their patients.

RY: And you know there must be a better way.

AS: That's right. Oddly enough, it was a situation of great conflict in reality – between the psychiatric social worker, who did specialist work on death and dying, and believed in allowing the feelings to be shared in an open way; and the nurses and doctors, who showed signs of needing to avoid this. It was the nurses who had the greatest difficulty in dealing with the whole situation.

RY: What did you do, by the way?

AS: I dissimulated and, of course, suffered greatly in my conscience, because my mother had said at the outset, on diagnosis, that she wanted to be told the whole truth about her illness. I have always valued the psychiatric social worker because subsequently, when I had had some months to begin to absorb the experience, she said to me: 'You know, your mother may well have been using denial herself. You may have thought that she wanted to know everything but of course there would have come a time when she *didn't* want to know everything.'

RY: There's a lot of this about.

AS: You really need that kind of input, and you need to be helped to process the experience. I also felt it had been sensitive of her to wait that time to plant the idea in my mind.

IML: This is what I think: if nurses were properly trained and supported they could be absolutely marvellous in this work.

RY: They get promoted away from seeing the patients.

IML: Well, yes, they didn't promote the ward sister [on the ward we worked in] at the RNOH [Royal National Orthopaedic Hospital]. She should have been promoted, and there was a vacant post, but the matron thought, perhaps rightly, that she would be unhappy as a nursing officer and that she might not be very good at it. If she was promoted the ward would have lost an unusually gifted ward sister, and she would have lost the children she was absolutely devoted to. The sad thing is that the Health Service had no way of giving status and reward commensurate with the quality of her work without taking her away from patients.

To go back to the question of nurses helping with death and bereavement: we had only two deaths in four years among the children at the Orthopaedic Hospital, and they were both in the same week. It was traumatic. The nurses in the Cot Unit talked to us first, and then they were in the ward talking to everybody, not just the families of the dead children but every family, because they were all terribly anxious. The nurses were able to talk to the mothers about it and face it with them and talk to the verbal children, and so the whole thing was talked through. The rest of the hospital put down the screen, and one of the senior sisters said she would never come to a seminar we ran again if we were going to deal with death the way the Cot Unit did. We hadn't had enough impact on the rest of the hospital at that point. The nurses in the Cot Unit were very young, but with good support they could face the issues. If you can get nurses like that, they are really the people to help patients and families, because they are on the spot, and known, and we all know the importance of being there when the person needs the help.

RY: But can you imagine, with the Health Service going the way it is, this way of thinking making headway? In fact, given the way things are going, it's more needed.

IML: Well, that's what's going to be the second half of that paper that I hope to write on the Aftermath of Disaster, when I've got time to write it [1987; see vol. 2]. People tend to ignore disaster, or threats of disaster, as you know. People knew the Aberfan tip was likely to come down. I spent my childhood among coal pits so I know about them too – and it was the same with the Zeebrugge disaster. People knew there was likely to be a disaster sooner or later. But the point I want to make is that we are living in the middle of disasters all the time and we've turned a blind eye to them, too – disaster areas like hospitals.

RY: Like Thatcherism.

IML: Well, yes, that's another issue.

RY: I'm serious. It is a disaster, just as I said.

IML: I wasn't disagreeing with you, I was just thinking that's a bit harder to cope with. But you get staff in the day nurseries and the hospitals and other places who actually are faced with disasters all the time – disasters like broken marriages, unemployment, dying children, little children who have psychotic mothers, or whatever. If they can learn to help better with these ongoing disasters, then they are better prepared to deal with the big disasters when they happen: they've got a certain amount of practice in it. It's useful but not enough to set up a great big disaster centre, which some experts like Colin Murray Parkes[30] want to do. What you need also is to get into the ongoing disasters and help the care-takers there to cope with them better, so that they not only cope with these disasters better at the time, but they actually learn to face death or loss or whatever it is. And you would have all these people in the community who would have skills and experience and who would be available. They are actually in a position to meet people hit by a major disaster and they know them already. And once again it's the same with Zeebrugge – a whole lot of strangers were working with that. It's better than nothing, but it's not as good as it could be. [To *AS*:] You heard me having a disagreement with Colin Murray Parkes about the identity problems of survivors at the press meeting during the Disaster conference, and I would like to get that out apart from anything else. If one feels that anyone as distinguished as Colin Murray Parkes is mistaken, as I believed, it is a good thing to say so.

RY: I'm going to let you off the hook in a minute, but I do want to ask you one more question and see if you want to say anything else. Is there anything about how this work has been received which you'd like to comment on?

IML: My work personally?

RY: Yes. Bowlby was quite eloquent on this subject!

IML: Of himself?

RY: About how Melanie Klein and Anna Freud and Spitz received his work [see Bowlby *et al.*, 1986].

IML: I haven't had much of that actually. The nursing paper was extremely well received by colleagues.

RY: Quite right.

IML: However, when I continued my work at the Tavi after I had qualified in psychoanalysis, I did come under a lot of pressure from senior Kleinian analysts who felt I was wasting my time and my gifts staying there when I could have been working full-time in psychoanalysis. That subsided a bit when my papers began to appear, which showed how I was using psychoanalysis, and also when I made fairly rapid progress in psychoanalysis, becoming a full member of the Society and a training analyst pretty quickly.

The paper was badly received by a nurse who perhaps should have known better than write the review she wrote for the *Nursing Times* [see below, pp. 89–94]. Although it was anonymous, we quickly found out who had written it. That kind of review you should not write anonymously. It was signed RMN, Registered Mental Nurse. The review said that it was patent that this was a badly run hospital, etc., etc., and the whole paper was rubbish. I wrote privately to the editor complaining about her editorial policy, in publishing such a severely critical and emotional review anonymously. She reacted quickly and positively and offered me space in the *Nursing Times* to publish a shortened version of the paper, so the nurses themselves could read it. I was pleased when another RMN, who might not have written had she known who the reviewer was, wrote to the editor criticizing the review and the reviewer for writing it. She felt the reviewer had let the [RMN] side down.

One can understand why the paper might upset nurses and why it has taken years for the nurses to revise their response to it, but that's OK now and I am asked a lot by nurses to do seminars. What is also interesting is that the editor said that my article had to be not more than 1,500 words because they never published an article which was more than 1,500 words, the implication being that nurses couldn't cope with anything more. The review was much longer! Anyway, this editor let me have three lots of 1,500 words, which was very reasonable.

The original paper is much used in nursing now, but it was used by a lot of other professions first, like social workers. I don't know if this made much difference to social workers in institutions, but it certainly gave a lot of intellectual kudos. I don't think it's got very far into medicine.

RY: How about into the mentality of the Department of Health and Social Security?

IML: No. I don't think so.

RY: Because this isn't just about nursing! It's about how people behave!

IML: Yes, the hospital was only the case material. No, it hasn't. I was thinking about the work I did with a World Health Organization Conference in Holland. We had a couple of senior medical officers there from the Ministry of Health, but I don't think they were really into this way of thinking.

RY: There is a chance . . . One of the things that happens with something that's done for professionals is that it stays on these tramlines, whereas if it's out in the general press then that's another matter. Bringing it out as a book may achieve a wider appreciation.

IML: That paper hasn't stayed on these tramlines; it has got out to other professions, and they have been more able to take it in because it's not about them. I think the nurses were terribly hurt and felt . . .

RY: It was a bull's-eye.

IML: . . . They felt terribly hurt and persecuted by it. Also, not only that: there was nothing very much they could do about it. Even if they had believed it implicitly, they could have done little about it. Not the nurses in the hospital.

AS: One related issue would be the language with which you present your findings. I think you also talk about this in the University College paper: there might be a meaning in the notion that a coal miner is tearing out the insides of his mother's body, but the interpretation isn't going to be put in that language [Menzies Lyth, 1986, p. 3; see vol. 2].

IML: Yes.

AS: I'd be interested to hear your comments on how findings are put, in situations where you may not be speaking to people who share a common language. I remember that one of the reactions of your supporter in the *Nursing Times* was along the lines: 'Yes, Melanie Klein's concepts are controversial, but, on the other hand, the notions of projection and sublimation precede psychoanalytic writing by a long way.' There is obviously a possibility of finding an entrée into that kind of language.

IML: That's right. You see what we did at the general hospital, when we got to a certain point in our explorations, was to set up a meeting of the matron – who was still a matron then – deputy matron, senior tutor, and the first and second assistant matrons – all the senior nurses in the hospital. And we met once a fortnight or thereabouts, for long meetings of about three hours in which I simply fed back what we had been discovering and let them talk about it. Now, that was fed back in perfectly ordinary language and they chewed it over, and sometimes they accepted it and sometimes they didn't, and sometimes they were right and sometimes they were wrong. When they were right we modified our views, and when they were wrong we had to get at the resistances. That went on for months before ever anything was written down.

The difficulty, you see, in other words, is not really the clients so much, because I would always work that way with the client. I would feed back in a situation where I could test out their reactions and work with their resistances if necessary. The difficulty is when you make it public, because one can't work it through with a wide audience beforehand.

RY: Are we going to have any problems with that?

IML: No, I don't think so. There are not many people, with any of these papers, who haven't had it worked through. I have a regret about some of my papers on children's institutions, though. I feel I have not sufficiently expressed my appreciation and gratitude to Richard Balbernie of the Cotswold Community for the enormous amount he taught me, nor perhaps sufficiently worked through with him what I have written about Cotswold. Unfortunately, it is too late; he died.[31]

RY: Well, you can do what you like in the beginning.

IML: That's right. I can still express the appreciation.

RY: Is there any crossover that you are aware of between your teaching as an analytic supervisor and this work?

IML: Not that I can put into words.

RY: I'll just tell you why I ask. An analyst I respect said that he would recommend you above all as a supervisor, and I just wondered what was so absolutely special about this.

IML: I think I've probably got something I share with Elizabeth Spillius, actually, in that I think I am fairly unanxious and not therefore likely to clamp down on somebody who is doing something different from what I would do. I hope I can help people to find their own way, not slavishly to follow mine. Perhaps that does link with my work in institutions – no blueprints.

RY: When you don't know what's going on, you don't know what's going on and you know you don't know what's going on.

IML: Yes, and I very often say to people I'm supervising if perhaps we don't agree about something, 'Well, it's your patient and you know him very much better than I do, and you were there and I wasn't.' I remember just one person I was rather fierce with, because she did some fantastically awful things, but I think I do, on the whole, let people go their own way. I don't mean I don't make suggestions or give advice. You know, I get an astonished reaction when I say at the end, 'Forget everything I've said!' People who think I'm an 'expert' look at me as though

36

I've gone slightly crazy at that point, but the point is I'm talking about what was happening last week in another situation when I actually wasn't present myself, and the student is going into a new situation where the things I've been saying may or may not be relevant. It's very tempting when you are a supervisee to think: 'Ah, my supervisor said that and I will say it at all costs.'

RY: I confess I have done this!

IML: We've all done this!

RY: No, I mean word for word and, I'm embarrassed to say, worse than that, an interpretation made to me in the morning goes into my own session in the evening.

IML: Yeah, especially when you're getting desperate and you can't understand what's going on.

RY: It's very embarrassing when you catch yourself at it.

IML: Yeah, but you know, I think this has got a lot clearer since Bion. I think Freud was there, too, but Bion has made it quite clear, so I think on the whole my supervisees don't feel too persecuted by me. I'm in tremendous demand in Oxford. People in seminars I have run are now turning up one by one saying, 'That's not enough', and want individual supervision as well.

RY: That must be nice.

IML: It is; I enjoy supervision. I think that may make a difference. I actually enjoy supervision. I think I also perhaps convey a good deal of Bion's work, and others find that exciting, just as I do.

RY: Maybe people understand it better.

IML: I got a lot from Bion the 'hard way'. I had two years in a group with him when I was a kind of semi-student, semi-staff at the Tavi, and then I had my second analysis with him, so he is present in me in a different way from only through his writing. And maybe it's because I'm more familiar with him as a clinician that I am making sense. I find his writing hard, as most people do, but find it very valuable, particularly his views on the analyst's situation and how you should prepare yourself to meet it.

RY: You mention it often: negative capability and suspension of memory and desire. I can see it's a kind of touchstone for you and, of course, you're right.

IML: Yes, I think that is important. He does literally say somewhere that it is helpful if you can regard each patient as a new patient each day. I found that very useful because it clears the vision of the patient. If you've never been in the habit of sitting down and thinking what the patient said yesterday, as I wasn't, it isn't too hard to follow Bion.

RY: We can stop in a minute. Is there anything you want to say that is profound for posterity?

IML: I've said more than enough already. Looking back, I begin to have quite a considerable list of people who have helped me get where I am, starting with Trist and, well, most of my Tavi colleagues. It was a superb place to work.

RY: Makes me nostalgic for something I've never experienced. The nicest kind of envy . . .

IML: It was quite disturbing as well. Almost everybody had just started with analysis, and inevitably there was feedback into the Tavi. Extraordinary, but it gradually calmed down as we got more settled.

RY: It's become much more professionalized and – well, it's less easy-going by quite a long way.

IML: The Tavi, or . . . ?

RY: I know someone who trained in the seventies where everything was easy-going and gentle and . . .

IML: At the Institute?

RY: No, at the Tavi.

IML: Are you talking about the Clinic?

RY: Yes. The Clinic has become much more professionalized, more curriculum-ridden.

IML: I think so, yes. Well, I was talking more of the Tavistock Institute, because of course in the early days there was no distinction anyway. It was a most inspiring group of people. I was just terribly lucky to have met Eric Trist in the first place. I often wonder what would have happened to me if I hadn't met Eric Trist. I might have ended up in the Civil Service or something.

RY: Ann, is there anything you want to end on?

AS: Well, it isn't related to the last few minutes but as we're talking I suppose my thoughts do keep coming back to the notion of 'disavowed knowledge', because of one remark in your [*IML*'s] original nursing paper. I won't be able to recall it exactly, but you say that nurses are aware of such and such a practice and they deplore it, but nevertheless it goes on. It reminded me of my own days as a medical student, when it was known that clinical students found it most stressful to witness an autopsy on a young person, a person of their *own* age who had died. That, for me, sums up disavowed knowledge in that something was known about but nothing was done about working it through. In the culture of the institution, an anxiety was avoided rather than taken up.

RY: When I was at medical school, I think the deaner [the person in charge at autopsies] loved it.

AS: Again it was the problem that such things, within an institution, are not psychologically attended ot.

IML: Yes, you can make a long list of these things, you're right. Student nurses find it extremely difficult to work in gynaecology – it's too close – and nurses often make very anxious patients themselves when it comes to hysterectomy and things like that. Nurses do need help with such problems, and there's no real record of how much nurses use patients as a means of getting psychotherapy. I quickly had a 'practice' when I spent about eight days as a patient in St Mary's, Paddington. A woman next door to me, who was just a nice, elderly lady, had as big a practice as I did; it was less to do with professional skills than the nurses' needs. We got a bit fed up with them in the end. We got tired easily. We were supposed to be the patients.

RY: I can understand that. Let's switch off and offer you a drink.

London, 10 July 1987

NOTES

1. Bernard Babington Smith, lecturer in psychology at St Andrews University.

2. G. D. H. Cole, socialist historian, economist and political thinker. The Nuffield College Social Reconstruction Survey (1940–44), of which he was Chairman and Director, was undertaken to examine the consequences

of the war for social and economic conditions, and the possibilities of political and social reorganization in the light of them.

3. J. D. Sutherland, founder member of the Tavistock Institute of Human Relations (TIHR) and later Medical Director of the Tavistock Clinic, 1947–68.

4. A. T. M. Wilson, H. Bridger and J. Harvard-Watts, founder members of TIHR. J. Harvard-Watts was the first Chairman of Tavistock Publications Ltd and then became Managing Director.

5. A fund-raising and educational initiative to support the training of child psychotherapists and increase understanding of the emotional factors in child development, launched in London in 1987.

6. Currently Senior Staff Member, TIHR.

7. Deputy Director of the Industrial Welfare Society, subsequently at TIHR, 1948–69.

8. Now the Industrial Society, London, and chiefly concerned with personnel matters.

9. Initially a member of the Kleinian group in the British Psycho-Analytical Society, and a colleague of W. R. Bion. He later became an Independent analyst.

10. Consultant at the Tavistock Clinic and TIHR, involved in group-relations work, and Associate Member of the British Psycho-Analytical Society.

11. Consultant psychiatrist. Chairman of the Professional Committee of the Tavistock Clinic, 1979–85. Honorary Affiliate of the British Psycho-Analytical Society.

12. Consultant psychiatrist. Currently Chairman of the Professional Committee of the Tavistock Clinic. Associate Member of the British Psycho-Analytical Society.

13. 'The Aftermath of Disaster: Survival and Loss', 13 June 1987, Tavistock Clinic. A multidisciplinary conference which brought together workers involved with those affected by a major disaster, members of the media, and other interested professionals.

14. 'Fruits of Attachment Theory: Findings and Applications across the Life Cycle – A Celebration of Dr John Bowlby's 80th Birthday', 26–27 June 1987, Regent's College, London.

15. Psychoanalyst. Member of the British Psycho-Analytical Society. Former Staff Member, TIHR.

16. Psychoanalyst. Associate Member of the British Psycho-Analytical Society. Senior Staff Member, TIHR, 1949–80.

17. Senior Staff Member, TIHR, and in private practice as a psychoanalyst. Later a professor at Brunel University and a management consultant. Member of the British Psycho-Analytical Society.

18. Senior Staff Member, TIHR, 1968–83. Now with the Australian Institute of Social Administration (AISA).

19. A London computer company with which Alastair Bain worked on a sociotechnical project in the 1970s. See Bain, 1982.

20. Staff Member, TIHR, 1970–6, and member of the team at the Royal National Orthopaedic Hospital, Stanmore.

21. Anthropologist and child psychotherapist, formerly at TIHR, now working in Exeter and teaching child development to postgraduate social work students at Exeter University.

22. The history of scientific management, the human-relations movement in industry and the links with 'depth psychology' and psychoanalysis – including the work of the Tavistock Institute of Human Relations – has not been written up in a comprehensive way. Here are some suggestive references: Baritz, 1965; Carey, 1967; Emery and Trist, 1962; Mayo, 1933; Taylor, 1947; Trist, 1973; Young, 1972, 1981. [Note by RY]

23. The Rockefeller charities intervened in many disciplines and many institutions – including the Tavistock Institute of Human Relations, the Yale Institute of Human Relations, the London School of Hygiene and Tropical Medicine, the creation of molecular biology, the developments in agriculture known as the 'Green Revolution', and the Trilateral Commission. There is, unfortunately, no single source describing these developments and the growing criticisms of the overall strategy of managerializing, palliating class conflict, controlling Third World rebellions and exporting models of knowledge and management to Third World countries. Here are some representative references: Brown, 1979; Fisher, 1978; Fitzgerald, 1986; Morowski, 1986.

The scholar who most ardently defends the Rockefeller Foundation's policies is Robert E. Kohler. His articles can be approached via his 'Science, foundations and American universities in the 1920s' (Kohler, 1987, especially pp. 157–63). See also Kohler, 1976. The 'official' histories are Fosdick, 1952, and Dicks, 1970 (especially chapter 9 by S. G. Gray on the Tavistock Institute of Human Relations). [Note by RY]

24. A two-week group-relations training, in existence since 1957, which now meets in Leicester. There are offshoots, called 'Mini-Leicester'.

25. Consultant, TIHR.

26. A psychiatric hospital in north London.

27. James Robertson, Member (retired from practice) of the British Psycho-Analytical Society. With his wife, Joyce Robertson, he is a specialist in child development, especially the effects of institutionalization and mother–child separation on development. The Robertsons have used film, especially *A Two-Year-Old Goes to Hospital* (1953), to communicate their findings.

28. Dame Cicely Saunders, Medical Director of St Christopher's Hospice, Sydenham, London.

29. Late Member of the British Psycho-Analytical Society, especially well known for his work on psychosis.

30. Consultant psychiatrist at The London Hospital, especially well known for his work on bereavement, which he started at the Tavistock Clinic.

31. Richard Balbernie was a specialist in the running of institutions for disturbed children and Principal of the Cotswold Community, an approved school and later a community children's home in Wiltshire.

2 The functioning of social systems as a defence against anxiety (1959, 1961 [1961b], 1970)

A report on a study of the nursing service of a general hospital[1]

INTRODUCTION

THE STUDY was initiated by the hospital, which sought help in developing new methods of carrying out a task in nursing organization. The research data were, therefore, collected within a sociotherapeutic relationship in which the aim was to facilitate desired social change.[2]

The hospital is a general teaching hospital in London. This implies that, in addition to the normal task of patient care, the hospital teaches undergraduate medical students. Like all British hospitals of its type, it is also a nurse-training school. The hospital has about 700 beds for inpatients and provides a number of outpatient services. Although referred to as 'the hospital' it is, in fact, a group of hospitals which, at the time of the study, included a general hospital of 500 beds, three small specialist hospitals, and a convalescent home. The group of hospitals has an integrated nursing service run by a matron located in the main hospital. Nursing staff and students are interchangeable between hospitals.

The nursing personnel of the hospital number about 700. Of these, about 150 are fully trained staff and the remainder are students. The nurse-training course lasts four years. For the first three years, the student nurse is an 'undergraduate'. At the end of the third year she takes the examination which leads to 'state-registration', effectively her nursing qualification and

43

licence to practise. In the fourth year, she is a postgraduate student.

The trained nursing staff are entirely deployed in administrative, teaching and supervisory roles, although those who are deployed in operational units working with patients also carry out a certain amount of direct patient care. Student nurses are, in effect, the nursing staff of the hospital at the operational level with patients, and carry out most of the relevant tasks. From this point of view, it is necessary that student nurses be deployed so as to meet the nurse-staffing requirements of the hospital. The student nurse spends comparatively little time undergoing formal instruction. She spends three months in the Preliminary Training School before she starts nursing practice, and six weeks in the nursing school in each of the second and third years of training. For the rest of the time she is in 'practical training': acquiring and practising nursing skills by carrying out full-time nursing duties within the limits of her competence. This practical training must be so arranged that the student has the minimal experience of different types of nursing prescribed by the General Nursing Council.[3] The hospital offers – and likes nurses to have – certain additional experience available in specialist units in the hospital. The hospital's training policy is that the student nurse has approximately three months' continuous duty in each of the different types of nursing. Each student nurse must be deployed in a way that fulfils these training requirements. There are many possibilities of conflict in this situation. The nursing establishment of the hospital is not primarily determined by training needs, which take second place to patient-centred needs and the needs of the medical school. For some considerable time before the start of the study, the senior nursing staff had been finding it increasingly difficult to reconcile effectively staffing needs and training needs. Pressures from patient care demanded that priority be given to staffing, and constant training crises developed. The policy of three-month training tours had in effect been abandoned and many tours were very short;[4] some nurses came almost to the end of their training without having had all the necessary experience, while others had a serious imbalance owing to too much of the same kind of practice. These crises created the more acute distress because senior staff wished to give increasing priority to training and to raise the status of the nurse as a student.

The senior staff began to feel that there was a danger of complete breakdown in the system of allocation to practical work and sought our help in revising their methods. My purpose in writing this paper is not, however, to follow the ramifications of this problem. I will make some reference to it at relevant points, and will consider later why the existing method persisted so long without effective modification in spite of its inefficiency.

The therapeutic relationship with the hospital was to some extent based on the belief that we would be wise to regard the problem of student-nurse allocation as a 'presenting symptom' and to reserve judgement on the real nature of the difficulties and the best form of treatment until we had done further diagnostic work. We began, therefore, with a fairly intensive interviewing programme. We held formal interviews with about seventy nurses, individually and in small groups, and with senior medical and lay staff; we carried out some observational studies of operational units; and we had many informal contacts with nurses and other staff. Respondents knew the problem we were formally studying, but were invited to raise in interview any other issue that they considered central to their occupational experience. Much further research material was collected in the later meetings with senior staff as we worked together on the findings from the interviewing programme.[5]

As our diagnostic work went on, our attention was repeatedly drawn to the high level of tension, distress and anxiety among the nurses. We found it hard to understand how nurses could tolerate so much anxiety and, indeed, we found much evidence that they could not. In one form or another, withdrawal from duty was common. About one-third of student nurses did not complete their training. The majority of these left at their own request, and not because of failure in examinations or practical training. Senior staff changed their jobs appreciably more frequently than workers at similar levels in other professions and were unusually prone to seek postgraduate training. Sickness rates were high, especially for minor illnesses requiring only a few days' absence from duty.[6]

As the study proceeded we came to attach increasing importance to understanding the nature of the anxiety and the reasons for its intensity. The relief of the anxiety seemed to us an important therapeutic task and, moreover, proved to have a close connection with the development of more effective techniques of student-nurse allocation. The remainder of this paper considers the causes and the effects of the anxiety level in the hospital.

NATURE OF THE ANXIETY

A hospital accepts and cares for ill people who cannot be cared for in their own homes. This is the task the hospital is created to perform, its 'primary task'. The major responsibility for the performance of that primary task lies with the nursing service, which must provide continuous care for patients, day and night, all the year round.[7] The nursing service, therefore, bears the full, immediate and concentrated impact of stresses arising from patient care.

The situations likely to evoke stress in nurses are familiar. Nurses are in constant contact with people who are physically ill or injured, often seriously. The recovery of patients is not certain and will not always be complete. Nursing patients who have incurable diseases is one of the nurse's most distressing tasks. Nurses are confronted with the threat and the reality of suffering and death as few lay people are. Their work involves carrying out tasks which, by ordinary standards, are distasteful, disgusting and frightening. Intimate physical contact with patients arouses strong libidinal and erotic wishes and impulses that may be difficult to control. The work situation arouses very strong and mixed feelings in the nurse: pity, compassion and love; guilt and anxiety; hatred and resentment of the patients who arouse these strong feelings; envy of the care given to the patient.

The objective situation confronting the nurse bears a striking resemblance to the phantasy[8] situations that exist in every individual in the deepest and most primitive levels of the mind.

46

The intensity and complexity of the nurse's anxieties are to be attributed primarily to the peculiar capacity of the objective features of her work situation to stimulate afresh these early situations and their accompanying emotions. I will comment briefly on the main relevant features of these phantasy situations.[9]

The elements of these phantasies may be traced back to earliest infancy. The infant experiences two opposing sets of feelings and impulses, libidinal and aggressive. These stem from instinctual sources and are described by the constructs of the life instinct and the death instinct. The infant feels omnipotent and attributes dynamic reality to these feelings and impulses. He believes that the libidinal impulses are literally life-giving and the aggressive impulses death-dealing. The infant attributes similar feelings, impulses and powers to other people and to important parts of people. The objects and the instruments of the libidinal and aggressive impulses are felt to be the infant's own and other people's bodies and bodily products. Physical and psychic experiences are very intimately interwoven at this time. The infant's psychic experience of objective reality is greatly influenced by his own feelings and phantasies, moods and wishes.

Through his psychic experience the infant builds up an inner world peopled by himself and the objects of his feelings and impulses.[10] In this inner world, they exist in a form and condition largely determined by his phantasies. Because of the operation of aggressive forces, the inner world contains many damaged, injured, or dead objects. The atmosphere is charged with death and destruction. This gives rise to great anxiety. The infant fears for the effect of aggressive forces on the people he loves and on himself. He grieves and mourns over their suffering and experiences depression and despair about his inadequate ability to put right their wrongs. He fears the demands that will be made on him for reparation and the punishment and revenge that may fall on him. He fears that his libidinal impulses and those of other people cannot control the aggressive impulses sufficiently to prevent utter chaos and destruction. The poignancy of the situation is increased because love and longing

47

themselves are felt to be so close to aggression. Greed, frustration and envy so easily replace a loving relationship. This phantasy world is characterized by a violence and intensity of feeling quite foreign to the emotional life of the normal adult.

The direct impact on the nurse of physical illness is intensified by her task of meeting and dealing with psychological stress in other people, including her own colleagues. It is by no means easy to tolerate such stress even if one is not under similar stress oneself. Quite short conversations with patients or relatives showed that their conscious concept of illness and treatment is a rich intermixture of objective knowledge, logical deduction, and fantasy.[11] The degree of stress is heavily conditioned by the fantasy, which is in turn conditioned, as in nurses, by the early phantasy situations. Unconsciously, the nurse associates the patients' and relatives' distress with that experienced by the people in her phantasy world, which increases her own anxiety and difficulty in handling it.

Patients and relatives have very complicated feelings towards the hospital, which are expressed particularly and most directly to nurses, and often puzzle and distress them. Patients and relatives show appreciation, gratitude, affection, respect; a touching relief that the hospital copes; helpfulness and concern for nurses in their difficult task. But patients often resent their dependence; accept grudgingly the discipline imposed by treatment and hospital routine; envy nurses their health and skills; are demanding, possessive and jealous. Patients, like nurses, find strong libidinal and erotic feelings stimulated by nursing care, and sometimes behave in ways that increase the nurses' difficulties: for example by unnecessary physical exposure. Relatives may also be demanding and critical, the more so because they resent the feeling that hospitalization implies inadequacies in themselves. They envy nurses their skill and jealously resent the nurse's intimate contact with 'their' patient.

In a more subtle way, both patients and relatives make psychological demands on nurses which increase their experience of stress. The hospital is expected to do more than accept the ill patient, care for his physical needs, and help realistically with his psychological stress. The hospital is implicitly expected to accept and, by so doing, free patients and relatives from certain aspects of the emotional problems aroused by the patient and his illness. The hospital, particularly the nurses, must allow the projection into them of such feelings as depression and anxiety, fear of the patient and his illness, disgust at the illness and necessary nursing tasks. Patients and relatives treat the staff in such a way as to ensure that the nurses experience these feelings instead of – or partly instead of – themselves: for example by refusing or trying to refuse to participate in important decisions about the patient and so forcing responsibility and anxiety back on the hospital. Thus, to the nurses' own deep and intense anxieties are psychically added those of the other people concerned. As we became familiar with the work of the hospital, we were struck by the number of patients whose physical condition alone did not warrant hospitalization. In some cases, it was clear that they had been hospitalized because they and their relatives could not tolerate the stress of their being ill at home.

The nurse projects infantile phantasy situations into current work situations and experiences the objective situations as a mixture of objective reality and phantasy. She then re-experiences painfully and vividly, in relation to current objective reality, many of the feelings appropriate to the phantasies. In thus projecting her phantasy situations into objective reality, the nurse is using an important and universal technique for mastering anxiety and modifying the phantasy situations. Through the projection, the individual sees elements of the phantasy situations in the objective situations that come to symbolize the phantasy situations.[12] Successful mastery of the objective situations gives reassurance about the mastery of the phantasy situations. To be effective, such symbolization requires that the symbol *represents* the phantasy object, but *is not equated* with it. Its own distinctive, objective characteristics must also be recognized and used. If, for any reason, the symbol and the phantasy object become almost or completely equated, the anxieties aroused by the phantasy object are aroused in full intensity by the symbolic object. The symbol then ceases to perform its function in containing and modifying anxiety.[13] The close resemblance of the phantasy and objective situations in nursing constitutes a threat that symbolic representation will degenerate into symbolic equation and that nurses will consequently experience the full force of their primitive infantile anxieties in consciousness. Modified examples of this phenomenon were not uncommon in this hospital. For example, a nurse whose mother had had several gynaecological operations broke down and had to give up nursing shortly after beginning her tour of duty on the gynaecological ward.

By the nature of her profession the nurse is at considerable risk of being flooded by intense and unmanageable anxiety. That factor alone, however, cannot account for the high level of anxiety so apparent in nurses. It becomes necessary to direct attention to the other facet of the problem – that is, to the techniques used in the nursing service to contain and modify anxiety.

DEFENSIVE TECHNIQUES IN THE NURSING SERVICE

In developing a structure, culture and mode of functioning, a social organization is influenced by a number of interacting factors, crucial among which are its primary task, including such environmental relationships and pressures as that involves; the technologies available for performing the task; and the needs of the members of the organization for social and psychological satisfaction and, above all, for support in the task of dealing with anxiety.[14, 15, 16] In my opinion, the influence of the primary task and technology can easily be exaggerated. Indeed, I would prefer to regard them as limiting factors – that is to say, the need to ensure viability through the efficient performance of the primary task and the types of technology available to do this set limits to possible organization. Within these limits, the culture, structure and mode of functioning are determined by the psychological needs of the members.[17]

The need of the members of the organization to use it in the struggle against anxiety leads to the development of socially structured defence mechanisms, which appear as elements in the organization's structure, culture and mode of functioning.[18]

An important aspect of such socially structured defence mechanisms is an attempt by individuals to externalize and give substance in objective reality to their characteristic psychic defence mechanisms. A social defence system develops over time as the result of collusive interaction and agreement, often unconscious, between members of the organization as to what form it shall take. The socially structured defence mechanisms then tend to become an aspect of external reality with which old and new members of the institution must come to terms.

In what follows I shall discuss some of the social defences that the nursing service has developed in the long course of the hospital's history and currently operates. It is impossible here to describe the social system fully, so I shall illustrate only a few of the more striking and typical examples of the operation of the service as a social defence. I shall confine myself mainly to techniques used within the nursing service and refer minimally to ways in which the nursing service makes use of other people, notably patients and doctors, in operating socially structured mechanisms of defence. For convenience of exposition, I shall list the defences as if they are separate, although in operation they function simultaneously and interact with and support each other.

Splitting up the nurse–patient relationship. The core of the anxiety situation for the nurse lies in her relation with the patient. The closer and more concentrated this relationship, the more the nurse is likely to experience the impact of anxiety. The nursing service attempts to protect her from the anxiety by splitting up her contact with patients. It is hardly too much to say that the nurse does not nurse patients. The total workload of a ward or department is broken down into lists of tasks, each of which is allocated to a particular nurse. She performs her patient-centred tasks for a large number of patients – perhaps as many as all the patients in the ward, often thirty or more. As a corollary, she performs only a few tasks for, and has restricted contact with, any one patient. This prevents her from coming effectively into contact with the totality of any one patient and his illness and offers some protection from the anxiety this arouses.

Depersonalization, categorization, and denial of the significance of the individual. The protection afforded by the task-list system is reinforced by a number of other devices that inhibit the development of a full person-to-person relationship between nurse and patient, with its consequent anxiety. The implicit aim of such devices, which operate both structurally and culturally, may be described as a kind of depersonalization or elimination of individual distinctiveness in both nurse and patient. For example, nurses often talk about patients not by name, but by bed numbers or by their diseases or a diseased organ: 'the liver in bed 10' or 'the pneumonia in bed 15'. Nurses themselves deprecate this practice, but it persists. Nor should one underestimate the difficulties of remembering the names of, say, thirty patients on a ward, especially the high-turnover wards. There is an almost explicit 'ethic' that any patient must be the same as any other patient. It must not matter to the nurse whom she nurses or what illness. Nurses find it extraordinarily difficult to express preferences even for types of patients or for men or women patients. If pressed to do so, they tend to add rather guiltily some remark like 'You can't help it'. Conversely, it should not matter to the patient which nurse attends him or, indeed, how many different nurses do. By implication it is the duty as well as the need and privilege of the patient to be nursed and of the nurse to nurse, regardless of the fact that a patient may greatly need to 'nurse' a distressed nurse and nurses may sometimes need to be 'nursed'. Outside the specific requirements of his physical illness and treatment, the way a patient is nursed is determined largely by his membership of the category patient and minimally by his idiosyncratic wants and needs. For example, there is one way only of bed-making, except when the physical illness requires another; only one time to wash all patients in the morning.

The nurses' uniforms are a symbol of an expected inner and behavioural uniformity; a nurse becomes a kind of agglomeration of nursing skills, without individuality; each is thus perfectly interchangeable with another of the same skill level. Socially permitted differences between nurses tend to be restricted to a few major categories, outwardly differentiated by minor differences in insignia on the same basic uniform: an arm stripe for a second-year nurse, a slightly different cap for a third-year nurse. This attempts to create an operational identity between all nurses in the same category.[19] To an extent indicating clearly the need for 'blanket' decisions, duties and privileges are allotted to categories of people and not to individuals according to their personal capacities and needs. This also helps to eliminate painful and difficult decisions, for example about which duties and privileges should fall to each individual (see p. 54). Something of the same reduction of individual distinctiveness exists between operational sub-units. Attempts are made to standardize all equipment and layout to the limits allowed by their different nursing tasks, but disregarding the idiosyncratic social and psychological resources and needs of each unit.

Detachment and denial of feelings. A necessary psychological task for the entrant into any profession that works with people is the development of adequate professional detachment. He must learn, for example, to control his feelings, refrain from excessive involvement, avoid disturbing identifications, maintain his professional independence against manipulation and demands for unprofessional behaviour. To some extent the reduction of individual distinctiveness aids detachment by minimizing the mutual interaction of personalities, which might lead to 'attachment'. It is reinforced by an implicit operational policy of 'detachment'. 'A good nurse doesn't mind moving.' A 'good nurse' is willing and able without disturbance to move from ward to ward or even hospital to hospital at a moment's notice. Such moves are frequent and often sudden, particularly for student nurses. The implicit rationale appears to be that a student nurse will learn to be detached psychologically if she has sufficient experience of being detached literally and physically. Most senior nurses do not subscribe personally to this implicit rationale. They are aware of the personal distress as well as the operational disturbance caused by over-frequent moves. Indeed, this was a major factor in the decision to initiate our study. However, in their formal roles in the hierarchy they continue to initiate frequent moves and make little other training provision for developing genuine professional detachment. The pain and distress of breaking relationships and the importance of stable and continuing relationships are implicitly denied by the system, although they are often stressed personally – that is, nonprofessionally – by people in the system.

This implicit denial is reinforced by the denial of the disturbing feelings that arise within relationships. Interpersonal repressive techniques are culturally required and typically used to deal with emotional stress. Both student nurses and staff show panic about emotional outbursts. Brisk, reassuring behaviour and advice of the 'stiff upper lip', 'pull yourself together' variety are characteristic. Student nurses suffer most severely from emotional strain and habitually complain that the senior staff do not understand and make no effort to help them. Indeed, when the emotional stress arises from the nurse's having made a mistake, she is usually reprimanded instead of being helped. A student nurse told me that she had made a mistake that hastened the death of a dying patient. She was reprimanded separately by four senior nurses. Only the headmistress of her former school tried to help her as a person who was severely distressed, guilty and frightened. However, students are wrong when they say that senior nurses do not understand or feel for their distress. In personal conversation with us, seniors showed considerable understanding and sympathy and often remembered surprisingly vividly some of the agonies of their own training. But they lacked confidence in their ability to handle emotional stress in any way other than by repressive techniques, and often said, 'In any case, the students won't come and talk to us.' Kindly, sympathetic handling of emotional stress between staff and student nurses is, in any case, inconsistent with traditional nursing roles and relationships, which require repression, discipline and reprimand from senior to junior.[20]

The attempt to eliminate decisions by ritual task-performance. Making a decision implies making a choice between different possible courses of action and committing oneself to one of them; the choice being made in the absence of full factual information about the effects of the choice. If the facts were fully known, no decision need be made; the proper course of action would be self-evident. All decisions are thus necessarily attended by some uncertainty about their outcome and consequently by some conflict and anxiety, which will last until the outcome is known. The anxiety consequent on decision-making is likely to be acute if a decision affects the treatment and welfare of patients. To spare staff this anxiety, the nursing service attempts to minimize the number and variety of decisions that must be made. For example, the student nurse is instructed to perform her task-list in a way reminiscent of performing a ritual. Precise instructions are given about the way each task must be performed, the order of the tasks, and the time for their performance, although such precise instructions are not objectively necessary, or even wholly desirable.[21]

If several efficient methods of performing a task exist – for example, for bed-making or lifting a patient – one is selected and exclusively used. Much time and effort are expended in standardizing nursing procedures in cases where there are a number of effective alternatives. Both teachers and practical-work supervisors impress on the student nurse from the beginning of her training the importance of carrying out the 'ritual'. They reinforce this by fostering an attitude to work that regards every task as almost a matter of life and death, to be treated with appropriate seriousness. This applies even to those tasks that could be effectively performed by an unskilled lay person. As a corollary, the student nurse is actively discouraged from using her own discretion and initiative to plan her work realistically in relation to the objective situation – for example, at times of crisis to discriminate between tasks on the grounds of urgency or relative importance and to act accordingly. Student nurses are the 'staff' most affected by 'rituals', since ritualization is easy to apply to their roles and tasks, but attempts are also made to ritualize the task-structure of the more complex senior staff roles and to standardize the task-performance.

Reducing the weight of responsibility in decision-making by checks and counterchecks. The psychological burden of anxiety arising from a final, committing decision by a single person is dissipated in a number of ways, so that its impact is reduced. The final act of commitment is postponed by a common practice of checking and rechecking decisions for validity and postponing action as long as possible. Executive action following decisions is also checked and rechecked habitually at intervening stages. Individuals spend much time in private rumination over decisions and actions. Whenever possible, they involve other nurses in decision-making and in reviewing actions. The nursing procedures prescribe considerable checking between individuals, but it is also a strongly developed habit among nurses outside areas of prescribed behaviour. The practice of checking and counterchecking is applied not only to situations where mistakes may have serious consequences, such as in giving dangerous drugs, but to many situations where the implications of a decision are of only the slightest consequence – for example, on one occasion a decision about which of several rooms, all equally available, should be used for a research interview. Nurses consult not only their immediate seniors but also their juniors and nurses or other staff with whom they have no functional relationship but who just happen to be available.

Collusive social redistribution of responsibility and irresponsibility. Each nurse must face and, in some way, resolve a painful conflict over accepting the responsibilities of her role. The nursing task tends to evoke a strong sense of responsibility in nurses, who often discharge their duties at considerable personal cost. On the other hand, the heavy burden of responsibility is difficult to bear consistently, and nurses are tempted to give it up. In addition, each nurse has wishes and impulses that would lead to irresponsible action – for example, to scamp boring, repetitive tasks or to become libidinally or emotionally attached to patients. The balance of opposing forces in the conflict varies between individuals – some are naturally 'more responsible' than others – but the conflict is always present. To experience this conflict fully and intrapsychically would be extremely stressful. The intrapsychic conflict is alleviated, at least as far as the conscious experiences of nurses are concerned, by a technique that partly converts it into an interpersonal conflict. People in certain roles tend to be described as 'responsible' by themselves and to some extent by others, and in other roles people are described as 'irresponsible'. Nurses habitually complain that other nurses are irresponsible, behave carelessly and impulsively, and in consequence must be ceaselessly supervised and disciplined. The complaints commonly refer not to individuals or to specific incidents but to whole categories of nurses, usually a category junior to the speaker. The implication is that the juniors are not only less responsible now than the speaker, but also less responsible than she was when she was in the same junior position. Few nurses recognize or admit such tendencies. Only the most junior nurses are likely to admit these tendencies in themselves and then justify them on the grounds that everybody treats them as though they were irresponsible. On the other hand, many people complain that their seniors as a category impose unnecessarily strict and repressive discipline, and treat them as though they have no sense of responsibility.[22] Few senior staff seem able to recognize such features in their own behaviour to subordinates. Those 'juniors' and 'seniors' are, with few exceptions, the same people viewed from above or below, as the case may be.

We came to realize that the complaints stem from a collusive system of denial, splitting and projection that is culturally acceptable to – indeed, culturally required of – nurses. Each nurse tends to split off aspects of herself from her conscious personality and to project them into other nurses. Her irresponsible impulses, which she fears she cannot control, are attributed to her juniors. Her painfully severe attitude to these impulses and burdensome sense of responsibility are attributed to her seniors. Consequently, she identifies juniors with her irresponsible self and treats them with the severity that self is felt to deserve. Similarly, she identifies seniors with her own harsh disciplinary attitude to her irresponsible self and expects harsh discipline. There is psychic truth in the assertion that juniors are irresponsible and seniors harsh disciplinarians. These are the roles assigned to them. There is also objective truth, since people act objectively on the psychic roles assigned to them. Discipline is often harsh and sometimes unfair, since the multiple projection also leads the senior to identify all juniors with her irresponsible self and so with each other. Thus, she fails to discriminate between them sufficiently. Nurses complain about being reprimanded for other people's mistakes while no serious effort is made to find the real culprit. A staff nurse[23] said: 'If a mistake has been made, you must reprimand someone, even if you don't know who really did it.' Irresponsible behaviour was also quite common, mainly in tasks remote from direct patient care. The interpersonal conflict is painful, as the complaints show, but is less so than experiencing the conflicts fully intrapsychically, and can more easily be evaded. The disciplining eye of seniors cannot follow juniors all the time, nor does the junior confront her senior with irresponsibility all the time.

Purposeful obscurity in the formal distribution of responsibility. Additional protection from the impact of specific responsibility for specific tasks is given by the fact that the formal structure and role system fail to define fully enough who is responsible for what and to whom. This matches and objectifies the obscurity about the location of psychic responsibility that inevitably arises from the massive system of projection described above. The content and boundaries of roles are very obscure, especially at senior levels. The responsibilities are more onerous at this level, so that protection is felt to be very necessary. Also the more complex roles and role-relationships make it easier to evade definition. As described above (p. 55), the content of the role of the student nurse is rigidly prescribed by her task-list. However, in practice she is unlikely to have the same task-list for any length of time. She may – and frequently does – have two completely different task-lists in a single day.[24] There is therefore a lack of stable person-role constellations, and it becomes very difficult to assign responsibility finally to a person, a role, or a person-role constellation. We experienced this obscurity frequently in our work in the hospital, finding great difficulty, for example, in learning who should make arrangements or give permission for nurses to participate in various research activities.

Responsibility and authority on wards are generalized in a way that makes them nonspecific and prevents them from falling firmly on one person, even the sister. Each nurse is held to be responsible for the work of every nurse junior to her. Junior, in this context, implies no hierarchical relationship and is determined only by the length of time a student nurse has been in training, and all students are 'junior' to trained staff. A student nurse in the fourth quarter of her fourth year is by implication responsible for all other student nurses on the ward; a student nurse in the third quarter of her fourth year for all student nurses except the previous one, and so on. Every nurse is expected to initiate disciplinary action in relation to any failure by any junior nurse. Such diffused responsibility means, of course, that responsibility is not generally experienced specifically or seriously.

The reduction of the impact of responsibility by delegation to superiors. The ordinary usage of the word 'delegation' in relation to tasks implies that a superior hands over a task and the direct responsibility for its detailed performance to subordinates, while he retains a general, supervisory responsibility. In the hospital, almost the opposite seems to happen frequently – that is to say, tasks are frequently forced upwards in the hierarchy so that all responsibility for their performance can be disclaimed. In so far as this happens, the heavy burden of responsibility on the individual is reduced.

The results of many years of this practice are visible in the nursing service. We were struck repeatedly by the low level of tasks carried out by nursing staff and students in relation to their personal ability, skill and position in the hierarchy. Formally and informally, tasks are assigned to staff at a level well above that at which one finds comparable tasks in other institutions, while these tasks are organized so as effectively to prevent their delegation to an appropriate lower level, for example, by clarifying policy. The task of allocating student nurses to practical duties was a case in point. The detailed allocation work was carried out by the first and second assistant matrons[25] and took up a considerable proportion of their working time. In our opinion the task is, in fact, such that if policy were clearly defined and the task appropriately organized, it could be efficiently performed by a competent clerk part-time under the supervision of a senior nurse, who need spend little time on it.[26] We were able to watch this 'delegation upwards' in operation a number of times as new tasks developed for nurses out of changes resulting from our study. For example, the senior staff decided to change the practical training for fourth-year nurses so that they might have better training than formerly in administration and supervision. This implied, among other things, that they should spend six months continuously in one operational unit, during which time they would act as understudy-cum-shadow to the sister or the staff nurse. In the circumstances, personal compatibility was felt to be very important and it was suggested that the sisters should take part in the selection of the fourth-year students for their own wards. At first there was enthusiasm for the proposal, but as definite plans were made and the intermediate staff began to feel that they had no developed skill for selection, they requested that, after all, senior staff should continue to select for them as they had always done. The senior staff, although already overburdened, willingly accepted the task.

The repeated occurrence of such incidents by mutual collusive agreement between superiors and subordinates is hardly surprising considering the mutual projection system described above (pp. 56–8). Nurses as subordinates tend to feel very dependent on their superiors, in whom they psychically vest by projection some of the best and most competent parts of themselves. They feel that their projections give them the right to expect their superiors to undertake their tasks and make decisions for them. On the other hand, nurses, as superiors, do not feel they can fully trust their subordinates in whom they psychically vest the irresponsible and incompetent parts of themselves. Their acceptance of their subordinates' projections also conveys a sense of duty to accept their subordinates' responsibilities.

60   *Idealization and underestimation of personal developmental possi-*

bilities. In order to reduce anxiety about the continuous efficient performance of nursing tasks, nurses seek assurance that the nursing service is staffed with responsible, competent people. To a considerable extent, the hospital deals with this problem by an attempt to recruit and select 'staff' – that is, student nurses – who are already highly mature and responsible people. This is reflected in phrases like 'nurses are born, not made' or 'nursing is a vocation'. This amounts to a kind of idealization of the potential nursing recruit, and implies a belief that responsibility and personal maturity cannot be 'taught' or even greatly developed. As a corollary, the training system is mainly orientated to the communication of essential facts and techniques, and pays minimal attention to teaching events orientated to personal maturation within the professional setting.[27] There is no individual supervision of student nurses, and no small-group teaching event concerned specifically to help student nurses work over the impact of their first essays in nursing practice and handle more effectively their relations with patients and their own emotional reactions. The nursing service must face the dilemma that, while a strong sense of responsibility and discipline are felt to be necessary for the welfare of patients, a considerable proportion of actual nursing tasks are extremely simple. This hospital, in common with most similar British hospitals, has attempted to solve this dilemma by the recruitment of large numbers of high-level student nurses who, it is hoped, are prepared to accept the temporary lowering of their operational level because they are in training.

This throws new light on the problem of the 30 per cent to 50 per cent wastage of student nurses in this and other British hospitals. It has long been treated as a serious problem, and much effort has been expended on trying to solve it. In fact, it can be seen as an *essential* element in the social defence system. The need for responsible semi-skilled staff greatly exceeds the need for fully trained staff – by almost four to one in this hospital, for example. If large numbers of student nurses do *not* fail to finish their training, the nursing profession risks being flooded with trained staff for whom there are no jobs. The wastage is therefore an unconscious device to maintain the balance between staff of different levels of skill while all are at a high personal level. It is understandable that apparently determined efforts to reduce wastage have so far failed, except in one or two hospitals.

Avoidance of change. Change is inevitably to some extent an excursion into the unknown. It implies a commitment to future events that are not entirely predictable and to their consequences, and inevitably provokes doubt and anxiety. Any significant change within a social system implies changes in existing social relationship and in social structure. It follows that any significant social change implies a change in the operation of the social system as a defence system. While this change is proceeding – that is, while social defences are being restructured – anxiety is likely to be more open and intense.[28] Jaques (1955) has stressed that resistance to social change can be better understood if it is seen as the resistance of groups of people unconsciously clinging to existing institutions because changes threaten existing social defences against deep and intense anxieties.

It is understandable that the nursing service, whose tasks stimulate such primitive and intense anxieties, should anticipate change with unusually severe anxiety. In order to avoid this anxiety, the service tries to avoid change wherever possible – almost, one might say, at all costs – and tends to cling to the familiar even when the familiar has obviously ceased to be appropriate or relevant. Changes tend to be initiated only at the point of crisis. The presenting problem was a good example of this difficulty in initiating and carrying through change. Staff and student nurses had long felt that the methods in operation were unsatisfactory and had wanted to change them. They had, however, been unable to do so. The anxieties and uncertainties about possible changes and their consequences inhibited constructive and realistic planning and decision. At least the present difficulties were familiar and they had some ability to handle them. The problem was approaching the point of breakdown and the limits of the capacities of the people concerned when we were called in. Many other examples of this clinging to the inappropriate familiar could be observed. For example, changes in medical practice and the initiation of the National Health Service[29] have led to more rapid patient turnover, an increase in the proportion of acutely ill patients, a wider range of illness to be nursed in each ward, and greater variation in the workload of a ward from day to day. These changes all point to the need for increasing flexibility in the work organization of nurses in wards. In fact, no such increase in flexibility has taken place in this hospital. Indeed, the difficulty inherent in trying to deal with a fluctuating workload by the rather rigid system described above has tended to be handled by increased prescription and rigidity and by reiteration of the familiar. As far as one could gather, the greater the anxiety, the greater the need for such reassurance in rather compulsive repetition.

The changing demands on nurses described above necessitate a growing amount of increasingly technically skilled nursing care. This has not, however, led to any examination of the implicit policy that nursing can be carried out largely by semi-qualified student nurses.

COMMENTARY ON THE SOCIAL DEFENCE SYSTEM

The characteristic feature of the social defence system, as we have described it, is its orientation to helping the individual avoid the experience of anxiety, guilt, doubt and uncertainty. As far as possible, this is done by eliminating situations, events, tasks, activities and relationships that cause anxiety or, more correctly, evoke anxieties connected with primitive psychological remnants in the personality. Little attempt is made positively to help the individual confront the anxiety-evoking experiences and, by so doing, to develop her capacity to tolerate and deal more effectively with the anxiety. Basically, the potential anxieties in the nursing situation are felt to be too deep and dangerous for full confrontation, and to threaten personal disruption and social chaos. In fact, of course, the attempt to avoid such confrontation can never be completely successful. A compromise is inevitable between the implicit aims of the social

63

defence system and the demands of reality as expressed in the need to pursue the primary task.

It follows that the psychic defence mechanisms that have, over time, been built into the socially structured defence system of the nursing service are, in the main, those which by evasion give protection from the full experience of anxiety. These are derived from the most primitive psychic defence mechanisms. Those mechanisms are typical of the young infant's attempts to deal, mainly by evasion, with the severe anxieties aroused by the interplay of his own instincts that are intolerable at his immature age.[30]

Individuals vary in the extent to which they are able, as they grow older, to modify or abandon their early defence mechanisms and develop other methods of dealing with their anxieties. Notably, these other methods include the ability to confront the anxiety situations in their original or symbolic forms and to work them over, to approach and tolerate psychic and objective reality, to differentiate between them and to perform constructive and objectively successful activities in relation to them.[31] Every individual is at risk that objective or psychic events stimulating acute anxiety will lead to partial or complete abandonment of the more mature methods of dealing with anxiety and to regression to the more primitive methods of defence. In our opinion, the intense anxiety evoked by the nursing task has precipitated just such individual regression to primitive types of defence. These have been projected and given objective existence in the social structure and culture of the nursing service, with the result that anxiety is to some extent contained, but that true mastery of anxiety by deep working through and modification is seriously inhibited. Thus, it is to be expected that nurses will persistently experience a higher degree of anxiety than is justified by the objective situation alone. Consideration in more detail of how the socially structured defence system fails to support the individual in the struggle towards more effective mastery of anxiety may be approached from two different but related points of view.

I will first consider how far the present functioning of the nursing service gives rise to experiences that in themselves

reassure nurses or arouse anxiety. In fact, as a direct consequence of the social organization, many situations and incidents
develop that clearly arouse anxiety. On the other hand, the
social system frequently functions in such a way as to deprive
nurses of necessary reassurance and satisfactions. In other
words, the social defence system itself arouses a good deal of
secondary anxiety as well as failing to alleviate primary anxiety.
I shall illustrate these points with some typical examples.

Threat of crisis and operational breakdown. From the operational
point of view, the nursing service is cumbersome and inflexible.
It cannot easily adapt to short- or long-term changes in
conditions. For example, the task-list system and minutely
prescribed task-performance make it difficult to adjust
workloads when necessary by postponing or omitting less urgent
or important tasks. The total demands on a ward vary considerably and at short notice according to factors like types and
numbers of patients and operating days. The numbers and
categories of student nurses also vary considerably and at short
notice. Recurrent shortages of second-year or third-year nurses
occur while they spend six weeks in the school; sickness or leave
frequently reduce numbers. The work/staff ratio, therefore,
varies considerably and often suddenly. Since work cannot easily
be reduced, this generates considerable pressure, tension and
uncertainty among staff and students. Even when the work/staff
ratio is satisfactory, the threat of a sudden increase is always
present. The nurses seem to have a constant sense of impending
crisis. They are haunted by fear of failing to carry out their
duties adequately as pressure of work increases. Conversely,
they rarely experience the satisfaction and lessening of anxiety
that come from knowing they have the ability to carry out their
work realistically and efficiently.

The nursing service is organized in a way that makes it
difficult for one person, or even a close group of people, to
make a rapid and effective decision. Diffusion of responsibility
prevents adequate and specific concentration of authority for
making and implementing decisions. The organization of
working groups makes it difficult to achieve adequate concen-

tration of necessary knowledge. For example, the task-list system prevents the breakdown of a ward into units of a size that allows one person to be fully acquainted with what is going on in them and of a number that allows adequate communication between them and to the person responsible for co-ordinating them. In a ward, only the sister and the staff nurse are in a position to collect and co-ordinate knowledge. However, they must do this for a unit of such size and complexity that it is impossible to do it effectively. They are, inevitably, badly briefed. For example, we came across many cases where the sister did not remember how many nurses were on duty or what each was supposed to do, and had to have recourse to a written list. Such instances cannot be attributed primarily to individual inadequacy. Decisions tend to be made, therefore, by people who feel that they lack adequate knowledge of relevant and ascertainable facts. This leads to both anxiety and anger. To this anxiety is added the anxiety that decisions will not be taken in time, since decision-making is made so slow and cumbersome by the system of checking and counterchecking and by the obscurity surrounding the localization of responsibility.

Excessive movement of student nurses. The fact that a rise in work/ staff ratios can be met only within very narrow limits by a reduction in the workload means that it is often necessary to have staff reinforcements – usually, to move student nurses. The defence of rigid work organization thus appears as a contributory factor to the presenting problem of student allocation. The unduly frequent moves cause considerable distress and anxiety. Denial of the importance of relationships and feelings does not adequately protect the nurses, especially since the moves most directly affect student nurses, who have not yet fully developed these defences. Nurses grieve and mourn over broken relationships with patients and other nurses; they feel they are failing their patients. One nurse felt compelled to return to her previous ward to visit a patient who, she felt, had depended a great deal on her. The nurse feels strange in her new surroundings. She has to learn some new duties and make relationships with new patients and staff. She probably has to nurse types of illness she has never nursed before. Until she gets to know more about the new situation she suffers anxiety, uncertainties and doubts. Senior staff estimate that it takes a student two weeks to settle down in a new ward. We regard this as an underestimate. The suddenness of many moves increases the difficulty. It does not allow adequate time for preparing for parting and makes the parting more traumatic. Patients cannot be handed over properly to other nurses. Sudden transfers to a different ward allow little opportunity for psychological preparation for what is to come. Nurses tend to feel acutely deprived by this lack of preparation. As one girl said, 'If only I had known a bit sooner that I was going to the diabetic ward, I would have read up about diabetics and that would have helped a lot.' Janis (1958) has described how the effects of anticipated traumatic events can be alleviated if an advance opportunity is provided to work over the anxieties. He has described this as the 'work of worrying', a parallel concept to Freud's concept of the 'work of mournng' (Freud, 1917). The opportunity to work over the anticipated traumata of separation is, in the present circumstances, denied to nurses. This adds greatly to stress and anxiety.

This situation does indeed help to produce a defensive psychological detachment. Students protect themselves against the pain and anxiety of transfers, or the threat of transfers, by limiting their psychological involvement in any situation, with patients or other staff. This reduces their interest and sense of responsibility and fosters a 'don't care' attitude of which nurses and patients complain bitterly. Nurses feel anxious and guilty when they detect such feelings in themselves, and angry, hurt, and disappointed when they find them in others: 'Nobody cares how we are getting on, there is no team spirit, no one helps us.' The resulting detachment also reduces the possibility of satisfaction from work well done in a job one deeply cares about.

Underemployment of student nurses. Understandably, since workloads are so variable and it is difficult to adjust tasks, the nursing service tries to plan its establishments to meet peak rather than average loads. As a result, student nurses quite often have too little work. They hardly ever complain of overwork and a

67

number complained of not having enough work, although they still complained of stress. We observed obvious underemployment as we moved about the wards, despite the fact that student nurses are apt to make themselves look busy doing something and talk of having to look busy to avoid censure from the sister. Senior staff often seemed to feel it necessary to explain why their students were not busier, and would say they were 'having a slack day' or they 'had an extra nurse today'.

Student nurses are also chronically underemployed in terms of work level. A number of elements in the defence system contribute to this. Consider, for example, the assignment of duties to whole categories of student nurses. Since nurses find it so difficult to tolerate inefficiency and mistakes, the level of duties for each category is pitched low – that is, near to the expected level of the least competent nurse in the category. In addition, the policy that makes student nurses the effective nursing staff of the hospital condemns them to the repetitive performance of simple tasks to an extent far beyond that necessary for their training. The performance of simple tasks need not of itself imply that the student nurse's role is at a low level. The level depends also on how much opportunity is given for the use of discretion and judgement in the organization of the tasks – which, when, and how. It is theoretically possible to have a role in which a high level of discretion is required to organize tasks that are in themselves quite simple. In fact, the social defence system specifically minimizes the exercise of discretion and judgement in the student nurse's organization of her tasks, for example through the task-list system. This ultimately determines the underemployment of many student nurses who are capable of exercising a good deal of judgement and could quickly be trained to use it effectively in their work. Similar underemployment is obvious in senior staff connected, for example, with the practice of delegating upwards.

Underemployment of this kind stimulates anxiety and guilt, which are particularly acute when underemployment implies failing to use one's capacities fully in the service of other people in need. Nurses find the limitations on their performance very frustrating. They often experience a painful sense of failure when they have faithfully performed their prescribed tasks, and express guilt and concern about incidents in which they have carried out instructions to the letter but, in so doing, have practised what they consider to be bad nursing. For example, a nurse had been told to give a patient who had been sleeping badly a sleeping draught at a certain time. In the interval he had fallen into a deep natural sleep. Obeying her orders, she woke him up to give him the medicine. Her common sense and judgement told her to leave him asleep and she felt very guilty that she had disturbed him. One frequently hears nurses complain that they 'have' to waken patients early in the morning to have their faces washed when they feel that the patients would benefit more by being left asleep. Patients also make strong complaints, but 'all faces must be washed' before the consultant medical staff arrive in the wards in the morning. The nurses feel they are being forced to abandon common-sense principles of good nursing, and they resent it.

Jaques (1956) has discussed the use of discretion and has come to the conclusion that the level of responsibility experienced in a job is related solely to the exercise of discretion and not to carrying out the prescribed elements. Following that statement, we may say that the level of responsibility in the nurse's job is minimized by the attempt to eliminate the use of discretion. Many student nurses complain bitterly that, while ostensibly in a very responsible job, they have less responsibility than they had as senior schoolgirls. They feel insulted – indeed, almost assaulted – by being deprived of the opportunity to be more responsible. They feel, and are, devalued by the social system. They are intuitively aware that the further development of their capacity for responsibility is being inhibited by the work and training situation, and they greatly resent this. The bitterness of the experience is intensified because they are constantly being exhorted to behave responsibly, which, in the ordinary usage of the word in a work situation, they can hardly do. In fact, we came to the conclusion that senior staff tend to use the word 'responsibility' differently from ordinary usage. For them, a 'responsible' nurse is one who carries out prescriptions to the letter. There is an essential conflict between staff and students that greatly adds to stress and bitterness on both sides. Jaques (1956) has stated that workers in industry cannot rest content until they have reached a level of work that deploys to the full their capacity for discretionary responsibility. Student nurses – who are, in effect, 'workers' in the hospital for most of their time – are certainly not content.

Deprivation of personal satisfactions. The nursing service seems to provide unusually little in the way of direct satisfaction for staff and students. Although the dictum 'nursing should be a vocation' implies that nurses should not expect ordinary job satisfaction, its absence adds to stress. Mention has already been made of a number of ways in which nurses are deprived of positive satisfactions potentially existent in the profession, for example the satisfaction and reassurance that come from confidence in nursing skill. Satisfaction is also reduced by the attempt to evade anxiety by splitting up the nurse–patient relationship and converting patients who need nursing into tasks that must be performed. Although the nursing *service* has considerable success in nursing patients, the individual nurse has little direct experience of success. Success and satisfaction are dissipated in much the same way as the anxiety. The nurse misses the reassurance of seeing a patient get better in a way she can easily connect with her own efforts. The nurse's longing for this kind of experience is shown in the excitement and pleasure felt by a nurse who is chosen to 'special' a patient, that is, to give special individual care to a very ill patient in a crisis situation. The gratitude of patients, an important reward for nurses, is also dissipated. Patients are grateful to the hospital or to 'the nurses' for their treatment and recovery, but they cannot easily express gratitude in any direct way to individual nurses. There are too many and they are too mobile. The poignancy of the situation is increased by the expressed aims of nursing at the present time – to nurse the whole patient as a person. The nurse is instructed to do that, it is usually what she wants to do, but the functioning of the nursing service makes it impossible.

Sisters, too, are deprived of potential satisfactions in their roles. Many of them would like closer contact with patients and more opportunity to use their nursing skills directly. Much of their time is spent in initiating and training student nurses who come to their wards. The excessive movement of students means that sisters are frequently deprived of the return on that training time and the reward of seeing the nurse develop under their supervision. The reward of their work, like the nurse's, is dissipated and impersonal.

The nursing service inhibits in a number of ways the realization of satisfactions in relationships with colleagues. For example, the traditional relationship between staff and students is such that students are singled out by staff almost solely for reprimand or criticism. Good work is taken for granted and little praise given. Students complain that no one notices when they work well, when they stay late on duty, or when they do some extra task for a patient's comfort. Work-teams are notably impermanent. Even three-monthly moves of student nurses would make it difficult to weld together a strong, cohesive work-team. The more frequent moves, and the threats of moves, make it almost impossible. In such circumstances it is difficult to build a team that functions effectively on the basis of real knowledge of the strengths and weaknesses of each member, her needs as well as her contribution, and adapts to the way of working and type of relationship each person prefers. Nurses feel hurt and resentful about the lack of importance attached to their personal contribution to the work, and the work itself is less satisfying when it must be done not only in accordance with the task-list system but also with an informal, but rigid, organization. A nurse misses the satisfaction of investing her own personality thoroughly in her work and making a highly personal contribution. The 'depersonalization' used as a defence makes matters worse. The implied disregard of her own needs and capacities is distressing to the nurse; she feels she does not matter and no one cares what happens to her. This is particularly distressing when she is in a situation fraught with risks and difficulty and knows that sooner or later she will have great need of help and support.

Such support for the individual is notably lacking throughout the whole nursing service within working relationships. Compensation is sought in intense relationships with other nurses off-duty.[32] Working groups are characterized by great isolation of their members. Nurses frequently do not know what other members of their team are doing or even what their formal duties are; indeed, they often do not know whether other members of their team are on duty or not. They pursue their own tasks with minimal regard to colleagues. This leads to frequent difficulties between nurses. For example, one nurse, in carrying out her own tasks correctly by the prescription, may undo work done by another also carrying out her tasks correctly by the prescription, because they do not plan their work together and co-ordinate it. Bad feeling usually follows. One nurse may be extremely busy while another has not enough to do. Sharing out of work is rare. Nurses complain bitterly about this situation. They say 'there is no team spirit, no one helps you, no one cares'. They feel guilty about not helping and angry about not being helped. They feel deprived by the lack of close, responsible, friendly relations with colleagues. The training system, orientated as it is to information-giving, also deprives the student nurse of support and help. She feels driven to acquire knowledge and pass examinations, to become 'a good nurse', while at the same time she feels few people show real concern for her personal development and her future.

The lack of personal support and help is particularly painful for the student nurse as she watches the care and attention given to patients. It is our impression that a significant number of nurses enter the profession under a certain confusion about their future roles and functions. They perceive the hospital as an organization particularly well equipped to deal with dependency needs, kind and supportive, and they expect to have the privilege of being very dependent themselves. However, because of the categorization they find that they are denied the privilege except on very rare occasions, notably when they go sick themselves and are nursed in the hospital.

I go on now to consider the second general approach to the failure of the social defences to alleviate anxiety. This arises from the direct impact of the social defence system on the individual, regardless of specific experiences – that is to say, from the more directly psychological interaction between the social defence system and the individual nurse.

Although, following Jaques, I have used the term 'social defence system' as a construct to describe certain features of the nursing service as a continuing social institution, I wish to make it clear that I do not imply that the nursing service *as an institution* operates the defences. Defences are, and can be, operated only by individuals. Their behaviour is the link between their psychic defences and the institution. Membership necessitates an adequate degree of matching between individual and social defence systems. I will not attempt to define the degree, but state simply that if the discrepancy between social and individual defence systems is too great, some breakdown in the individual's relation with the institution is inevitable. The form of breakdown varies, but in our society it commonly takes the form of a temporary or permanent break in the individual's membership. For example, if the individual continues to use his own defences and follows his own idiosyncratic behaviour patterns, he may become intolerable to other members of the institution who are more adapted to the social defence system. They may then reject him. If he tries to behave in a way consistent with the social defence system rather than his individual defences, his anxiety will increase and he may find it impossible to continue his membership. Theoretically, matching between social and individual defences can be achieved by a restructuring of the social defence system to match the individual, by a restructuring of the individual defence system to match the social, or by a combination of the two. The processes by which an adequate degree of matching is achieved are too complicated to describe here in detail. It must suffice to say that they depend heavily on repeated projection of the psychic defence system into the social defence system and repeated introjection of the social defence system into the psychic defence system. This allows continuous testing of match and fit as the individual experiences his own and other people's reactions.[33]

The social defence system of the nursing service has been described as a historical development through collusive interaction between individuals to project and reify relevant elements of their psychic defence systems. However, from the viewpoint of the new entrant to the nursing service, the social defence system at the time of entry is a datum, an aspect of external reality to which she must react and adapt. Fenichel makes a similar point (1946). He states that social institutions arise through the efforts of human beings to satisfy their needs, but that social institutions then become external realities comparatively independent of individuals which affect the structure of the individual. The student nurse is faced with a particularly difficult task in adapting to the nursing service and developing an adequate match between the social defence system and her psychic defence system. It will be clear from what I have said above that the nursing service is very resistant to change, especially change in the functioning of its defence system. For the student nurse, this means that the social defence system is to an unusual extent immutable. In the process of matching between the psychic and social defence systems, the emphasis is heavily on the modification of the individual's psychic defences. This means in practice that she must incorporate and operate the social defence system more or less as she finds it, restructuring her psychic defences as necessary to match it.

An earlier section described how the social defence system of the hospital was built of primitive psychic defences, those characteristic of the earliest phases of infancy. It follows that student nurses, by becoming members of the nursing service, are required to incorporate and use primitive psychic defences, at least in those areas of their life-space which directly concern their work. The use of such defences has certain intrapsychic consequences. These are consistent with the social phenomena already referred to in other contexts in this paper. I will describe them briefly to complete the account. These defences are orientated to the violent, terrifying situations of infancy, and rely heavily on violent splitting which dissipates the anxiety. They avoid the experience of anxiety and effectively prevent the individual from confronting it. Thus, the individual cannot bring the content of the phantasy anxiety situations into effective contact with reality. Unrealistic or pathological anxiety cannot be differentiated from realistic anxiety arising from real dangers. Therefore, anxiety tends to remain permanently at a level determined more by the phantasies than by the reality. The forced introjection of the hospital defence system, therefore, perpetuates in the individual a considerable degree of pathological anxiety.

The enforced introjection and use of such defences also interferes with the capacity for symbol formation (see also p. 49 above). The defences inhibit the capacity for creative, symbolic thought, for abstract thought, and for conceptualization. They inhibit the full development of the individual's understanding, knowledge and skills that enable reality to be handled effectively and pathological anxiety mastered. Thus the individual feels helpless in the face of new or strange tasks or problems. The development of such capacities presupposes considerable psychic integration, which the social defence system inhibits. It also inhibits self-knowledge and understanding, and with them realistic assessment of performance. The deficient reality sense that follows from the defence system also interferes with judgement and provokes mistakes. The individual is confronted with them when it is too late and a sense of failure, increased self-distrust and anxiety ensue. For example, mistakes, guilt and anxiety arise from following out the prescriptions rather than applying the principles of good nursing. This situation particularly affects belief and trust in positive impulses and their effectiveness to control and modify aggression. Anxiety about positive aspects of the personality is very marked in nurses: for example fear of doing the wrong thing, expectation of mistakes, fear of not being truly responsible. The social defences prevent the individual from realizing to the full her capacity for concern, compassion and sympathy, and for action based on these feelings which would strengthen her belief in the good aspects of herself and her capacity to use them. The defence system strikes directly, therefore, at the roots of sublimatory activities in which infantile anxieties are reworked in symbolic form and modified.

In general, one may say that forced introjection of the defence system prevents the personal defensive maturation that alone allows for the modification of the remnants of infantile anxiety and diminishes the extent to which early anxieties may be re-evoked and projected into current real situations. Indeed, in many cases it forces the individual to regress to a maturational level below that which she had achieved before she entered the hospital. In this, the nursing service fails its individual members desperately. It seems clear that a major motivational factor in the choice of nursing as a career is the wish to have the opportunity to develop the capacity for sublimatory activities in the nursing of the sick, and through that to achieve better mastery of infantile anxiety situations, modification of pathological anxiety, and personal maturation.

It may be interesting, in view of this, to add one further comment on wastage. It seems more serious than number alone suggests. It appears to be the more mature students who find the conflict between their own and the hospital defence system most acute and are most likely to give up training. Although the research objectives did not permit us to collect statistics, it is our distinct impression that among the students who do not complete training are a significant number of the better students: those who are personally most mature and most capable of intellectual, professional and personal development with appropriate training. Nurses often talked of students who had left as 'very good nurses'. No one could understand why they had not wanted to finish their training. We had the opportunity to discuss the matter with some students who were seriously considering leaving. Many said they still wanted to nurse and found it difficult to formulate why they wanted to leave. They suffered from a vague sense of dissatisfaction with their training and the work they were doing and a sense of hopelessness about the future. The general content of the interviews left little doubt that they were distressed about the inhibition of their personal development. There is also a striking difference in the personalities of groups of students at different stages of training. We do not attribute all of this difference to the effects of training. Some of the differences appear to arise from self-selection of students who give up training. If we are correct in this impression, the social defence system impoverishes the nursing service for the future, since it tends to drive away those potential senior staff whose contribution to the development of nursing theory and practice would be greatest. Thus the wheel turns full circle and the difficulty in changing the system is reinforced. It is the tragedy of the system that its inadequacies drive away the very people who might remedy them.

SUMMARY AND CONCLUDING COMMENTS

This paper has presented some data from a study of the nursing service of a general teaching hospital. Its specific purpose was to consider and, if possible, account for the high level of stress and anxiety chronic among nurses. In following through the data, it was suggested that the nature of the nurse's task, in spite of its obvious difficulties, was not enough to account for the level of anxiety and stress. Consequently, an attempt was made to understand and illustrate the nature of the methods the nursing service provided for the alleviation of anxiety – its social defence system – and to consider in what respects it failed to function adequately. The conclusion was that the social defence system represented the institutionalization of very primitive psychic defence mechanisms, a main characteristic of which is that they facilitate the evasion of anxiety but contribute little to its true modification and reduction.

In concluding, I wish to touch briefly on a few points that space does not permit me to elaborate. I have considered only incidentally the effect of the defence system on the efficiency of task-performance, apart from stating that it does permit the continuing performance of the primary task of the service. It will have been apparent, however, that the nursing service carries out its task inefficiently in many respects – for example it keeps the staff/patient ratio unduly high, leads to a significant amount of bad nursing practice and excessive staff turnover, and fails to train students adequately for their real future roles. There are many other examples. Further, the high level of anxiety in nurses adds to the stress of illness and hospitalization for patients and has adverse effects on such factors as recovery rates. Revans's investigation (Revans, 1959) connected recovery rates of patients quite directly with the morale of nursing staff. Thus the social structure of the nursing service is defective not only as a means of handling anxiety, but also as a method of organizing its tasks. These two aspects cannot be regarded as separate. The inefficiency is an inevitable consequence of the chosen defence system.

This leads me to put forward the proposition that the success and viability of a social institution are intimately connected with the techniques it uses to contain anxiety. Analogous hypotheses about the individual have long been widely accepted. Freud put forward such ideas increasingly as his work developed (1926). The work of Melanie Klein and her colleagues has given a central position to anxiety and the defences in personality development and ego-functioning (1948b). I put forward a second proposition, which is linked with the first: namely, that an understanding of this aspect of the functioning of a social institution is an important diagnostic and therapeutic tool in facilitating social change. Bion (1955) and Jaques (1955) stress the importance of understanding these phenomena and relate difficulties in achieving social change to difficulty in tolerating the anxieties that are released as social defences are restructured. This appears to be closely connected with the experiences of people, including many social scientists, who have tried to initiate or facilitate social change. Recommendations or plans for change that seem highly appropriate from a rational point of view are ignored, or do not work in practice. One difficulty seems to be that they do not sufficiently take into account the common anxieties and the social defences in the institution concerned, nor provide for the therapeutic handling of the situation as change takes place. Jaques (1955) states that 'effective social change is likely to require analysis of the common anxieties and unconscious collusions underlying the social defences determining phantasy social relationships.'

The nursing service presents these difficulties to a high degree, since the anxieties are already very acute and the defence system both primitive and ineffectual. Efforts to initiate serious change were often met with acute anxiety and hostility, which conveyed the idea that the people concerned felt very threatened, the threat being of nothing less than social chaos and individual breakdown. To give up known ways of behaviour and embark on the unknown were felt to be intolerable. In general, it may be postulated that resistance to social change is likely to be greatest in institutions whose social defence systems are dominated by primitive psychic defence mechanisms, those which have been collectively described by Melanie Klein as the paranoid-schizoid defences (Klein, 1952a, 1959). One may compare this sociotherapeutic experience with the common experience in psychoanalytic therapy, that the most difficult work is with patients whose defences are mainly of this kind, or in phases of the analysis when such defences predominate.

Some therapeutic results were achieved in the hospital, notably in relation to the presenting symptom. A planned set of courses has been prepared for student nurses, which jointly ensures that the student nurses have adequate training and that the hospital is adequately staffed. Interestingly, it was in preparing these courses that objective data were calculated for the first time about discrepancies between training and staffing needs. For example, to give adequate gynaecological training the gynaecological wards would have to carry four times too many staff; to keep the operating theatres staffed, the nurses would have to have one and a half times too much theatre experience for training. Before this time the existence of such discrepancies was known, but no one had collected reliable statistical data (a simple matter) and no realistic plans had been made to deal with them. To prevent emergencies from interfering with the implementation of the planned courses, a reserve pool of nurses was created whose special duty was to be mobile and deal with them. A number of other similar changes were instituted to solve other problems that emerged in the course of the investigation.[34] The common features of the changes, however, were that they involved minimal disturbance of the existing defence system. Indeed, it would be more correct to say that they involved reinforcing and strengthening the existing type of defence. Proposals were made for more far-reaching change, involving a restructuring of the social defence system. For example, one suggestion was that a limited experiment be done in ward organization, eliminating the task-list system and substituting some form of patient assignment.

However, although the senior staff discussed such proposals with courage and seriousness, they did not feel able to proceed with the plans. This happened despite our clearly expressed views that unless there were some fairly radical changes in the system, the problems of the nursing service might well become extremely serious. The decision seemed to us quite comprehensible, however, in view of the anxiety and the defence system. These would have made the therapeutic task of accomplishing change very difficult for both the nursing service and the therapist.

The full seriousness of the situation is not perhaps clear without considering this hospital in the context of the general nursing services in the country as a whole. The description of the hospital makes it seem a somewhat serious example of social pathology, but within the context of other general hospital nurse-training schools it is fairly typical. Nothing in our general experience of hospitals and nursing leads us to believe otherwise (Skellern, 1953; Sofer, 1955; Wilson, 1950). There are differences in detail, but the main features of the structure and culture are common to British hospitals of this type and are carried in the general culture and ethic of the nursing profession. The hospital studied has, in fact, high status. It is accepted as one of the better hospitals of its type.

The nursing services in general have shown a similar resistance to change in the face of great changes in the demands made on them. There can be few professions that have been more studied than nursing, or institutions more studied than hospitals. Nurses have played an active part in initiating and carrying out these studies. Many nurses have an acute and painful awareness that their profession is in a serious state. They eagerly seek solutions, and there have been many changes in the expressed aims and policy of the profession. There have also been many changes in the peripheral areas of nursing – that is to say, those which do not impinge very directly or seriously on the essential features of the social defence system. Against that background, one is astonished to find how little basic and dynamic change has taken place. Nurses have tended to receive reports and recommendations with a sense of outrage and to react to them by intensifying current attitudes and reinforcing existing practice.

An example of a general nursing problem that threatens crisis is the recruitment of nurses. Changes in medical practice have increased the number of highly technical nursing tasks. Consequently, the level of intelligence and competence necessary for a fully trained and efficient nurse is rising. The National Health Service has improved the hospital service and made it necessary to have more nurses. On the other hand, professional opportunities for women are expanding rapidly and the other professions are generally more rewarding than nursing in terms of the opportunity to develop and exercise personal and professional capacities as well as in financial terms. The increasing demand for high-level student nurses is therefore meeting increasing competition from other sources. In fact, recruiting standards are being forced down in order to keep up numbers. This is no real solution, for too many of the recruits will have difficulty in passing the examinations and be unable to deal with the level of the work. Many of them, on the other hand, would make excellent practical nurses on simpler nursing duties. So far, no successful attempt has been made in the general hospitals to deal with this problem, for example, by splitting the role of nurse into different levels with different training and different professional destinations.

It is unfortunately true of the paranoid-schizoid defence systems that they prevent true insight into the nature of problems and realistic appreciation of their seriousness. Thus, only too often, no action can be taken until a crisis is very near or has actually occurred. This is the eventuality we fear in the British general hospital nursing services. Even if there is no acute crisis, there is undoubtedly a chronic state of reduced effectiveness, which in itself is serious enough.

NOTES

1. This study is one of a number of projects that the Tavistock Institute of Human Relations and associated workers have undertaken in recent years in general and mental hospitals, and with nurses in other settings (Menzies, 1951; Skellern, 1953; and Wilson, 1950). Miss O. V.

Bridgeman, BA, (now Mrs Golding) assisted me in this study. I greatly appreciate her help in this field work and in the analysis of the data.

2. I wish to express my appreciation of the research opportunities provided by the hospital. I am grateful to many members of the medical and lay staff who gave us freely of their time and ideas. I am especially grateful to the nursing staff and students. They admitted us generously into close contact with their work, their satisfactions and their difficulties, although this sometimes involved disclosing painful professional and personal matters. Senior nursing staff spent many hours with me studying data and their interpretation, so that together we might formulate conclusions and plans for action. For them, this was a difficult and distressing process which required considerable courage. It challenged their personal and professional ethics, often led to their feeling personally and professionally criticized, and seemed to point to directions of development that they found impossible to follow. I appreciate greatly their co-operation in this difficult task and am grateful for the insights they helped to develop. Finally, I am indebted to the hospital for permission to publish the research material in this paper.

3. The nursing body that then controlled nurse training.

4. A sample check of actual duration showed that 30 per cent of student moves took place less than three weeks after the previous move and 44 per cent less than seven weeks.

5. It is a feature of a therapeutic study of this kind that much of the most significant research material emerges in its later stages, when the emphasis of the work shifts from diagnosis to therapy. Presentation and interpretation of data, and work done on resistances to their acceptance, facilitate the growth of insight into the nature of the problem. This extends the range of information seen to be relevant to its solution, and helps overcome personal resistances to the disclosure of information. An impressive feature of the study reported here was the way in which, after a spell of working on the data, the senior nursing staff themselves were able to produce and execute plans directed towards dealing with their problems.

6. There is much evidence from other fields that such phenomena express a disturbed relation with the work situation and are connected with a high level of tension. See, for example, Hill and Trist (1953).

7. My colleague, G. F. Hutton, in analysing the data from another hospital study (as yet unpublished) drew attention to the descent of modern hospitals from orders of nursing sisters. These early hospitals were entirely administered by the nurses. Doctors and priests were necessary and

important visitors, but visitors only. They met special needs of patients but had no administrative responsibility. The tradition of what Hutton called 'nurse-directed communities' remains strong, despite the complexity of organization of modern hospitals and the number and diversity of patient-centred staff.

8. Throughout this paper I follow the convention of using fantasy to mean conscious fantasy, and phantasy to mean unconscious phantasy.

9. In my description of infantile psychic life I follow the work of Freud, particularly as developed and elaborated by Melanie Klein. A brief but comprehensive summary of her views may be found in her papers 'Some theoretical conclusions regarding the emotional life of the infant' (Klein, 1952b) and 'Our adult world and its roots in infancy' (Klein, 1959).

10. For a further description of the process of building the inner world, see Klein (1952b, 1959).

11. For a description of some patients' concepts of illness, see Janis (1958), where there is also an account of how working through the fantasy may relieve the anxiety.

12. Klein (1948b) stresses the importance of anxiety in leading to the development of symbol formation and sublimation.

13. Segal (1957) uses the terms symbolic representation and symbolic equation. In developing this distinction, she stresses the acute anxieties experienced by patients in whom the symbol does not merely represent the phantasy object but is equated with it. She illustrates from the material of two patients for both of whom a violin was a phallic symbol. For one patient the violin *represented* the phallus and violin-playing was an important sublimation through which he could master anxiety. For the other more deeply disturbed patient, the violin was *felt to be* the phallus and he had had to stop playing because he could not touch a violin in public.

14. Bion (1955) has put forward a similar concept in distinguishing between the sophisticated or work group concerned with a realistic task and the basic-assumption group dominated by primitive psychological phenomena; the two 'groups' being simultaneously operative aspects of the same aggregation of people.

15. The importance of anxiety and defences against it have been much stressed in psychoanalytical theories of personality development. Freud's earliest works show his interest and he develops his theory in later work (Freud, 1893–5, 1926). The central developmental role of anxiety and

defences has, more recently, been much stressed by Melanie Klein and her colleagues (Klein, 1948b, 1952b).

16. For a fuller discussion of the primary task and related factors, see Rice (1958).

17. The different social systems that have developed under long-wall coal-mining conditions, using the same basic technology, are a good example of how the same primary task may be performed differently using the same technology when social and psychological conditions are different. They have been discussed by Trist and Bamforth (1951).

18. Jaques (1955) has described and illustrated the operation of such socially structured defence mechanisms in an industrial organization. The term is his.

19. In practice it is not possible to carry out these prescriptions literally, since a whole category of nurses may temporarily be absent from practical duties on formal instruction in the nursing school or on leave.

20. See below, pp. 56–8, for an account of how these roles and relationships arise.

21. Bion (1955), in describing the behaviour of groups where the need to be dependent is dominant, has commented on the group's need for what he calls a 'bible'. It is not perhaps surprising to find that in the hospital, whose primary task is to meet the dependency needs of patients, there should be a marked need for just such definitive prescription of behaviour.

22. This has long been a familiar complaint in British hospitals and emerged as a central finding in a number of nursing studies.

23. A staff nurse is a fully qualified nurse who is the sister's deputy.

24. There are usually three different lists of tasks in a ward, numbered 1, 2 and 3, and a student nurse may well be Number 1 in the morning and Number 2 in the afternoon, e.g. if the Number 2 of the morning goes off duty in the afternoon.

25. The nurses third and fourth in seniority in administration.

26. Arrangements are almost complete for the restructuring of the task along such lines.

27. This is connected also with the attempt to eliminate decision-making as far as possible. If there are no decisions to be made, the worker simply needs to *know* what to do and how to do it.

28. This is a familiar experience while the individual's defences are being restructured in the course of psychoanalytic therapy.

29. These trends have continued and intensified.

30. I will enumerate briefly here some of the most important of these defences. In doing so, I follow the work of Freud as developed by Melanie Klein (1952b, 1959). The infant makes much use of splitting and projection, denial, idealization, and rigid, omnipotent control of himself and others. These defences are, at first, massive and violent. Later, as the infant becomes more able to tolerate his anxiety, the same defences continue to be used but are less violent. They begin to appear also in what are perhaps more familiar forms, e.g. as repression, obsessional rituals, and repetition of the familiar.

31. Or, expressed otherwise, the capacity to undertake sublimatory activities.

32. By tradition a nurse finds her closest nurse friends in her 'set', i.e. the group with which she started training. Friendship between nurses in different sets is culturally unacceptable, but nurses in the same set spend little working time together except in their short spells in formal instruction.

33. Paula Heimann (1952) gives a description of these important processes, through which both psychic and external reality are modified.

34. For example the revised training programme for fourth-year students; see p. 60 above.

Responses to 'The functioning of social systems'

Defence mechanisms in nursing: a review by a Registered Mental Nurse*

T HIS IS a very interesting article, it says important things and gives an unusual slant on nursing, but I do not agree with it. I also found it confusing and difficult to read.

WHAT THE ARTICLE IS ABOUT

A general hospital called in the author to help work out a new duty rota for student nurses. The existing system of work was studied and changes in the rota were made. None of these – the system, the study or the changes – are described in full, but a theory is set out to explain the findings. The only data given by which to judge the theory are those chosen to support it.

THE THEORY

The theory is that of Miss Melanie Klein, which has attracted a considerable following, but is hotly debated even among psychoanalysts.

As I understand it the theory is as follows. Infants have strong feelings which give rise to fantasies about other people and themselves. They fear the strength of these feelings and anxiety is generated which is controlled in a primitive way by crediting others with the dangerous feeling (projection), or in a more

---

* This review was published in *Nursing Times*, 2 September 1960 and was preceded by the following remarks: 'This is a review of an article which appeared recently in *Human Relations*, the journal of the Tavistock Institute of Human Relations. The article, which deserves to be widely read by senior members of the nursing profession, is a devastating criticism of the nursing service of a general hospital as seen by a psychoanalyst.'

mature way by facing the fear and substituting an activity which uses up the emotional energy in a socially and personally acceptable way (sublimation).

Nurses need to sublimate emotions of both love and hate, but they deal with situations reminiscent of those which evoke primitive anxiety; therefore, says Miss Menzies, nursing may not only activate primitive anxiety but primitive defences also.

Shared anxiety leads to similar ways of dealing with it. These ways become traditional. In nursing, traditional defences are of a primitive type with which new nurses have to come to terms if they are to succeed in training.

THE DEFENCES

To experience the full weight of patients' anxieties and to carry responsibility for them would arouse anxiety, so the hospital tries to avoid this in three main ways: by preventing nurses becoming too intimate with any one patient, by restricting both nurses' and patients' individuality, and by avoiding responsibility.

Splitting up the nurse–patient relationship is achieved by task-assignment and frequent moving of nurses. Patients' individuality is minimized by referring to them by bed numbers, by procedures such as bed-making being performed in a uniform way, by carrying out orders blindly and contrary to common sense (for example, waking a patient to give a sedative). Nurses' individuality is minimized by uniforms, by putting nurses into grades and treating all in the same grade alike, by ignoring nurses' feelings, and by the failure to provide personal counselling for them.

Making decisions arouses painful conflict, so responsibility is avoided by checking and counterchecking of orders, by displacement of responsibility upwards (passing the buck), by passing blame downwards (scapegoating), and by lack of definition of responsibilities, particularly in the higher grades.

Giving responsibility involves trusting people and accepting their individuality. Nurses are not given responsibility equal to their potential ability. They are not allowed to arrange their own work, but carry out their task-lists like a ritual. Praise is withheld.

In the hospital this kind of defence fails to alleviate or control anxiety because crises cannot be dealt with efficiently, staff movement is cumbersome, too many nurses are employed and for much of the time are doing no useful work. Personal satisfaction is not achieved.

Anxiety can be overcome only by facing it realistically, but the system prevents this. Ritual performance of tasks takes the place of acting on principle. Evidence suggests that it is the more mature staff who leave; thus the system is self-perpetuating.

Miss Menzies applies the theory not only to the hospital but to nursing as a whole. Weaknesses in nursing organization have frequently been pointed out, but remedies have been rejected with a sense of outrage and no radical changes have been made, because they do not deal with anxiety in a therapeutic way.

CRITICISM

Although I am not trying to excuse the silly things Miss Menzies has shown up, and although I agree with a good deal of what she says about neurotic anxiety underlying individual behaviour, I cannot accept her main theory. If it were true, then periods of greatest carnage would lead to breakdown in nursing services because of inflexibility and inefficiency. The contrary is the case. When death and disaster are greatest, as in war, nursing is most adaptable and successful.

There are several weaknesses in the theory.

Miss Menzies says that in nursing it is easy to exaggerate the importance of the primary task – that is, the care of the sick – and that *above all* defence against anxiety is crucial in deciding how nursing is organized. Miss Menzies derides standardization of methods and equipment, and explains the use of task-assignment as a defence technique to prevent the impact of a patient's anxiety on a nurse from becoming too great. Now these devices are ordinary ways of getting jobs done efficiently in the least possible time. Standardization of method is to a ward what habit is to an individual – an economy of effort. Keeping equipment in the same place is like being tidy – everyone knows where to find things And job-assignment goes on because it happens to be the quickest and easiest way of getting work done.

Unlike most professional workers, nurses do not control their own workload. Doctors arrange admissions, administrators speed up turnover and the workload rises relentlessly. No – it is not anxiety which determines the method of work, but the amount of work which creates the method and rouses normal anxiety.

FALSE ANALOGY

The second point in which the theory fails is in argument by analogy. Analogies are often picturesque but not accurate. They. can be used to make a point but not to develop a theory. Miss Menzies takes a theory worked out with individuals and spreads it over the pattern of ward work, the administration of the hospital and British nursing as a whole. I do not believe it is valid except as it applies to individuals.

The third weakness is in the choice of a frame of reference. In making a study, facts should be gathered in a neutral way and a theory should conform to the facts. Miss Menzies reverses this procedure. She calls the study a case-history; data were *'collected within a sociotherapeutic relationship'*; diagnosis and therapy are referred to throughout. Since the frame of reference is one used for pathological states, it is not surprising that the result is a diagnosis of pathology.

A further weakness in the article is the presentation. The study is not described but we are told that seventy nurses, a 10 per cent sample, were interviewed. We are not told of any precautions to ensure that the sample was a random one, nor do we know how many showed the kind of anxiety described. As a rule great pains are taken to make sure that the staff understand and are not threatened by the study itself. This natural worry is not mentioned at all, nor what was done to avoid it.

Since I cannot accept Miss Menzies's theory, it is up to me to state my own from the data given.

DISCOVERING THE OBVIOUS

When the facts are sifted from the theory, a simple explanation suggests itself.

The hospital described had been incompetently run for some time. The lack of responsible leadership and the practice of blaming others for the faults of management had led to extensive scapegoating and passing the buck. Poor administration made it difficult to carry out the primary task of caring for the sick. The staff were worried about this. Those who had a pride in their work, who could not stand the muddle and the unhappy atmosphere, and who were able to do so, left. The increased turnover of senior staff brought to administrative posts junior and inexperienced people who had no one competent to guide them. Instead of looking into the efficiency of matron's office, a psychoanalyst was called in who worked within a sociother-

---

The following comments were printed by Nursing Times *with this review:*

Nurses are among our best allies. They have grasped more thoroughly than any other professional group the importance of extended training in mental health principles. This might be expected of a profession who, by and large, are even more closely in touch with patients and their feelings than are doctors. I hesitate to give any advice on their training because it has become so obvious that they know where they are going and that nursing superintendents, nurse tutors and professors of nursing will demand from all the disciplines that can provide it the kind of instruction which they feel they need. It is a heart-warming experience for a psychiatrist to join in a discussion with a group of nurses. Their enthusiasm and their ready insight into the problems of patients suggests that they are ready to be leaders and teachers in the field of mental health. In the education of the public and in extending mental health activities in the field of public health, the public health nurse has a great task to perform. It is up to those of us who can to provide the opportunities for theoretical and practical training which will do justice to this dynamic spirit.

Professor T. Ferguson Rodger, Professor of Psychological Medicine, Glasgow, speaking at the annual meeting of the World Federation for Mental Health, Edinburgh, August 1960

---

apeutic relationship – in itself a stressful situation for the staff.

My solution for the difficulties of the hospital would be to appoint a matron of known competence whom the nurses knew and trusted, who could restore their self-confidence by re-establishing order in the nursing service.

RMN

Letter from Isabel Menzies Lyth to
Nursing Times *

ADAM – I wish to comment on one section of
your review, 'Defence mechanisms in nursing'
(2 September). In the final section, your
reviewer puts forward her own 'simple explanation' of the facts described in my paper 'The functioning of
social systems as a defence against anxiety'. In this section she
writes: 'The hospital described had been incompetently run for
some time.' There were certainly a number of ways in which
the nursing service was not functioning effectively. I give
examples in my paper. It was the senior nursing staff's own
awareness of this fact and their eagerness to improve matters
which led them to request the professional help of a social
science organization, the Tavistock Institute of Human
Relations. One could not subject any social organization to
such detailed scrutiny without finding some ways in which its
functioning is ineffective. However, to conclude that the hospital
was incompetently run and to attribute the responsibility for this
to a few individuals is, to say the least, stretching the evidence.
Failure to reach 100 per cent effectiveness does not constitute
incompetence.

Your reviewer also seems to me to imply that the hospital
differs in some significant respect from other hospitals. With
that I cannot agree. My paper states:

> The full seriousness of the situation is not perhaps clear
> without considering this hospital in the context of the general
> nursing services in the country as a whole ... within the

context of other general hospital nurse-training schools it is fairly typical . . . The hospital studied has, in fact, high status.

I would like to elaborate this statement. The data which I gave in my paper can be matched, point by point, with data from other hospitals which show the widespread existence of similar phenomena. Such data are quoted in the reports of many other hospital investigations, to some of which I referred in my paper. They are frequently described in medical and nursing journals, in the public press and elsewhere. The high wastage of student nurses, for example, is unfortunately a problem which affects the majority of nurse-training schools. There are, of course, differences in the details of the phenomena in different hospitals, but not in their general nature and implications. The phenomena do not, as I try to show in my paper, arise from such factors as personal incompetence or irresponsibility. They arise from the prevailing type of organization of nursing services into which individuals must fit and within which they must behave in certain ways regardless of personal preference and ability.

Further, the study reported in my paper is not a single study. It forms part of a programme of hospital studies undertaken by colleagues and myself over a number of years. I am also familiar with the results of many other hospital studies. Nothing in my experience gives me any reason to suppose that the hospital studied is significantly less competently run than many other hospitals of its type. Nor was there a 'lack of responsible leadership'. Our experience in working with the hospital was quite the contrary – indeed, again, their asking for social science help and their collaboration with us in a difficult study is to be taken as evidence of the nurses' sense of responsibility.

Our experience in the Tavistock Institute of Human Relations has been that our services in helping with organizational problems are rarely sought by organizations which can be described as 'incompetent' or 'badly run'. On the contrary, the organizations which seek our help tend to be among the better of their type, forward-looking and serious about improving their functioning. The hospital studied proved no exception to this rule.

In concluding, I should like to take this opportunity to express again, to the nurses concerned, my gratitude and my admiration for the courage and seriousness with which they pursued this study, often at considerable personal cost. Not only did they collaborate fully in the study but they also generously gave their permission for the publication of my paper, without which permission it would not have been published. This they did in the hope, which I share, that the study would be useful not only to them but to the nursing profession as a whole.

Isabel E. P. Menzies, The Tavistock Institute of Human Relations

Letter from 'Another RMN', *Nursing Times*

MADAM – I have not yet been able to read Miss Menzies's article in the journal *Human Relations* on the subject of defence mechanisms in nursing which is described by the *Nursing Times* as 'a devastating criticism of nursing' and which is reviewed in the *Nursing Times* for 2 September over the signature RMN. The original article should be read before any detailed comments can be made, but while the review of the article is still fresh in our minds it seems worthy of some general discussion in these columns.

It is interesting to see that, apart from RMN's remark 'although I agree with a good deal of what she says about neurotic behaviour ['neurotic anxiety' in the original; see p. 91] underlying individual behaviour' there is no other indication that the writer of this review has done a course of training which includes a study of our mental processes. For, after the remark quoted, RMN goes on to deal with Miss Menzies's investigation by rationalizing each of the defence mechanisms she has described! And rationalizing, as RMN will recall, is the attempt by people everywhere to justify their beliefs and actions on logical grounds, whereas in most cases our beliefs and actions are determined by our emotions.

Some of Melanie Klein's theories are indeed controversial among psychoanalysts, but of course the defence mechanisms of projection and sublimation are considerably older than Mrs Klein's contribution to psychology and are widely accepted. One has only to consider one's own and other people's behaviour in everyday situations, by no means only in hospital and army life, to see how frequently they operate.

Psychiatric nurses should surely be among the first to be aware of the unconscious thought processes which are active all the time – otherwise they will have much difficulty in understanding the behaviour of the patients in their care. To rationalize as RMN has done is to suggest that our behaviour, with the exception of neurotic individuals, is usually logical and governed by our reason – in fact, RMN writes as one who denies the existence of the unconscious mind which is accepted by all the important schools of psychology.

As psychiatric nurses we should not shy away from the effects of our own defence mechanisms but be ready to face them as honestly as we can. Hospitals and their staff are doing important and valuable work and this is widely recognized, as the quotation from Professor Rodger's address, which is inset into RMN's review, illustrates. So we should have nothing to fear from investigation and criticism which may lead to the work being better still.

(Mrs) Doris Message, another RMN, Bexleyheath

3 Nurses under stress (1961 [1961a])*

I *Nursing Times*, 3 February

THE MATRON of a general teaching hospital asked us to assist her colleagues and herself in developing a new method of allocating student nurses to practical work.

While engaged on this task we became interested in other aspects of the nurses' experience. The nurses appeared to experience a great deal of stress in their work: for example, worry, fear, guilt, depression, shame, embarrassment, strain, distrust, disappointment. They made frequent references to such feelings when they talked to us. In addition, they behaved in ways which were familiar to us from working with normal people in situations where they experience stress.

Further, wastage among student nurses was heavy and sickness rates were high, mostly minor illnesses requiring only short spells of absence from duty. Social and medical research strongly suggests that such phenomena are an expression of a disturbed relationship between people and the organization in which they work, and are connected with stress. Such feelings may arise even when people have, in other respects, a good deal of satisfaction in their work, as the nurses did.

We have also noticed stress among nurses with whom we have worked in other hospitals and elsewhere. Phenomena such as high student wastage and sickness rates are common in British hospitals. Stress seemed to us, therefore, to be a problem

* This paper is based on the study of the nursing service analysed in Chapter 2 but is here presented specifically for the nursing profession.

of the profession arising from the professional situation, rather than a matter of the individual nurse's personality. We set ourselves the task of trying to account for the stress in the hope that this might indicate steps which could be taken to change the professional situation and so relieve stress.

SOURCES OF STRESS

The sources of stress may seem so obvious as hardly to merit comment. For example, nurses confront suffering and death as few other people do. They work with ill people also under stress. They face heavy demands for pity, compassion and sympathy. They are often expected to do the impossible in the way of providing comfort or cure. Many nursing tasks are by ordinary standards disgusting, distasteful and frightening. Physical contact with patients may be over-stimulating and disturbing. Patients are sometimes difficult and nurses find themselves getting irritable or resentful. Such feelings seem unworthy of their profession and arouse guilt and anxiety. Indeed, there is no scarcity of situations which expose nurses to stress.

However, the fact that nurses are in a stressful situation is not a sufficient explanation of why they actually experience so much stress. One must consider also how they deal with stress. A nurse, like everyone else, has her personal defences, but these were not our concern. However, social organizations as such also develop defence mechanisms: that is, established methods of helping their members to deal with disturbing emotional experiences – methods which are built into the way the organization works. This is an extension of the familiar idea that a social organization must work in such a way as to provide adequate psychological satisfactions for its members as well as performing its tasks with reasonable efficiency. We could presume, therefore, that the nursing service would have set up social defences to protect its members against the stress arising from their work, although this would not, of course, have been the result of an explicit decision.

We examined the way the service worked with a view to evaluating the protection it gave against stress, while facilitating also the performance of the tasks of patient care and nurse training. This meant that we considered such questions as how the service was organized; how the task of patient care was actually carried out; what sort of behaviour was prescribed for nurses; traditional attitudes to work, patients or colleagues; and interpersonal relationships.

I will confine myself in these articles mainly to phenomena within the nursing service, although I am aware that there are other important relationships, notably with doctors.

NURSE–PATIENT RELATIONSHIPS

The core of the anxiety lies in patient care and in the relationship with the patient. An examination of the ways in which the nursing service mediates the relation between patient and nurse, formally and informally, shows that they reduce the impact of patient on nurse and offer some protection from the subsequent anxiety. In general, the organization of the nursing service militates against close and prolonged contact between the individual patient and nurse, although nurses often want such contact and teaching emphasizes its importance. In a typical ward a group of about eight to ten student nurses with a sister and staff nurse look after about thirty patients. Consequently, the student nurses – and, indeed, the qualified nurses – perform a few tasks for each of a fairly large number of patients and it is difficult to establish close personal contact.

The service also reduces in various ways the direct impact of person on person. This amounts to a sort of depersonalizing of both nurse and patient. Patients tend to be described by bed numbers or illnesses. The nurses in this hospital, like other nurses, deprecate this practice, and senior nurses teach emphatically against it. But the practice continues by custom among student nurses because it alleviates stress. Nor is it easy to learn the names of patients, especially in large wards with a rapid change of patients and nurses. A common attitude among nurses, shown in behaviour rather than words, is that any patient is the same as any other patient. On the positive side, this implies that all must receive the same careful nursing. As a corollary, it implies that personalities should not matter, nor be taken overmuch into account. This implication is being fought, but persists. Preferences for particular patients or even types of patient are discouraged and nurses find it hard to admit to them.

Much the same depersonalization is true about nurses. They are treated as 'categories' – for example, 'second-year' – rather than as individuals. Duties, responsibilities and privileges are, on the whole, accorded to categories rather than to individuals with their own capacities and needs. If all patients are the same and all nurses are the same, at least by seniority, it follows that it should not matter to the patient which nurse or how many nurses nurse him, or to the nurse which patient she nurses. The nursing service functions as though this were true, although both patients and nurses know it is not. Patients are nursed by many nurses at one time, and even more over a period of time. The expression of the nurse's individuality in work is discouraged. The nurse tends to be an agglomeration of nursing skills of a certain level depending on her phase of training, rather than a person doing a job according to her own capacities and skills.

The nursing service also helps in achieving detachment from patients, a necessary objective for all professions working with people. Thus, student nurses were constantly being literally 'detached' from one work situation, their colleagues and patients, and sent to another, as though these should not matter. In time one could say they learned by bitter experience not to become too 'attached' because that made the distress of constant parting too severe. The nursing service, as such, seemed to act as though that kind of 'detachment' was helpful, although most individuals were quite well aware of its painful effects and disliked it.

PROTECTING NURSES FROM STRESS

The nursing service tries, therefore, to protect nurses from stress by fostering nurse–patient relationships which are often short and always rather tenuous. This does not prevent nurses from suffering great distress on occasion. Warm personal feelings still develop between nurses and patients; nurses care deeply about the welfare of their patients. They can be very upset by what happens to patients, by deaths, doctors' or nurses' mistakes, pain and emotional stress. Such feelings are hard to bear. There are certain accepted attitudes and behaviour in relation to such distress, at least while the nurse is on duty and in a working relationship with close colleagues. The emotional disturbance is denied as far as possible and dealt with by brisk, though kindly, remonstrances of the 'pull yourself together' variety. Expressions of strong feelings are discouraged. Comfort, reassurance or help from an understanding colleague or superior in the work situation are not usual, although nurses give each other much support in off-duty friendships. This learned attitude of denial of stress offers some protection against its conscious experience. Further, the restraint on expressing feelings offers some protection against spread of the distress among nurses who work closely together.

II *Nursing Times*, 10 February

MAKING DECISIONS is always stressful because it implies making a choice and committing oneself to a course of action without full knowledge of the outcome. The resultant stress is likely to be particularly acute when decisions directly or indirectly affect the well-being, health or even life of patients, as many nursing decisions do.

The nursing service seems to offer some protection against such stress by reducing the number of possible decisions that must actually be made, and substituting precise instructions. Nurses are implicitly or explicitly forbidden to make decisions about certain things The reduction of decisions has been carried farthest in the work of the student nurse. Very precise instructions are given about the order and timing of her tasks, and the way they must be performed. The service expects her to follow these instructions exactly: she must not, for example, decide that a change in the workload of the ward merits a change in the order of her tasks or even the omission of some less necessary tasks. Similar attempts have been made to eliminate decisions made by senior staff, although this has inevitably not been carried so far, since their roles are more complex and precise instructions less possible. For example, they are not expected to decide what each student can and should do. This is determined by her category, except in unusual circumstances.

When decision-making cannot be avoided several techniques are used, both formally and informally, to minimize its impact on any one person. Decisions are checked and counterchecked, as are the executive actions consequent on them. Consultation about decisions is a deeply ingrained habit. This is not only true of certain obviously dangerous procedures such as the administration of dangerous drugs. It affects all kinds of decisions, including many that are neither important nor dangerous.

RESPONSIBILITY AND CONFLICT

Taking responsibility may be satisfying and rewarding but always involves some conflict. Nurses experience this conflict acutely. The responsibilities of the nursing profession are heavy and nurses usually have a strong sense of personal responsibility. They often discharge their responsibilities at considerable personal cost. However, the very weight of the responsibility makes it difficult to bear consistently over long periods and nurses are sometimes tempted to escape from it, and to behave irresponsibly.

We observed a customary but implicit technique through which nurses handled the painful conflict over responsibility. Briefly, this amounted to turning the personal conflict into an interpersonal one. The nurses tended to refer to nurses junior to themselves as 'irresponsible', and treated them as though this were true. On the other hand, most nurses referred to themselves and their seniors as 'responsible', the implication being that they were not only more responsible than their juniors now but always had been. In addition, they tended to regard their seniors as unduly harsh disciplinarians.

A PSYCHOLOGICAL TIDYING-UP

What happens seems to be a kind of psychological 'tidying-up' through which one's own irresponsible impulses and those of one's equals and superiors are not perceived where they really are but are attributed to juniors. Thus one need not feel unduly guilty or critical of oneself, but takes action to discipline the 'irresponsible' juniors. Likewise, one's own burdensome sense of responsibility and often harsh self-criticism are attributed to seniors. One therefore expects to be criticized harshly by seniors and may behave so as to provoke their criticism, but one avoids some painful self-criticism. This makes for rather tense relations between categories of nurses, but spares each individual a good deal of her personal conflict.

In a more formal sense, the burden of responsibility is avoided by a considerable vagueness in the definition of responsibilities throughout the nursing hierarchy. The student nurse's task-lists look very specific, but students often exchange task-lists and not infrequently have two in the course of a single day, since nurses come on and go off duty at different times. So it becomes difficult to find out who has done or even who should have done what, and who is responsible for its being well or badly done. It is possible to be increasingly less specific about responsibility as the roles become more complex, and as the actual responsibilities become heavier. This prevents responsibility from falling fully and clearly on one person and protects nurses against the resultant conflict.

There also seemed to be a tendency to force responsibilities upwards through the nursing hierarchy, to try to hand over responsibility to people who are older or more experienced and who, because of the customary attitudes to seniors, are regarded as 'more responsible'. This seems to result in senior nurses having actually less responsibility than would be expected from comparing their hierarchical positions with similar positions in other organizations, and from an estimate of their personal capacities. Many nurses are better than their jobs. We were able to watch responsibility being pushed up the hierarchy in this way as new nursing tasks and responsibilities grew out of changes resulting from our study.

RESISTANCE TO CHANGE

Change, like decision-making, arouses stress since it implies giving up a familiar present for a relatively unknown future. The nursing service seems to cope with this by avoiding change whenever possible and clinging to familiar ways of doing things, even when these are becoming demonstrably inappropriate. The case of student allocation was an example: the old method had long been a source of stress and the decision that it must be changed came very late. It is surprising to an outsider how little the service has changed to meet the increasing demands made by the introduction of the National Health Service and radical changes in medical practice.

III *Nursing Times*, 17 February

I WILL NOW CONSIDER why the social defences of which I have given some typical examples in the first two parts of this article were inadequate, as shown by the persisting unduly high level of stress.

It has long been known that the individual whose psychic defences are based on evasion remains a prey to emotional disturbances and is vulnerable to stress. He cannot experience painful feelings fully enough and cannot, therefore, discharge them. On the other hand, the person who can face painful feelings and difficult situations more fully grows in psychic strength. He can understand better the nature of the stress and of the situations which evoke it. He can reduce the degree of stress by developing greater capacity to deal with stressful situations. But if he is a member of an organization which relies heavily on evasive social defences, he is in much the same plight as an individual who uses evasive psychic defences because he cannot develop his own defences.

EVASION INHIBITS GROWTH
This is the situation of the nurse. While on duty she has little choice but to accept protection against stress by evasion, since her attitudes and behaviour must conform closely to those required by the service, implicitly or explicitly, formally or informally; that is, she must accept the social defences and use them as her own. The evasive social defence system actually inhibits the development of the nurse's capacity to deal with her stress and to experience it less acutely.

An example may make the point clear. A student nurse is

'protected' against the stress arising from making decisions by having the decisions she is allowed to make reduced to a minimum. This deprives her of many opportunities to learn how to make decisions effectively, to test them and to experience their consequences. This slows the development of her skill in making decisions and her ability to reduce stress through the reassurance of decisions well made and growing confidence in the skill to make them. Instead, since decisions cannot always be eliminated, nurses come to face them without sufficient assurance from experience that they can make effective decisions, and therefore stress continues. One had the impression that few nurses were really secure about their ability to make wise decisions. In other words, one may say that the social defence system protects nurses, to some extent, from experiences of stress at the moment, but at the expense of its more permanent reduction.

THE 'RESPONSIBLE' NURSE

In some ways the social defence system protects students and qualified nurses against stress and difficulties which many of them are quite capable of handling successfully. There seems little doubt that many student nurses could take and enjoy more responsibility than the service now allows.

To give point to this, it may be necessary to clarify what is meant by responsibility. It seems that in nursing circles a 'responsible' student nurse is one who loyally and faithfully carries out her prescribed tasks. This is a departure from ordinary usage, where responsibility is closely linked with using *discretion*. That is, a 'responsible' person is one who is capable of using discretion wisely in doing his job, 'discretion' being just what the student nurse may not use. Many student nurses are capable, given appropriate help, of making, maintaining and enjoying continuous relationships with patients. They want to do this and are taught that it is desirable, but the system of work organization prevents them from doing it.

People enjoy facing difficulties and enjoy and need the challenge they present, provided the difficulites are not beyond their capacities. Success can be a great reassurance. Overprotection makes it impossible for many nurses to deploy fully in their jobs their personal capacities and professional skills, and experience real success. Indeed, the more mature and capable the nurse, the greater the problem. This situation is extremely frustrating to nurses who feel inhibited from doing their best for their patients and colleagues. Student nurses tend to feel this most keenly, but the feeling is shared to some extent at all levels in the hierarchy. Nurses feel guilty and anxious about it. Thus the overprotection built into the social defence system itself evokes stress.

EFFICIENCY AND RESPONSIBILITY

There are other ways in which the service itself gives rise to stress. For example, it is not very efficient as a method of organizing work. In this the nursing service is not at all unusual. Similar phenomena are to be observed in other kinds of social organization. They stem from the fact that in establishing a way of operating, a social organization cannot be concerned only with efficiency but must take into account the psychological needs of its members. Because of the high element of real danger in the nursing situation, care for the psychological needs of nurses tends to play a relatively large part *vis-à-vis* technical efficiency in determining the structure and method of functioning of the service. Some efficiency has had to be sacrificed, though not by conscious decision, to evasion of anxiety. Inefficiency in this sense is determined by the organization and is not a matter of an individual behaving inefficiently. Indeed, people who are behaving in one sense 'efficiently' – that is, carrying out instructions carefully and well – feel 'inefficient' because they consider they are violating the general principles of good nursing or of common sense.

I can give only a few examples of such service-determined inefficiency which increases stress. The fact that student nurses and staff cannot deploy their personal capacities fully, as described above, is one example. It is very wasteful of human resources. Further, nurses, at least student nurses, are on occasion not fully occupied. This arises from the rather rigid system of work organization which makes it difficult to adjust to changing demand in a ward by reorganizing their work. Ward establishments tend to be aimed at peak rather than average workloads and wards seem somewhat overstaffed. Nurses feel guilty about being underemployed whether in respect of time or capacity, and this increases stress. The system is also cumbersome and inflexible in a situation which increasingly demands flexibility: for example, decision-making tends to be slow. This makes nurses anxious lest decisions are not made in time and irritable about delays in important matters.

SATISFACTION BALANCING STRESS

This account would be incomplete without referring to the satisfaction which nurses experience in their work; such satisfactions are a very important counterbalance to stress. The potential rewards of nursing are great in terms of such things as the recovery of patients, suffering relieved, and satisfying relationships with patients and colleagues. The nurses in this hospital clearly experienced their work as rewarding.

However, they did not seem to be experiencing the full potential reward because of certain features of the social system. For example, while the nursing service had considerable success in nursing patients, it was difficult for any one nurse to experience this in a personal way. The task-list system makes the contribution of one nurse to the nursing of one patient rather small. The reward is dissipated as well as the stress. Patients are grateful to 'the hospital' or 'the nurses' – that is, rather impersonally – and the individual nurse misses the personal gratitude which is part of her reward. For student nurses an important satisfaction is the development of their knowledge and skill in nursing patients. The training and work situations quite definitely slow down this development. The better the student the less satisfaction she finds in the rate of development of her nursing skills. Indeed, our feeling was that the better students suffered a good deal in this respect and a significant number of them could not tolerate it and gave up training.

Nor is it possible, under present conditions, to realize at all fully the potential satisfactions in working with colleagues. Student nurses feel this particularly. For example, the traditional relationship between juniors and seniors described above means that the student nurse feels herself singled out more for blame than praise. This she finds very distressing, as she has a particular need for encouragement in settling down to her difficult profession. The student nurse tends to feel she does not matter as a person. They complain: 'nobody cares what happens to you', 'nobody helps you', 'you have no individuality'. They say the senior staff neither understand nor help them when they are in trouble – indeed, when they are worried and guilty about a mistake they are reprimanded instead of being comforted.

It was not, however, our experience that the senior staff did not understand or care. They understood only too well, many of them having vivid and still agonizing memories of their own training. They expressed their understanding and sympathy to us, but felt unable to do so within *operational* relationships. They were often uncertain about the wisdom of entering into a close emotional relationship with their students, and uncertain of their skill in handling it. Their training had not prepared them for this.

They tended to fall back on the only behaviour they knew – the discipline and severity they experienced in their own training. In any case, it is not easy for student nurses to approach their seniors for that sort of help, since by tradition they expect seniors to be disciplinarians. However, as a result of this situation, many senior staff feel they are not helping their colleagues and juniors enough and, in turn, miss the satisfaction which comes from really helping colleagues in need.

CONCLUSION

We have little doubt that some action to remedy the situation described is desirable, especially since we have no reason to believe that this hospital differs in any significant way from other hospitals. It is clear that there is no simple solution; if there were, it would have been introduced long ago. The ultimate solution must be a restructuring of the system of work organization and nurse training, so that it incorporates a different kind of social defence system based less on evasion. For example, one might try systems of ward organization which give nurses more continuous and intensive contact with patients; this would require new techniques for dealing with the stress that would arise initially, especially among the junior student nurses. Together these would mean an earlier confrontation of stressful situations and, if successfully handled, would lead to an ultimate alleviation of stress.

In our opinion, blueprints for change are not possible although one has a general idea of direction. The most hopeful approach to the problem of change at this stage would seem to be to tackle it in a concrete rather than an abstract way: for example, to work in one hospital or even a part of a hospital and try to build a working model. This approach, through model-building and progressive modification of models followed by dissemination of successful models, has proved successful in building and rebuilding other kinds of social organizations. It is our hope that we have been able to contribute to the understanding of the nursing situation and so to the design of such new models.

We began our study four years ago and our description of the hospital refers to that period. Since then a number of important developments have taken place partly as a result of the study. These can be regarded as attempts at partial new models. For example, a new system for allocation of student nurses is now in operation which gives longer continuous duty tours; new training has been introduced for the post-certificate student to give more experience of administration and more real responsibility; an attempt is being made to develop a closer and more supportive relationship between the teaching staff and the student. We are very grateful to the hospital which gave us the opportunity to carry out the study and permission to publish this paper. We are particularly grateful to the nurses for their serious and courageous co-operation with us in what proved to be a long and arduous investigation and for their sincere efforts to use the research findings.

4 Some methodological notes on a hospital study (1969)*

THE SOCIOTHERAPEUTIC APPROACH

THIS PAPER selects for comment some aspects of a particular research method and gives as illustration a brief account of a study in a hospital. The research method may be called sociotherapeutic or 'clinical'. The research serves towards the solution of a practical ongoing problem that a social organization is attempting to tackle. It is primarily aimed, therefore, at elucidating the nature of the problem and seeking information on the basis of which the organization may reach a better solution. The main objective of the research is therapy. The research worker's dominant role is as therapist or consultant to the organization. However, it has frequently been the experience of consultants that such studies also produce research findings of a more general nature, which are of practical and theoretical interest beyond the narrow boundaries of the client organization.

Although there are wide variations in the detail of such socio-therapeutic studies, those with which the author has been most closely concerned have tended to follow roughly the same general pattern. The study tends to be initiated by the client organization when one or more of the management affected by the problem make contact with a potential consultant to inquire about the possibilities of getting some help. Before the decision is made to carry out the work, there is a period of initial exploration with a number of objectives.

1. The consultant and the client organization try together to

* Published in (eds) S. H. Foulkes and G. Stewart-Price, *Psychiatry in a Changing Society*. Tavistock Publications, 1969, pp. 99–112.

clarify the problem. The consultant will also clarify with the client what research and therapeutic methods are available and may be used. This enables the client organization and the consultant to decide together whether the problem presented is one with which the consultant can help and whether the methods of working are acceptable to the client organization.

2. The initial contacts enable the client organization and the consultant to explore each other as personalities, with their own particular orientations to the problems of social organizations. This is an important exploration, since sociotherapeutic studies of this kind usually involve lengthy and intimate contact between the client organization and the consultant. Any serious incompatibility on the personal level might well jeopardize the work.

3. The client organization and the consultant must mutually explore practical problems such as possible time commitment on both sides, the amount and nature of the work both will be required to undertake, and costs and sources of finance.

If these mutual explorations lead to a decision to work together on the problem, the work proceeds as a variable mixture of research and therapy. Although theoretically separable, research and therapy are likely to be constantly mingled in various degrees at different stages of the study. In the earlier stages emphasis is likely to be on the research side; in the later stages on the therapeutic side.

The emphasis on research in the early stages of the work can perhaps be more properly described as an attempt to define more accurately the nature of the 'dis-ease' of the organization and to arrive at a more refined diagnosis. The problem that precipitated the approach for help would tend to be treated as a 'presenting problem' rather analogous to a presenting symptom. It may reflect merely the area of the organization's functioning where the 'pain' is most severely felt or can be most easily formulated. Or it may be used as a 'displacement area' because the real disorder is felt to be too close to the core of the organization's being to be easily disclosed either to the self or to others. It is also important to get to know as much as possible about the social organization that is host to the dis-ease.

The need to make a proper diagnosis is as essential in social as in individual therapy. Failure to achieve effective diagnosis might well jeopardize attempts at therapy. There is usually little to be gained by treating a social symptom in isolation: indeed, it may even be harmful. Unless one is reasonably well informed of the real nature of the organization, its dis-ease and its total functioning, there is a danger that one may devise solutions to the presenting problem whose main achievement is the precipi-tation of other serious problems in other parts of the organiz-ation. It is useful to be in a position both to predict and to control the total effects of possible solutions.

In carrying out the more diagnostic or research phase of the work, the main objective is to range as widely as possible with the people concerned around the topics of the general structure and functioning of the organization, its culture, its traditions, its conventions, its formal and informal communication systems, the practical and emotional experiences of its members, the rewards and problems it presents to its members, the formal and informal elements of the interpersonal relationships, formal and informal authority systems, and so on. All is grist to the mill of achieving understanding of the organization and of the presenting problem in its organizational setting.

Because of the width of the canvas, techniques such as highly structured questionnaires do not usually seem particularly appropriate. Unstructured intensive interviews, either with single individuals or with groups, have generally been found more useful. Individuals may be either 'key informants', such as people in key management positions, or individuals selected to represent significant categories of people involved in the problem, for example a random 10 per cent sample of all the workers in a certain department. Similarly, the groups may be made up of functioning groups in the organization, or of individ-uals selected to represent important categories. The aim of the group discussions and interviews is to achieve as free and undirected communication from the informants as possible, and to subject their communications to as little influence as possible from any views or preconceptions the consultant has about the organization, its members, structure, functioning, and problems. At first, at any rate, the consultant has no specific questions in mind which he wants answered. He wants only to learn as much as possible about the organization. This is, of course, a very different research approach from one that sets out to study defined aspects of a defined topic and uses questions prepared in advance.

It is in the group discussions that structure and interviewer/informant interaction may be reduced to their absolute minimum, and for this reason a diagnostic survey is always initiated with group discussions when the field conditions allow this. Careful briefing of such groups makes it possible to establish a quasi-free-associative process of communication and of interaction between group members. To this end the consultant briefs the groups somewhat as follows. The consultant introduces himself and any colleagues to the group and reminds the group of the present problem, but he also tells the group members that he does not wish them to confine themselves to that topic, and that he is interested to hear about anything that seems to them significant and important in terms of their own experience as members of the organization. A few very general leads are given as to topics that might be raised. The group members are then asked to hold a discussion among themselves and let the consultants listen to it. A senior consultant sits with the group, ready to intervene if the group gets into any difficulty and needs help, but mainly just listening and observing. A junior colleague records significant aspects of the group's discussion and behaviour.

Such group discussions have a number of advantages in addition to that of minimizing consultant guidance to communication. They give freer access to personal and institutional unconscious phantasy systems than do other easily usable techniques, because of the quasi-free-associative element. Alternative ways of getting such access to unconscious phantasy systems – for example by means of individual projective techniques like Rorschach or thematic apperception tests – seem to us inappropriate both because of their clinical pathological overtones and because they are individually orientated, whereas the consultant's 'patient' is the organization. However, delineating the unconscious phantasy systems on an institutional basis seems very important. One's understanding of a social organization, as of a person, is likely to be seriously limited if one cannot gain access to unconscious or implicit elements as well as to the more overt ones.

Further, one can often find in such groups a miniature version of the total organization. One can, for instance, watch patterns of interaction between members, which reflect patterns in the total organization. One can observe modes of behaviour, speech and thought habitual among members of the organization, which would show less clearly in one-to-one interaction with an outsider. By these means, again, development of understanding of the organization may be greatly facilitated.

The group discussions are not, therefore, used for fact-finding in the ordinary sense of the word: that is, for providing – or for providing only – so-called objective facts, overt easily verifiable data – for example about the formal hierarchical structure of the organization – or data that would lend themselves to statistical analysis. They are used rather to enable the consultant to build up an account of the 'patterning' of the organization, its structure and its functioning, its culture, tradition and conventions, the occupational and personal experiences of its members in both conscious and unconscious terms. The result is a dynamic account of the nature of a social system rather than a statement of facts; not only what goes on but how, and above all why, it goes on; 'depth anthropology' would not be a bad description of this operation.

The group discussions also serve as a useful background to the individual interviews, which must inevitably involve more informant/interviewer interaction and more interviewer-based structure, however much one may try to develop an interview out of the leads given by the informant. The group data give some knowledge of significant areas to be explored and probed more intensively in the individual interviews; thus the interviewer has some assurance that the structure and topics he introduces are relevant to the study and likely to be so to the informant. However, the individual interviews are also informant-directed to a considerable extent. It is not important that an informant should cover all aspects of a topic, since we are not interested in statistical analysis; nor is it important that informants confine themselves to topics regarded now as significant by the consultant. The interviews facilitate checking, elaboration and refinement of the dynamic picture of the organization that has begun to emerge from the group discussions.

In working with both groups and individuals, the consultant gives certain guarantees in advance about his professional behaviour. He undertakes to report nothing outside the interviewing situation except anonymously and to maintain absolute confidence about any information if the informant so wishes. Such guarantees place restraints on the consultant which may be somewhat hampering. The comments of certain informants cannot be anonymous: for example, some remarks could be made only by the managing director and would be immediately recognized as coming from him. It is burdensome and frustrating to have information one cannot use explicitly. However, it is our feeling that such behaviour is essential if one is to gain and hold the trust of the people concerned. It is doubtful if much reliance is placed on such guarantees early in a study, but the opportunity to test the sincerity of the guarantees against the consultant's behaviour over time, if he honours the guarantees, builds up trust. This in turn encourages the frankness and sincerity of informants. The data so given are available for the development of the consultant's own understanding, even if they cannot be directly disclosed to members of the client organization.

I should like to make a number of comments on the use of such research techniques before going on to describe other aspects of consultancy studies:

1. I should like to take up further the question of the professional behaviour and ethics of the consultant. By intent, the consultant creates a research situation that aims at making it possible for informants to discuss with him intimate and personal aspects of their experiences in the organization and at

allowing the consultant to penetrate deeply into these experiences with them. From the nature of the work, many of the topics discussed are painful and evoke emotional disturbance in informants. The consultant has a professional responsibility to try to anticipate such disturbances and prevent or minimize them, and to deal with disturbances therapeutically when they develop. The possibility of such disturbance is one reason why a consultant cannot necessarily cover all aspects of a topic with all informants. Some areas may be too painful for certain informants easily to expose in a relationship which is basically fact-finding and not therapeutic for them and where the consultant does not, therefore, have the therapeutic sanction to cause pain. It is important that consultants should have enough intuitive understanding and the necessary experience to be able to assess such situations and work them through reasonably well with informants.

2. The process of analysing and interpreting the data collected by these methods is a complex one and has many potential difficulties. The data do not lend themselves to the use of statistical techniques, or to related techniques for testing validity and reliability. Reaching conclusions depends rather on the clinical and sociological acumen of the consultant and on the soundness of the psychological and organizational theories he uses as a background to analysis and interpretation. Ultimate conviction as to reliability and validity depends on a many-times-repeated process of establishing hypotheses and returning to concrete situations in the organization to test and retest them and to refine and elaborate them. Ultimate assurance of their validity depends also on the final test of whether action based on the findings in fact leads to a more effective solution of the organization's problems.

3. In communicating the diagnostic findings to the client organization, one finds oneself in a situation similar to that of the psychotherapist. The clinical data permit a variety of interpretations, all of which may represent correct insights into the problem. The consultant, like the psychotherapist, has to select which interpretation should be communicated to the client, at

what time and in what circumstances, in order to maximize the therapeutic effectiveness of the client/consultant relationship. Many of the data collected may never be communicated to the client, or indeed to anyone else, although they may have been helpful in increasing the consultant's understanding.

A point is reached in the diagnostic phase when the consultant decides that he has enough data and enough understanding of the organization to move with the client into the more therapeutic phase of the study. He will then begin to report back the diagnostic findings and explore their implications with the client. Decisions need to be made now about the form reporting back should take and to whom the reporting will be done. The main choice about the form of reporting is between written and verbal reports. My own preference is for verbal reporting, at least initially, if the situation makes this possible, and perhaps a written report later for reference purposes. The preference for verbal reporting stems from the nature of the therapeutic process. In conveying the results of the study to the client and exploring their implications, one inevitably comes up against resistance to their acceptance which must be dealt with if effective action is to be achieved. It has been our experience that this can best be done in a face-to-face situation when the client and the consultant share the data, explore them together, and face the resistances as they come up. This is an important situation also for continuing the testing, elaboration and refinement of hypotheses about the organization and its problems. It has been our experience that, as client and consultant work together, many further valuable data are fed into the study, since the client increasingly realizes the relevance of his own experience in the organization and recognizes the potential therapeutic benefits of frank communication. Quite significant reorientations tend to take place, during such work, in the views of individuals about themselves, their colleagues and the organization, and in their relationships to the organization and each other.

As to the choice of people to whom to report, one would wish to report to all who are likely to be involved in the problem and in change subsequent to the report. In the case of large organizations, of course, it is often impossible to work directly with all those concerned and one may have to work with representatives. The experience behind this preference for direct reporting is connected not only with the belief that, in principle, people should have some share in decisions that affect them, but also with the practical point that this again facilitates working through resistance to the acceptance of data and their implications and of changes that may be based on them.

In working towards some resolution of the organization's problems, it would not be usual for the consultant to make specific recommendations about what changes should be initiated. Rather, the consultant would try to help the people concerned in the organization to evolve new solutions for themselves, based on their own experience and on the research findings and their implications, and accepting the existing restraints in the nature of the organization and of the people in it. In other words, the process involved is essentially one whereby the organization itself is enabled to find new and more constructive ways of dealing with its tasks and problems: on the basis of improved information and increased insights on the one hand, and the lessening of barriers to effective communication and of resistance to change on the other.

In such circumstances the solutions found are not likely to be 'ideal' in the blueprint sense. As in individual or group psychotherapy, the changes will go only as far as the client organization and the consultant can take them in the current circumstances. It is pointless to try to impose solutions that the organization could not operate or that its environment would not permit. Such an attempt would be likely only to increase resistance to change.

Finally, there is the question of the termination of the therapeutic relationship between the client organization and the consultant. It is, in our experience, important for the successful completion of the work that the relationship continue throughout the difficult phase of planning change and dealing with the disturbances inevitable in accomplishing it. It seems to us inappropriate that the consultant should behave as too many do: that is, write his prescription for social change and leave the organization alone to face the consequences of trying to implement the prescription. When the consultant *should* withdraw is much harder to define than when he should not. When he does is partly a matter of his socioclinical judgement as to when the organization is sufficiently stabilized to carry on without further help; partly it is a matter of meeting and dealing with the organization's own wishes. It is not uncommon for the relationship of client and consultant to go on intermittently for an indefinite period, to give support and help with problems as they arise. The consultant walks a tightrope between withholding desirable help and colluding with overdependency, which may arise in an organization just as in individual patients.

THE HOSPITAL STUDY AS AN ILLUSTRATION OF THESE METHODS

The initiative for this study came from the hospital itself, the matron having been advised by a nursing colleague that the Tavistock Institute might be able to help her to deal more effectively with problems in the nurse-training system – namely, in the allocation of student nurses to practical training and nursing duties. The study stemmed, therefore, from the practical needs of the hospital rather than from the consultant's wish to study hospitals, although in fact the Institute was very glad to have the opportunity to do research in a hospital.

There followed a series of exploratory discussions between the matron, the deputy matron, the assistant matrons, and the principal tutor for the hospital and members of the senior staff of the Tavistock Institute. This group decided provisionally to go ahead with the study under the direction of the author. However, the group felt that it would be desirable, before making a final decision, to consult other nurses who would be involved in the study. Accordingly, meetings were held with other nursing staff and with representatives of the student nurses. The aim of these meetings was to explain the purpose and methods of the proposed study, to allow the nurses to express their views, doubts and questions, and to seek their support and collaboration. Such support being forthcoming, a final decision was made to go ahead.

It would be idle to suppose that much more than formal support was given at that stage. It would not, in fact, have been easy for either staff or student nurses to challenge the tentative decision of the senior staff to undertake the study. Such a challenge would not have been in line with nursing tradition. On the other hand, the meetings did allow the people concerned to get to know a little about the study and the consultant, and gave them some feeling that we were prepared to be influenced by the social field in which we worked. This facilitated later, more comprehensive working through of doubts and difficulties about the study.

The next task was to plan and to carry out the diagnostic survey. We interviewed, either individually or in small groups, almost all the qualified nurses in the hospital, some of them many times. We interviewed individually and in small groups a 10 per cent sample of the student nurses. We also interviewed a few of the senior medical staff and the senior lay administrators. We carried out observational studies of four contrasting wards. In addition, we collected a good deal of statistical data relevant to the problem of allocation of student nurses to practical training and nursing duties.

As we became known and our guarantee of anonymity and confidentiality became reasonably well trusted, we found that our informants were prepared to talk very frankly and fully about their experiences and we could begin to build a relatively comprehensive picture of the nursing situation in the hospital. As soon as we felt fairly well informed about the situation, we initiated the more 'therapeutic' activities. We began by reporting verbally to the matron, but very soon, with her agreement, we broadened the basis of this reporting to a group consisting of the five senior nurses in the hospital. This group met at approximately fortnightly intervals over some months, each meeting lasting two to three hours. At first the meetings consisted largely of verbal reporting by the consultant, but later they became much more a general pooling of experience and views by all the members of the group. Much valuable diagnostic material emerged from the contributions of the nurses from their long and rich experience in nursing.

These meetings were an exciting and moving therapeutic experience. The process in the group resembled the process in a therapeutic group, although its objective was social change and was not directly concerned with the individual members. A great deal of the work was concerned with working through resistance to the acceptance of the contributions made both by individual members and by the study, and with following up the implications of these contributions. The group worked on the material provided within itself; examined contributions; checked and rechecked their validity in the light of its combined experience; contradicted, elaborated and refined them. Quite significant reorientation took place in the group and in individuals with regard to the problems we were tackling together, and in the relationships between the members of the group. In particular, the group developed a greater capacity for free interchange of views than is usual in a senior nursing group. The courage and sincerity of its members in tackling the difficult problems of change in a notably rigid profession were most impressive.

The group gradually crystallized, out of its discussions, several plans for change in the system of allocating student nurses to practical training and nursing duties and in surrounding areas of their work. The implementation of such plans obviously involved other nursing staff and students, and they now began to be involved also in the sociotherapeutic process. The suggested plans were put to their representatives and were explored by them and modified in certain ways before finally being put into operation.

The therapeutic process was not, of course, confined to formal situations in which the consultant took part. A vast amount of work was also done by nursing staff and students in other situations and then fed back into the formal planning meetings. This work was sometimes done in formal meetings or in the carrying out of various preparatory tasks such as devising a plan for student-nurse allocation, but a great deal of it was informal talking, done in off-duty periods and as the nurses went about their ordinary duties. One of the notable things about this sort of study is the extent to which it stimulates thinking and exploration in the client organization itself.

There was a gradual reduction in frequency of contact between the consultant and the nursing staff as the plans evolved and the nurses themselves took over their implementation. The study proper stopped when the plans were implemented and the new situation around them seemed to have stabilized, although some casual contact between the senior nursing staff and the consultant continued for some time afterwards.

In concluding this account of the study, I should like to mention a particular serious limitation from which it suffered. It did not prove possible for a number of reasons effectively to involve in the study the other two main social subsystems in the hospital: medical and lay. This meant, in effect, that change in the nursing system was limited to such changes as could be introduced without requiring any major balancing adjustments in the other subsystems. It would not have been possible, for example, to bring about any major change in ward organization without the full co-operation of the medical staff because of its effect on the medical subsystem.

CONCLUDING REMARKS

This paper has described one particular research approach out of many possible approaches. My choice of this method is partly a matter of personal preference. I prefer to work in an organization which has delineated a problem in its own functioning and has a real drive towards social change. In other words, I personally prefer a clinical and therapeutic relationship with the organization being studied. To achieve this, I am prepared to be directed by the field as regards the organization and its problem.

As a research method, this clinical approach has both advantages and disadvantages compared with other available methods. To comment only briefly on this point: our experience has been that the therapeutic relationship with the client organization tends to facilitate access to significant data in their full complexity and depth. This is connected with informants' motivation for communication, which stems to a considerable extent from the drive towards the resolution of problems and social change. Such motivation creates a very different situation from that in which the motivation stems from the research worker's need to do research. It has been our experience that as the relevant connections are made between communication and problem-solving, the clinical approach encourages frankness in the informants and helps them to disclose intimate and painful facts in very much the same way as happens in individual or group psychotherapy. The informants' perspectives are also broadened and they begin to see the relevance of a wide range of experiences to the problem being tackled, and to be able to communicate on a broad front and in depth. These developments become particularly evident in the therapeutic phases of the study, which often provide the most significant research data.

A difficulty of the clinical approach lies in the very depth and complexity of the data it provides, factors that may make the analysis and interpretation of the data a hazardous task compared with the analysis and interpretation of data from more structured research approaches. Understanding depends greatly on what the consultant can himself make of the data, and is therefore subject to the risk of his misunderstanding because of subjective factors in himself. Checks can be provided, however, to minimize this risk, for example in the form of constant interchange between members of the consultant team or 'supervision' from other experienced colleagues outside the study, and of constant checking and rechecking in the field. The understanding of the data is also a stressful task for the consultant, since it depends so much on his internalizing the data and on his emotional, as well as his intellectual, sifting processes. The data have to be 'felt' inside oneself; that is, one has to take in and experience the stress in the organization, much as one does in individual and group psychotherapy. This is very different from a situation which has all the external supports of such devices as structured questionnaires and sophisticated statistical techniques for analysing data.

A disadvantage of the method lies also in the limitation it

imposes on the choice of research problems. This obviously makes it necessary to devise and use other methods of approach to problems where, from the social point of view, research patently needs to be done but the chances that anyone will bring the matter to a research worker are not great. Many of the more diffuse problems of our society – for example geriatric difficulties or road accidents – do not lend themselves to such an approach, since the people who need help are not organized to seek it.

On the other hand, the disadvantages are to some extent balanced by the valuable and sometimes unexpected by-products that emerge from such studies. The access so gained to an organization has on a number of occasions enabled the consultant to increase the general understanding and theoretical formulations about the functioning of social systems. In the hospital study we were fortunate in working in an organization the nature of whose task, caring for the sick, stimulated a great deal of anxiety and stress in its members. The data collected around this situation enabled us further to develop theoretical formulations put forward by other authors in relation to one particular aspect of the functioning of social systems: their use by their members as socially structured systems of defence against anxiety. These socially structured defence systems not only affect the emotional satisfactions and difficulties of the members of the organization, but can be shown to affect also the efficiency and viability of the organization itself. An understanding of the anxieties and the social defence systems adds an important dimension to the total understanding of social organizations and to diagnostic and therapeutic work within them.

5 Action research in a long-stay hospital

Two papers (1973, 1982, revised 1987)

THE TWO PAPERS that follow were written at different points in an action research study carried out by the Royal National Orthopaedic Hospital at Stanmore, Middlesex, and a team from the Tavistock Institute of Human Relations between 1971 and 1975. The object of the study was to explore the experiences and problems of young children in long-stay hospitals; to consider how the method of care of the children could be modified to alleviate immediate distress and to prevent or mitigate long-term damage; and to attempt to introduce such modifications.

The first paper, 'Action research in a long-stay hospital', was written some eighteen months after the beginning of the project and represents a distillate of experiences in the RNOH and other hospitals, of the experience of colleagues with whom I have worked and talked and whose publications I have read, and of my work as a children's psychoanalyst. It attempts to describe experiences of child patients and their families and so to lead to consideration of what action could be taken to improve matters. The paper also considers why action research seems preferable at this time to fact-finding research as a way of facilitating action.

The second paper, 'The psychological welfare of children making long stays in hospital', was written after the study ended and is the final account of the work done. It considers the position of the children, particularly in the light of attachment theory and the effects of early mother–child separation; it describes in detail the objectives at the start of the study and how these were modified; finally, it considers what was accomplished in the study, what remained undone when it ended and the effect of the changed methods of care on the children, their families and the hospital staff.

I would like to express my gratitude to many people who collaborated in the work described in this paper and to others who supported it, although not directly involved:

1. The Department of Health and Social Security, who funded the study and gave much encouragement and support through their interest in it.

2. The Project Steering Committee, which was closely associated with the work of the study. The hospital members of the Steering Committee were:

Miss A. H. Allen	Nursing Officer
Mr S. H. J. Blake	(Chairman) Hospital Secretary
Mr A. Catterall	Consultant surgeon
Dr J. J. Fleminger	Consultant psychiatrist
Dr S. S. Herman	Consultant paediatrician
Mrs R. J. Kverndal	Principal social worker
Mr C. W. Manning	Consultant surgeon
Miss E. Noble	Headmistress of the hospital school
Miss M. A. O'Hare	Principal nursing officer
Miss M. Young	Ward sister (Sir William Coxen Ward)

The degree of their interest and involvement is indicated by the fact that there was almost always full attendance at Committee meetings. They were most generous of time and effort, unfailing in their concern for the child patients and their families, constructively critical and always supportive. In addition to their work on the Committee, they helped greatly to sustain a climate of concern among their colleagues and a willingness to consider and implement changes.

3. Many other hospital staff also gave generously of time and effort to improve the care of children and families, both in collaboration with the research team and on their own initiative. I acknowledge gratefully their willingness to face the disturbance of change and their concern for the patients and families.

4. My colleagues who at some time worked with me on the project, all with much enthusiasm, and who made important contributions both to the ongoing work and to the thinking about it: Tim Dartington, Gianna Henry, Richard Jones, James Robertson, Sheila Scott and Elizabeth Wolpert. I am especially grateful to James Robertson, who put at the team's disposal his vast knowledge of children in institutions; and to Tim Dartington and Gianna Henry for their contributions to evaluating the final results of the study. My secretary, Joan Hackett, contributed much more than her normal secretarial work, sharing in the concern of hospital staff and the team for the patients and families.

The author takes full responsibility for the views and statements made in these papers.

I Action research in a long-stay hospital

THE LONG-STAY CHILD POPULATION

TWENTY YEARS AGO, Bowlby and his co-workers regarded long-stay as over three months, this being about the length of time Robertson had observed it took young patients in a tuberculosis sanatorium to pass through the phases of protest and despair and reach the final phase of detachment (Bowlby, 1951, 1969, 1973; Robertson, James, 1958a). Robertson described these children at a time when the mother was little present with the child in hospital or might not be present at all. The child would be grief-stricken, confused and frightened, would protest, perhaps throw himself about, cry and scream as though to attract his absent mother's attention, and would clearly be seeking for her. After several days when this behaviour failed to summon the mother, or summoned her only for short visits, the behaviour would change as though the child was giving up, the crying and seeking would cease; the child becomes apathetic and withdrawn, and despair sets in. Later still comes detachment when the child seems to stop caring, may take little notice of mother if she visits, is more interested in the gifts she brings, appears cheerful and happy and is indiscriminate in his relationships. By now, the child is seriously and possibly permanently disturbed.

The length of time children spend in hospital has decreased for a number of reasons: a change in the illnesses that take them into hospital, and because hospital practice has been influenced by the work of Bowlby, Robertson and others and by the National Association for the Welfare of Children in Hospital. For the purpose of this study we regarded long-stay as a single stay of one month or more or a number of short stays at fairly frequent intervals amounting together to one month or more for the same condition. This was the situation for the great majority of children in the RNOH. This was still long enough to cause damage if the children were inadequately cared for in hospital, especially as there seemed to be additional risks for these children and their families. Children who came into long-stay hospitals and their families often seem to be under considerable stress apart from the hospitalization.

As far as I know no figure has been put on the incidence of psychiatric disturbance in this group, but there is evidence from people who have worked with them which suggests that it is significantly higher than in the population as a whole. For example, accidents are often not true accidents but the precipitate of a temporary or permanent disturbance leading to a failure in family protection for a child or inadequacy in his own self-protectiveness. Stress in family relationships may lead to unconsciously based attacks by one member of a family on another.

Helen Martin's work (1970) in the Burns Unit of the Hospital for Sick Children, Great Ormond Street, London, provides excellent illustration of these points, with moving and dramatic case-histories of the antecedents to accidents. A number of children were scalded in a fight for food. She notes a jealous eighteen-month-old girl scalded while grabbing a bottle being heated for her eight-month-old sister. Helen Martin makes the point that there was a significantly high proportion of disturbed families in her random research sample. In addition, an accident is likely to exacerbate disturbances in family relationships: Helen Martin describes how the child may painfully experience the accident as the loss of a loving and protective mother. Other members of the family may feel guilty about the accident, or angry with the victim for being injured; the mother may experience painful inadequacy or failure. Such disturbance is by no means always worked through to a positive outcome, especially since hospitalization may restrict or prevent the family interactions necessary to accomplish this.

Psychogenic and psychosomatic illnesses reflect and express psychosocial disturbances in child and family. There may be a vicious circle in which the effects of the illness increase the disturbance – for example the alarming impact of a serious asthma attack, or violent scratching at eczema. It may be difficult for parents to sustain adequate love and care for such children in view of the children's demands, interference with normal family life, the hopelessness sometimes generated by the relative ineffectiveness of treatment. Some children remain free of physical symptoms only when separated from their families and it may be difficult to keep them at home. I well remember a severely asthmatic boy who was symptom-free in hospital, but relapsed into a severe asthmatic state as soon as he was sent home. He had been months in the hospital and had become an effective supernumerary member of staff. Robertson's attention was drawn to an illegitimate boy admitted from the Midlands to a London hospital suffering from eczema. He had been eight years in hospital, longer than most of the medical and nursing staff.

The psychologically disturbing effect of deformity and disability is well known and may be especially marked where the condition is congenital and discovered at birth or shortly afterwards. Experience of such children in psychotherapy frequently shows a particular developmental feature: the effect on the child of interaction with a mother who is guilty, anxious and depressed about her child and unable to respond in a normal, relaxed motherly way. She may not be able effectively to accept and deal with his communications of distress but instead subtly communicates her own feelings to a baby who does not have the psychological equipment to deal with them. The overburdened baby fails to develop an adequate organization to cope with such feelings and this leads to features like restless discharge activity, indiscriminate aggression or marked obsessional defences, along with strong psychotic undertones which may make such children a difficult therapeutic proposition.

Children who come to analysis may not be typical, but experience of children in hospital reinforces the psychotherapeutic experiences. The children and families are subject to a great deal of pressure; the care of the disabled child may make exorbitant demands on the mother, who may neglect husband

and other children; there may be bitter undertones of resentment or recrimination about the child's condition between husband and wife; tension may develop about the wisdom of having other children. The child may suffer from restricted activities resulting from his condition and from the taunts of other children.

I am postulating, therefore, that a significant number of the children and families who enter into long-stay hospitalization show psychosocial disturbances and are therefore particularly unsuited to cope with the problems of such hospitalization, which are a severe burden even for those children and families who are psychologically normal on admission.

PROBLEMS OF LONG HOSPITALIZATION FOR YOUNG CHILDREN

Crucial among the problems of lengthy stays in hospital is the separation of the child from his mother and family. The fact that the pathological conditions are comparatively rare and few hospitals treat them often means that children are hundreds or even thousands of miles from their families, home and normal environments. Sustaining adequate visiting under such circumstances is always difficult and may be virtually impossible. At worst, some children in long-stay hospitals have no family visiting and no common language with hospital staff. This was true in the RNOH of children from the Middle East who spoke only Arabic. Interpreters were not always available. By the time the children left they had sometimes apparently forgotten their Arabic and spoke only English. At best, it is difficult for the mother to be present as much as the child needs, and if she is, it may well be at excessive expense to herself and the family, both in disrupted family life and financial cost. Families sometimes put themselves voluntarily into stressful situations in order to sustain support for the hospitalized child. In two families the husband voluntarily became unemployed so that he could support the family situation while the wife stayed with the child in hospital. Hospitals vary tremendously in the extent to which they co-operate in easing the problems of visiting and family contact. The best restrict neither hours nor numbers and categories of visitors. Others restrict hours, for example, to times outside the hours of the hospital children's school, or forbid parents to be present during ward rounds. Some hospitals allow only parental visiting. This interferes with the child's maintaining other important relationships, for example with siblings, and it may be more difficult for parents to visit if they cannot bring other children with them.

The length of stay may also affect the number of visitors. One may contrast the support that can be mobilized for short-stay or emergency admissions and the obstacles to visiting throughout a lengthy hospitalization. In short stays, generally in a local hospital, temporary disruption of ordinary family life is tolerable or even welcomed for the child's sake, but as time goes on it becomes emotionally and practically increasingly difficult to sustain, and visiting may be sacrificed to the needs of the family at home and ordinary family life. Support systems for the family tend to become less effective as time goes on. Relatives, friends and neighbours mobilize effective support at first, but their support is likely to diminish as the situation passes from the acute to the chronic.

Another disturbing result of long hospitalization may be the attrition of the significance of the child to his family. The family has to deal with the wound caused by the child's absence and, unless robust and sensitive to the child's problems, may do so by closing its ranks: the child loses his place. When he is ready to return, temporarily or permanently, it may be difficult for him to get in and the family may use all kinds of methods to avoid having him. This is especially so in psychiatrically disturbed families. For example, during her third spell of several months' hospitalization a seven-year-old girl was given her first weekend leave. The family made an extraordinary mistake. Although the ward sister was certain she had made it clear to the parents that Diana could go home on Saturday, her father turned up to visit without his car for the first time ever. There was apparently no particular reason why he came by train, but Diana could not be taken home and the father had to return to fetch her on the Sunday. Diana's account to me of the visit was distressing. She told me in a sad, empty voice that she had not enjoyed it. When asked what she had done she said nothing much; the rest of the family had all gone about their normal occupations on the Monday. Her next youngest sister had gone to school as usual, her still younger brother had played with friends in the garden as usual, her mother had gone about her normal household duties. Diana was left to amuse herself as best she could. Diana's account was probably not factually correct, but the emotional undertones could not be ignored. Diana's mother, challenged by other mothers in the ward about why she did not visit more often, said in a persecuted and sad voice that she did not love her any more.

One can see the damage to the family and how this shows in their attitudes to the child. Diana's illness had been expensive and disruptive to family life; Diana had turned into a difficult child, cheeky and physically aggressive, sparing neither adults nor children from her destructiveness and teasing. Physically her progress was disappointing. It was hard to spend much time with her unless one could contact her utter despair. The family was not basically a disturbed family but they had been through an experience with this girl which had been too much to manage well. This was not the worst case. Some children are totally, or almost totally, rejected by their families; weekend leaves are refused, discharge to the family is difficult or impossible, the plight of both child and family is terrible. A healthy family which sustains a child's place may welcome back a child so affected by hospitalization as to be unable to fit into family life. Robertson described a girl with infective tuberculosis who became so 'detached' that she was a permanent misfit in her normal healthy family (Robertson, James, 1958a).

Further, the young patient is likely to be subjected to stressful diagnostic and remedial interventions, only too often in the absence of his natural protector and comforter, his mother. Irrational but intense fears are easily stimulated: for example the fear of bleeding to death or being bled to death when blood samples are taken; the fear of further deformity. The situation is particularly painful when children feel healthy before admission and may be relatively unaware of their condition and when their parents, too, regard them as healthy, as for example in infantile idiopathic scoliosis, a lateral curvature of the spine. The child may feel no disability and may be unaware – or relatively so – of his deformity and the parents regard him as healthy. As one mother said, 'I could stand it if he was ill – but he is healthy!' To the child, diagnosis and treatment can feel like a devastatingly disruptive, inexplicable intrusion through the body-boundaries, a terrible punishment for he does not know what. Disruption of the body-image and of the only partially established identity is another hazard. The body may be added to by plasters, disguised under bandages, subtracted from or significantly changed by the treatment of deformities, such as club feet. The familiar – albeit pathological – image of the body is altered.

In some accidents or illness the new resulting body-image may be, by any standards, horrifying, and mobilize massive defensive techniques in the child. Some of the burned or scalded children described by Helen Martin were almost unable to discern the state of their own bodies and could only concentrate their attention on other children. Anxiety about ultimate recovery may be acute, and one should not be deceived by the young patients' apparent calm or even gaiety. Thesi Bergman has described boys in a Cleveland orthopaedic ward who denied fear and discomfort and maintained a gay stoicism. One day a large buzzing fly entered the ward and the boys panicked. The fly was not dangerous, but the unfamiliar intrusion touched off all their latent terror (Bergman, 1965).

Young patients may be disturbed by the illness, disability and treatment from which other children suffer. I well remember a long conversation with a boy awaiting an appendicectomy about another boy who had had an eye operation. His fantasies were bizarre and lurid. Even allowing for the displaced anxiety about himself, he was enormously disturbed by what happened to the other boy. Healthy siblings sometimes refuse to visit because they cannot stand the sight of the patients.

An important aspect of hospitalization and treatment for many children is immobilization. This deprives the child of a normal means of dealing with feelings and problems: by activity. Anna Freud has commented on the increase in verbal aggression in such children, a feature on which I have also remarked, especially among immobilized adolescent boys (Freud, A., 1952).

We perhaps too easily take for granted aspects of hospitalization that are immediately distressing and may cause lasting damage. Children are often nursed in large, open wards where there is an almost total lack of opportunity for withdrawal and privacy. Where can a child go to be alone? Where can he go for a quiet think, or to read if he is old enough: where can he be quietly alone with a trusted person to talk to, or to cry? Living almost one's entire life in public is far from being a normal developmental experience. Noise is a related problem in a large, busy children's ward where there can be little of the daytime that is really quiet. Unfortunately, this is sometimes made worse by conditions which are themselves desirable: for example, unrestricted visiting. The young patients adjust to the noise level; they learn to disregard it; they learn to shout above it when they want to be heard; they develop a certain selfishness and disregard for other people's need for quiet. This may be a good adaptation to the ward situation but if it goes on too long it becomes permanent and is a bad adaptation to normal life.

Being always in such a large space tends to disorientation: to a feeling of the too-bigness of the space around one: a deprivation of the child's normal need to withdraw into 'something or someone'. This situation may be just tolerable for a short stay in hospital, especially since the child is then more likely to have his mother present for long periods emotionally providing some of the boundaries and withdrawal opportunities that ward design physically removes, but is likely to be damaging to the less maternally protected long-stay child.

The opposite is also true. Hospital can be like a prison from which there is little hope of escape until the sentence is over. Mobile children sometimes abscond if they think they are not being observed; children taken on outings in hospital grounds plead to be taken outside the gates – not far, just so long as the boundary is breached. A cry taken up all round a children's ward after lights out was 'Hospital burn down, Hospital burn down, then we can all go home.'

that the views of such people have had so little effect on the care of these children.

I also accept this recommendation. Such a change could make a crucial difference to the future mental health of these children. It would provide the basic things children need in the absence or insufficient presence of their mother and their ordinary family environment. Nursing qualifications do not seem strictly necessary for the head of this kind of unit, although they are certainly not a disadvantage provided the person concerned is highly skilled in coping with the emotional needs of children and also of her staff, since the work would be very stressful. This person, and the house staff, would then mediate the relationship between the child and other hospital staff as an ordinary mother does with the family doctor, child welfare clinic, schools, and so on.

A consultant paediatrician to the children's home is also important. The Department of Health and Social Security, in giving advice on hospital facilities for children in general, said that the general responsibility for the management and oversight of a children's department should rest with a children's physician (DHSS and Welsh Office, 1971). Individual responsibilities for the treatment of individual children would rest with consultants in various specialities.

That it is possible to change a children's institution providing conventional group care into one run on family-group systems has been demonstrated by Anna Freud and her co-workers at the Hampstead Nurseries (Burlingham and Freud, 1948). The transition resulted in an upsurge of demanding and other normal family-type behaviour, usually suppressed in institutional children, and also in an improvement in the state of the children. In this case the child had a second foster-mother, always the same one, when his own foster-mother was off-duty, rather like a home-based child cared for by a well-known aunt or close friend when his mother is 'off-duty'. The nurse/foster-mothers felt enormous strain in their restructured roles and needed great support, a point to which I will return later.

An important difference between the hospital situation and the ordinary children's home is in fact the much greater avail-

Finally, I want to return to the psychiatric hazards of long hospitalization for young patients stemming from the relatively low level of visiting, particularly by mothers; in extreme cases none at all, or monthly, or occasionally for special events such as operations. Some children may be very much in the position of John in the Robertsons' film, only worse, because they are ill or injured, whereas John was physically healthy (Robertson, James and Robertson, Joyce, 1967–71). Like John, the child admitted to a conventionally run long-stay ward may not find the mother-substitute he needs – a single adult with whom he can build up a close and meaningful relationship, stable and lasting – a disastrous situation for the young child and difficult even for older children. Children's wards usually have few permanent staff, sometimes only the sister and a relatively permanent staff nurse, while the rest of the 'staff' are transitory student nurses. In more fortunate children's wards there are qualified and permanent nursery nurses. Ward organization is commonly such as to lead to multiple indiscriminate care-taking of the kind shown in John's residential nursery, which defeated all his efforts to become 'attached'. The great kindness shown by many nurses does not counteract the lack of the one meaningful relationship.

Besides, multiple indiscriminate care-taking implies that no nurse has direct responsibility for any one child. Responsibility is disparate and therefore not acutely felt, and may not be discharged in a fully effective way. Nurses cannot build up the close, caring relationship with individual children that would help them become sufficiently sensitive and responsive to the child's needs. Closeness of tie and intimate experience are necessary to evoke the deep sense of responsibility and concern which helps them become effective mother-substitutes. This unfortunately means that there is system-based neglect of the child even when the staff are well disposed to children in general and the ward is efficiently run. Children cry and nobody responds for too long, if at all. Children learn that smiling, charming behaviour is more likely to evoke a friendly response than crying: they are well on the way to the last devastating stage of the Robertson 'syndrome' – detachment, with superficial charm and an attrition of their capacity for close, deep and meaningful relationships.

Under this system, the young patient may spend quite long periods alone and bored while nurses are busy about other duties and inattentive to quiet patients who are not their own particular business, and are not a nuisance. In *The Empty Hours* Maureen Oswin has described well the painful periods of boredom children can suffer (Oswin, 1971). Any observant person can see this for themselves. Hospital schools, when they exist, are an enormous help but they operate for school hours and school terms. Long-term children so often lack not only the means but also the people who normally help them occupy their time.

By contrast, children may also suffer from too much stimulation, particularly perhaps those who respond charmingly to contact and play imaginatively, thus giving pleasure to staff. Mothers frequently complain that they find their children do not settle down into a normal pattern of mother/child interaction when they get home but demand constant company and attention.

Children in hospital are outside the scope of the Curtis Committee Report and of the Children Act, which followed it, and in any case these did not cover children under two (Curtis Committee, 1946). These set up concepts and objectives for the care of other children who are deprived of normal family life: for example, the importance of providing effective substitutes for mother and family such as care in small, family-type units with effective foster-mothering. These concepts are largely absent in the training of hospital staff who care for children. The Community Home Design Guide published by the Department of Health and Social Security also advised on the physical layout of community homes for such children, including a degree of privacy and an allocation of space denied to the hospital child.

DIRECTIONS FOR ACTION

One has by now some sense of the kind of action necessary to alleviate distress in such children and their families and to prevent or mitigate damage. One may challenge the notion that

an ordinary hospital setting is appropriate for long-stay cl as against a children's home with the relevant medical, n and auxiliary services visiting or seeing the child elsev Having said that, however, one has to acknowledge tha majority of children's homes do not themselves pr adequately for what the separated and distressed childr them really need, in spite of the Curtis recommendations. ing the film *John* would cure one of any idea that such h provide adequate care for children out of their families. C dren's homes, like hospitals, may need considerable mo cation before they become an adequate substitute for a nor home and ensure the healthy development of the children. W is needed is a children's home as like a normal home as possi Relevant considerations would include: size – it needs to small, say six to eight children with the minimum number staff to look after them, so as to minimize the danger of multi indiscriminate care-taking as in *John*, and to promote closen and intimacy; case-assignment, so that there is a possibility real attachment; staff who can understand children and promo natural expressiveness, especially when the child is distresse well-managed boundaries to protect against intrusion as in good home, and so on. In addition, the hospital/children's hom must help to maximize the participation of mothers and othe family care-takers in the care of the child. To establish such home would be quite a daunting proposition, as indeed i discussed in the second RNOH paper.

J. C. Spence adumbrated this idea when he said it would be better if the children lived in small groups under a house mother and from there went to their lessons in a school, to their treatment in a sick bay, and their entertainment in a central hall (Spence, 1947). He added: that 'there would be no *dis*advantage in the house mother's having nursing training, but that in itself is not a qualification for the work she would have to do; her duty is to live with her group of children and attempt to provide those things of which they have been deprived.'

James Robertson also has many times put forward the idea that what is needed is a children's home. The striking thing is

ability of significant visitors, especially mothers, to hospitalized children even in long-stay hospitals and the fact that they are – and should remain – home- and family-based children. This raises an important issue about the 'unit of care'. In common with most children's institutions, children's hospitals or wards tend (at least implicitly), to see the unit of care as the child, a view which orientates them to caring for the child and often thereby increasing the psychological and social distance between a child and his family. A young child cannot be thus isolated from his family without risk. The proper unit of care is the child and his family, especially his mother, as is well illustrated in Robertson's film *Going to Hospital with Mother* (Robertson, James, 1958b). Some wards have moved implicitly towards operating that concept; others can only be described as freezing the mother out in spite, often, of having ostensibly 'unrestricted visiting'.

Mothers, if given training and support, can become very skilled when nursing their own hospitalized children. I have seen this demonstrated and I have seen nurses taking great pains to work with mothers to care for children as nearly as possible in their natural way and to teach mothers and fathers such basic nursing skills as giving bedpans, lifting, bed-bathing and so on. But I have also seen mothers look on while nurses did simple mothering tasks for children such as brushing and combing their hair. I need not add that the first method helps mothers to sustain a relatively high level of visiting and good contact with their children, while the second makes them suffer from feelings of futility and uselessness so that visiting tends to fall off and contact with children becomes less effective.

To return to my main point: women carrying the substitute-mother role for ill or disabled long-stay children need to add something to their role in addition to that of the substitute mother in institutions for healthy children – that is, to learn to combine support and sustenance for the mother/child and family/child unit when the whole unit is present, with effective substitution when it is absent. It has also been our observation that children accept and are more helped by mother-substitutes when they have been observed by the child in a good relationship

145

with the mother and helping her, than when the child has to make a relationship with the substitute on his own.

Unfortunately this complicated, combined role is not always welcome to the staff of children's hospitals who see themselves as caring for children; *they* feel deprived by the mothers. For example, Brain and Maclay reported, in an experimental study of mothers rooming-in with children, that the nurses conceded that mothers were often a great comfort to children but were unanimous in preferring children to be admitted on their own, among their reasons being that *they*, the nurses, made more personal contact with unaccompanied children (Brain and Maclay, 1968).

There are important issues about how the child's own nurse could establish the 'own' relationship with him, especially in view of the fact that she cannot give a twenty-four-hour service. A crucial point is availability, as is well illustrated by the Robertsons in their films and papers (Robertson, James and Robertson, Joyce, 1967–71). When she is there the mother-substitute must really be 'there' as a mother would, in touch with the child although not necessarily actively interacting all the time: alert to his communications, sensitive to his needs, appropriately responsive, the person who must be there when he needs something. Tasks, too, have their priorities: for example, receiving the child and those who come to hospital with him on admission, helping them settle, letting the child see the nurse in helpful interaction with the parents; doing everything for the child at times when the absence of the mother is particularly stressful, waking him and getting him up, putting him to bed, bathing him, feeding him, talking and playing with him when he wants to; mediating between the child and others and protecting his boundaries; helping the child keep alive his ties with his mother and family when they are absent; dealing with all potentially disturbing interventions necessary for the treatment, being the person through whom all others make a relationship with the child. It is truly astonishing in hospital wards how many strangers – or comparative strangers – go straight up to a child and start doing things: this is very unlikely to happen to a small, home-based child and is most disturbing when it does.

Desirably the nurse would be present during any particularly stressful periods, for example pre- and post-operatively and accompanying the child to theatre. Lastly – and very important for repeat-stay children – the child should if possible have the same nurse/mother-substitute on each admission.

There are a number of options that can be exercised by people treating these young patients and making decisions on their behalf, and the interacting exercise of these options makes a great difference to the hospitalization experiences of child and family.

There is the option to treat or not to treat; the decision is sometimes self-evident, but there are borderline cases where this may not be so. How does one balance the beneficial effects of treatment, psychologically as well as physically, against the potentially damaging effects of hospitalization? Achieving effective diagnosis and prognosis is not easy and long-stay hospitals do not always have the resources to make effective psychological and social diagnoses.

Secondly, there is a possible option about *which* treatment, if treatment there must be. Some treatments are psychologically and socially more damaging than others, more painful, more frightening, more immobilizing, causing more interference with the normal handling of the child, involving more separation from home, family and environment. Spence sent children home in orthopaedic appliances: you can send children home in some orthopaedic appliances but not in others, which may be alternative treatments for the same condition. A complication here, of course, is that the treatments are not necessarily seen as alternatives by any one doctor.

The third option is when to treat. From the viewpoint of the potentially damaging effects of hospitalization the later the better, so that the child has as long as possible to develop independence and the internal resources to help him tolerate and cope with pain, anxiety and separation, to acquire interests that will help him fill the 'empty hours'. Obviously this has to be balanced against physical considerations and the psychological and social effects of waiting for treatment.

Fourthly, there is the option about where to treat. Optimally, of course, not in hospital at all. Spence says:

I have experimented in the domestic care and treatment of children with active abdominal tuberculosis, of children immobilized by orthopaedic appliances, of children with chronic disease which required frequent observation and examination, and from these experiments I am convinced that too often and too lightly is a decision made to confine children in long-stay hospitals. (quoted in Bowlby, 1951)

Many people since Spence have supported this view and things have improved, but his last statement is still unfortunately only too true. There is no doubt that more children could be nursed at home more of the time, especially if effective domiciliary aids – nursing and home helps in particular – were provided. There are, of course, physical risks in having such children at home, risks which Spence knowingly took, and thought worthwhile. Robertson reports a conversation in which Spence told him of such a child who broke an ankle in an accident – Spence still thought it worthwhile to have him at home and, according to Robertson, was unperturbed by possible accusations of negligence.

Besides this option of home or hospital, there is sometimes an option about which hospital. From a psychosocial point of view, the nearer to home and the ordinary environment the better; but how does one balance this advantage against that of highly skilled and specialized medical, nursing and other care given in the specialist and teaching hospitals? It is a difficult issue, but again it seems likely that children are unnecessarily sent to distant hospitals when hospitals nearer home would provide good enough physical treatment for at least some of the time; for example for some of the nursing care, for follow-up X-rays and for other conditions that do not require the specialist hospital.

Lastly, there are often options about the patterning of hospitalization – for example the planning of home leave. How often and when in relation to the child's and family's capacities and needs? How much of the treatment could be done on a day-admission basis? At what point in the child's convalescence or recovery should he be discharged? Here one meets again the problems I have discussed earlier. There are differences of opinion between doctors that are not factually based. Some surgeons, successfully and without undue anxiety, carry out minor operations on a day-admission basis; others will not take what they feel to be an unjustifiable medical risk.

The decision cannot necessarily be effectively made on the basis of the child's physical condition alone; the psychological and social state of the child and family are crucial. It can be difficult and not necessarily helpful to force a child back into a family which does not want him or is not yet ready to receive him – remember Diana. The capacity of different families to cope differs. I well remember two boys of about the same age who had had similar accidents and were discharged at about the same physical stage of recovery. One went back to a family characterized by love and concern and good relationships; the accident and the temporary disturbance which led to it had been well coped with psychologically, the family was integrated in its community and mobilized a great deal of support to help with the convalescent child at home. It seemed possible that his discharge had been unduly delayed. The other boy went home to a family with a distraught mother, an inadequate father, and a mongol sister cared for at home. It was a permanently disturbed family which had not worked through the stress antecedent to or consequent on the accident. Within a few days the boy had had another accident and was back in hospital.

A thread running through the whole discussion of the exercise of options is the need for total diagnosis and prognosis, the use in the team of people capable of making a psychosocial assessment of child and family, who would work with other staff to relate this effectively to treatment plans. A child psychiatrist would make a useful contribution as a back-up for other members of the team and in helping them assess the significance of their observations With the social worker, the child psychiatrist could intervene with children and families under severe stress, to give treatment and try to prevent some of the problems that arise, such as closing up the family gaps. Some of the roles and tasks I have discussed above, especially substitute mothering, are certainly very stressful, bringing staff into more continuous and intimate contact with the child's distress than is the case with multiple indiscriminate care-taking, increasing demands for affection and availability and giving less possibility of evading the meaning of the situation to the child. A child psychiatrist would also have a contribution to make in increasing sensitivity among staff to the distress of patients and families and supporting staff in the distress this will cause them, a task mainly being undertaken at the time of writing by the Tavistock team with the help of the ward sister and social worker.

WHY ACTION RESEARCH?

In concluding this paper I return to the necessity for *action* research. It is not hard to draw up a blueprint, a theoretical model, for a long-stay children's hospital or ward. A general model has been available, with authoritative support, for many years. So why has appropriate action not been taken by people with great concern for their young patients, and how could one effectively proceed to change?

It is in fact difficult for organizations to change themselves from within on their own initiative and with their own resources. Very occasionally it has happened with inspired leadership and a membership that could accept it. Major institutional change cannot be effected by decision-making alone, or even mainly: it inevitably involves a slow, gradual and often painful evolutionary process. This process is in many ways akin to analytical forms of psychotherapy and has some of the same difficulties and rewards. In particular, achieving major institutional change involves a challenge to what Jaques has called the socially structured defence mechanisms which is a major undertaking for all concerned (Jaques, 1953).

As I have described in a paper on action research in a general teaching hospital (Menzies, 1970; see above, pp. 43–85), members of an organization use it in their struggle against the experience of anxiety – especially, though not only, anxiety directly evoked by their membership. The social defence system develops over time as members try to externalize and give substance, in reality, to their own characteristic psychic defence mechanisms. There is collusive interaction and agreement, often unconscious, between the members as to what form it shall take. Once established the social defence system becomes an aspect of objective reality which may be hard to change, for practical as well as emotional reasons.

The indiscriminate multiple care-taking so common in our hospitals is one such defensive device. It splits up the nurse's relation with patients and tends to prevent her from coming into contact with the totality of any one patient; thus it protects her from the depth and intensity of feeling that would arouse. Multiple indiscriminate care-taking dissipates responsibility often rather vaguely among nurses, thus reducing its impact in a situation where it can be frightening and distressing to carry full responsibility.

A long-stay children's hospital generates a great deal of stress for staff. The members of the research team are aware of this from our own experience of the stress that is generated in us. We are also aware of the temptation to build up defences, to become less sensitive to what is going on, to discount the evidence of suffering before our eyes and ears. It is not easy. We are not surprised, therefore, to find that long-stay hospitals have built up massive social defence systems to protect staff from the stress and pain. Part of the answer to why desirable changes have not taken place in long-stay hospitals lies, therefore, in the fact that they would present an enormous challenge to the existing social defence system. Even in prospect, people are intuitively aware of the anxiety and stress that would be released and understandably find this difficult to confront. Take, for example, the change from multiple indiscriminate care-taking to small family groups with house mothers. Gone is the defence of dissipated contact and responsibility; the nurse would be subjected to enormously more strain in her relationship with children, would be much more deeply involved, and would have more defined responsibility. The institution – or rather its members – often need help in challenging defences, tolerating the resultant stress and working towards new, improved defences and adaptive techniques.

The action part of an action research study is very much located in this area of work, while the organization and the research team together consider data and plan action. It is not an easy process for anyone. My first experience of such a process was in a long series of meetings with the senior nursing staff in the general teaching hospital. The nurses were very co-operative and showed courage and honesty in facing the task, but it was very hard and stressful for them. It was also some of the hardest and most stressful work I had ever done (Menzies, 1970; see above, pp. 43–85).

II The psychological welfare of children making long stays in hospital: an experience in the art of the possible

THE EXPERIENCE this paper discusses took place in the Sir William Coxen Ward of the Royal National Orthopaedic Hospital in the course of a four-year study carried out by a team from the Tavistock Institute of Human Relations, directed by the author. The objective was to collaborate with the hospital in:

1. exploring the particular problems of young children making long or repeated stays in hospital;

2. considering what modifications in the method of care might be possible to alleviate both immediate distress and possible lasting damage to personality development;

3. introducing such modifications.

BACKGROUND TO THE STUDY

Neither the hospital nor the research team deemed it necessary to establish that the distress among such children is very great or that its effect may be permanent. We[1] had all experienced the effects on young children of institutionalization in hospitals and in day and residential nurseries for ourselves. Moreover, there are well-established research findings on the subject which we accepted as the background theory for the study (Bowlby, 1951; Robertson, James, 1958a; Heinicke and Westheimer, 1965). These findings are widely known and have gained considerable intellectual acceptance both generally and among the various professions concerned with the care of young children in hospital. However, real emotional understanding of their

153

meaning is less widespread and adoption into hospital practice has been patchy (Report of the Court Committee; see Court, 1976).

The findings are centrally concerned with the conditions that facilitate the healthy psychosocial development of the child and with factors that may interfere with this. They agree that the conditions provided in the early years of life are crucial and that the child's experience then has a lasting effect and is the matrix from which later development springs. Bowlby, for example, stresses the importance of the child's opportunity to form attachments, the most significant among those attachments being that with his mother (I will talk of the 'mother' as the attachment figure, although in rare cases it may be another woman or a man). The quality, consistency and stability of the early attachment experiences greatly influence both the immediate experiences of the young child and his personality growth. The process of developing attachment is at its height during the first six to seven months of life and its success depends focally – albeit among other things – on there being fairly continuous interaction between the mother and child without any major separations. The fact that the baby may not show great distress if separated from his mother at this period, since strong attachment is not yet formed, may blind the observer to the seriousness of the separation: that it is likely to interfere with successful attachment.

It is noteworthy that successful attachments are not formed only, if at all, through the efficient performance of 'service' functions for the child: feeding, bathing, nappy-changing, potting. This is a sobering thought for child-care institutions which too often provide 'service' and little else. More important are the 'social' functions: play, 'talk', touching or smiles, sometimes but not only while 'service' is being provided; and the evident delight and joy these give both mother and infant. Most important, too, is the mother's capacity to deal with the infant's distresses, to understand and react sensitively to his cries, to soothe his fears, to comfort and reassure him. The mother acts as a stimulus control system for the baby, controlling the situation around him and protecting him from disruptive intrusions.

Each mother–infant pair develops its own idiosyncratic pattern of interaction familiar to both. This familiarity is of great mutual benefit, speeding effective response and helping to make the world feel a safe place for the infant.

The ensuing period, up to about the age of three, sees the full blossoming of attachment: evident strong preference for the mother; need for her presence even if she is ostensibly ignored; she the first person to whom the child turns in his joys and his sorrows; immense distress often at parting and certainly about prolonged separation. Nobody else will do. Reunions may be far from joyful; the child angry, rejecting and with diminished trust. Separation at this stage, then, is not lightly to be contemplated if one is concerned about the child's present welfare and his future development.

After three, attachment begins to diminish in intensity, longer separations from the mother are tolerable, the child's relationships broaden and other attachment figures increase in significance. The child's internal resources grow in strength: his store of good memories, his capacity to keep important people firmly in his mind in their absence, his hopes for their return. But the mother is likely to remain the single most important figure for a long time and to continue to be the first resource when the child is in trouble. Regression is a normal reaction to stress and the older child in trouble may well behave like a younger one; hence the 'mummyishness' of many older children, adolescents or even adults in hospital.

Normally the focal mother–child attachment is embedded in a system of other attachments, notably in nuclear and extended families. These figures are also important both in giving and sharing pleasures and in providing additional comfort to both partners in distress. A mother and baby left alone together a great deal may become too much for each other – as is seen, for example, among single mothers who bring their babies to day nurseries. The mother needs to escape to a job and adult companionship from the intolerable stress of caring for a baby without support. It should be noted too, in our context, that these other attachment figures are usually the most effective mother-substitutes should the separation of the baby or small child from his mother be inevitable.

All in all, then, the best developmental situation for the pair to develop their attachment and bring it to fruition is one in which they can be together, or available to each other, most of the time and where their relationship is embedded in relationships with other people who have or develop attachments to them separately and together.

These findings are further supported by direct research into the effects of separation of the young child from his mother, notably when the child is put into an institution. Immediate and often inconsolable distress is almost universal. Indeed, its absence may itself be a pathological sign; for example, in children who have not formed a successful primary attachment. Most children after even a short stay in an institution with significant separation from the mother are, on return home, anxious and difficult to manage, their relationship with their mother being usually a focus of disturbance (Robertson, James, 1969a,b). The extent and speed of recovery in the child vary enormously. Some appear to recover quickly and completely, some retain various degrees of minor impairment; a proportion remain seriously impaired and in a characteristic way well described by Robertson. The capacity for meaningful attachments is impaired; relationships are superficial and may be promiscuous; emotional responses are frequently inappropriate, in particular cheerfulness and an apparent lack of anxiety in situations which would normally evoke distress and fear. There may be an avid interest in material objects as a compensation for the poverty of human relationships. Intellectual development and the capacity for concentration may be impaired.

This variability in recovery would appear to be a function of several interacting factors:

1. *The child's capacity to manage the experience of separation from his mother and normal setting.* Age is clearly an important factor. Other things being equal, the older the child the better. Of crucial importance are the child's early attachment experiences and the inner strength and resources he has built up in conse-

quence. The deeply attached child may initially show more distress but is likely to recover better.

2. *Factors in the institutional setting.* Broadly, the more the institution differs from the normal home setting, the worse the effects are likely to be. The ways in which institutions vary from home are many and will be discussed in some detail later, but most relevant here and most significant for the ultimate effect on the child is the nature of the care-taking supplied as an alternative to the mother and other natural attachment figures. It seems clear that it is best when a child is cared for by one person to whom a significant attachment can be formed. This is not usually possible in institutions, which only too often go to the other extreme and provide multiple indiscriminate care-taking, where the child has no figure he can in any way call his own but has a succession of transitory care-takers who look after all the children indiscriminately (Robertson, James, 1969 a,b). This effectively prevents the child from forming a new attachment and may well permanently impair his capacity for forming attachments and meaningful relationships.

3. *The length of stay in the institution and of the separation.* The longer this is, the worse the effects are likely to be: a point of central concern for long-stay hospitals.

What has perhaps been less well documented in previous research, but we have found to be of great importance, is that separation may also have detrimental effects on the mother's capacity to remain attached to her child and to care for him well. She, too, may become estranged. She misses the idiosyncratic interactions, intimacy and familiarity and so may lose sensitivity. The child will develop in a way she does not know and may find it hard to relate to. She begins to need him less for her own fulfilment. She closes up the gap his absence has left. She may be guilty at failing him in a crisis, and feel inadequate because she has had to hand him over to 'experts'. Indeed she, too, may never develop attachment if the baby is very young (as, for example, in a premature-baby unit). The result may be that the child, himself damaged by separation, may return to a

mother also damaged and thus less able to restore the relationship and to help him in his recovery from hospitalization.

DEFINITION OF THE OBJECTIVES IN DETAIL

With this background in mind, the hospital and research team
together could define the general approach to the problem
of relieving immediate distress in the children and providing
prophylaxis against lasting damage through hospitalization.
Stated in general terms, the research objective became to give
the child a setting as near to normal home conditions as a
hospital and the needs of treatment permitted. Within this
general objective, three main sub-objectives were delineated
although, as will be seen, they were highly interrelated.

1. *Sustaining the mother–child relationship.* This was regarded as
the most important single objective. It posed a difficult problem
in a long-stay hospital with a national and international catchment area. Mothers could not in general be with the child
continuously, as they can in a short-stay local hospital. A
different balance would need to be struck between the child's
need for his mother and hers for him, and the mother's other
responsibilities to her husband, home and possibly other children. Consideration had to be given to the mother's needs for
rest, relaxation and support from her own natural care-takers.
The objective then was defined as working towards optimal
maternal presence for each child and family, taking all the
relevant factors into account.

2. *Alternatives to maternal care.* It will be clear from the previous
paragraph that there was no expectation that the mother would
be available for the whole of a child's stay. In some cases,
maternal presence might not be even remotely adequate. So the
second objective was to explore how far, within a hospital
setting, effective alternative care-taking could be provided. Two
sources of such care-takers were available:

(a) Other attachment figures from the child's home
environment.

(b) Care-takers from the hospital staff.

3. *The hospital setting.* The hospital setting itself was to be explored to examine ways in which it differed from the normal home setting and how far these could be modified.[2]

RESEARCH AND ACTION STRATEGY

I will conclude this Introduction with a comment on the research and action strategy deployed towards these objectives, referring back to the subtitle of this paper. Basic to the whole strategy was the need to take a fresh look at the situation, to try to set aside habitual ways of looking at things, to blind oneself to the obvious, to become questioning and constructively critical, to think again. This implied the need to stand back and cultivate some detachment, which is not easy and can be distressing. For example, such a fresh look can show that procedures considered best or even essential are neither, and may indeed be harmful, so that guilt and anxiety may be stimulated. Taking another look at the patient may show him to be very different from one's previous conception of him: more anxious, more distressed, more in need of care and comfort. This causes more distress to the observer.

Central to our theme is that such a fresh look may give a different perspective to judgements of the possible and imposs-ible – showing, for example, that things are quite possible which had been thought impossible because 'they have never been done before here' and often that the so-called impossible may in fact be preferable. One cannot therefore responsibly refrain from trying to do the previously 'impossible', and then one is precipitated into the stress and uncertainties of change. Or it may emerge that existing procedures have developed for the benefit of staff rather than patients, a situation which responsible and devoted staff would find difficult to sustain once it became obvious to them (Menzies, 1970; see above, pp. 43–85). Perhaps most painful of all is when the fresh look challenges existing beliefs and traditions, often strongly held. In our case one such area was perception of the child and his development – sometimes painful for staff to explore.[3]

The use of the word 'art' also implies something important about the process of study and change. This was often highly intuitive, depending on the development of new insights, sometimes slowly and painfully, 'playing it by ear' with emphasis on the significance of feelings, although facts and theories were also used. It depended on skills and experience. Above all, it was not aimed at scientific fact-finding that would produce a definitive model to be neatly described on paper but at changes which gradually evolved, piecemeal, one thing leading to another – an ongoing process of change, often almost imperceptible but in the end bringing about very significant modifications in the way the children and families were cared for.

The presence of the research team certainly facilitated this process. It was easier for them to stand back and to take a fresh look since they were not an integral part of the hospital setting and, indeed, at first were completely new to it. Further, they brought to the task experience of other similar settings, of what had been useful there and what could be done. It is difficult to go on saying that something is impossible if someone else is doing it. Most important was the team's function in giving support in the stress and anxiety evoked by the fresh look and by consequent changes; in helping to develop the new skills which the changes required and to elucidate developments in roles and relationships; in acting as advocate for change.

But although the research team facilitated the process, it does not seem that the presence of such a team is a *sine qua non* for such a process to take place. Indeed, it would be dangerous to think so, since it would inhibit self-help – that is, the undertaking of such a task by hospitals on their own initiative with local resources, through contact with other institutions operating different procedures and through publications. The main requirements are the willingness to do so and the courage and strength to tolerate the stress. Many institutions have indeed implemented significant changes on their own initiative. The RNOH is itself a good example of self-help in this respect for, since the ending of the study some seven years ago [1975], the hospital has continued to implement significant changes on its own account both in the care of the small children and by carrying the principles developed there into other wards and departments, for example into the rest of Coxen Ward and into the adolescent wards. During the study, indeed, the relevant staff quickly became deeply involved in the process themselves and often took initiatives independently in introducing modifications in practice.

INITIAL AREAS OF EXPLORATION

This section will discuss examples of how the work proceeded following the three main areas of concern as delineated at the beginning of the study.

First, however, a brief note about the setting for the care of the young children. They were cared for in a Cot Unit which took up to twelve children, from birth to the age of four. The Cot Unit occupied the 'foot' of an L-shaped ward, the Sir William Coxen Ward, the 'leg' of which took some twenty children between four and eleven years of age. There was a sister in charge of the whole ward with one or two staff nurses, three nursery nurses and five or six student nurses There were several teachers from the hospital school, including a nursery teacher in the Cot Unit. At first there was no very clear distinction between the two parts of the ward, although the nursery nurses worked almost exclusively in the Cot Unit.

The level of concern for the children and their families was very high both in the staff who worked in the Unit and among other staff who worked with the children and families. The research team's first impression was that this was among the best children's wards they had ever seen. There was a liberal visiting policy that placed no restrictions on the number or category of visitors, thus facilitating the maintenance of significant attachments and helping sustain the child's contacts with the outside world. Mothers were genuinely welcomed and were actively engaged in the care of their own and sometimes other children. Staff saw the support of the mothers as part of their role. The teaching staff helped enormously in sustaining education, in keeping children constructively occupied and in maintaining outside contacts, especially with schools. They were well in touch with the children's distress. The social workers were very much a part of the life of the ward, spending a great deal of time there, available to both children and families. They also worked in the outpatient clinics whenever possible. There they interviewed children and families to help prepare them for admission and to plan as effectively as possible for the child's hospitalization. These efforts in the Cot Unit were also well supported by the management of the various professions concerned. There was a tradition of thinking about and rethinking methods of care.

Much might remain to be done in the study, but all in all it was a very good setting for what the hospital and the research team hoped to accomplish.

THE PRESENCE OF THE MOTHER WITH HER CHILD
The way the Cot Unit operated seemed to have contributed to maternal presence that was high for a long-stay hospital with a national and international catchment area, but we agreed that it was probably not yet 'optimal' and could be increased. We began, therefore, to look again at possibilities. It was clear that the presence of even devoted mothers could not necessarily be taken for granted. There can be obstacles in the mother herself and in her home situation which may interfere and which she may not be able to overcome without help. For example, a hospital is a strange place to the mother as well as to the child; she may have a confused idea of what she can do there and how she can help her child. She may be anxious at the idea of being away from home on her own without her usual adult support figures. She may be in conflict about her other responsibilities, especially other children. Moreover, other people may also put obstacles in her way; for example, other family members may compete with the hospitalized child for her attention and become more demanding at the threat of some withdrawal of her concern for them. There can also be obstacles from the hospital side which interfere with the mother's deploying her concern for her child. For example, ambivalence about the presence of mothers may be only too clearly, if subtly, expressed. On the one hand mothers may be told they may be in the hospital as much as they wish; but this is then contradicted by the stating of situations where their presence would not be welcome – during ward rounds, for example.

Nor did we place much faith in the efficacy of exhortation as a means of increasing maternal presence. It does not necessarily contribute to the removal of obstacles on either side; indeed, it may be a means whereby a hospital puts all the responsibility on the mother and family without acknowledging its own responsibilities, and leaves it to them to do the right thing. It may only, therefore, succeed in increasing the anxiety and guilt of the mother about her child without helping her in any way to deploy them effectively in his care.

We felt it important, therefore, to consider what help, support and encouragement could be given to the mother to deploy her natural concern by optimizing her presence with her child in the hospital. How was the mother's own wish to be with her child to be supported, especially in the face of sometimes rather daunting obstacles? Exploration showed that there were a number of fairly crucial points in the process of the child's hospitalization where appropriate interventions might help the mother to move closer to the optimal situation for herself, the child, and the rest of the family and others involved.

(a) Outpatient clinics

Procedures at outpatient clinics were reviewed – these being where, with a few exceptions, the decision to admit the child is made and communicated to his parents. Although parents may have considered the possibility of hospitalization earlier, with variable success in confronting it and preparing for it, this is, in a sense, the point at which it becomes a reality that has to be faced and coped with. This is therefore a situation in which the future pattern of relationship between the hospital and its staff and the parents and child begins to be set. The parents have to begin to think seriously about the implications of hospitalization for their child and themselves and to see them in the wider context of their family and other relationships. These beginnings of planning unfortunately have to be done when the parents are not necessarily in the best state to do it effectively. They may often be in a state of considerable shock, the admission being experienced as a confirmation of the seriousness of the child's illness, injury or deformity and as disruptive to their familiar ways of living and relating to each other.

We then reconsidered the resources available to help parents in this situation. It did not seem reasonable or practicable to expect the surgeons during the outpatient clinics to do more than explain carefully the nature of the child's physical problem and the likely process of treatment and hospitalization. They could not be expected to take the necessary time, nor did it seem reasonable to expect them automatically to have the skill and knowledge to go further with the family at this point. Nor were the nurses at outpatients usually available or skilled at such work. The hospital social workers attached to the surgical teams seemed the obvious people. They had the relevant skills and knowledge and a serious commitment to optimizing maternal presence, and attached great importance to work in outpatient clinics.

Attention was given to strengthening the role the social workers had already developed in outpatient clinics, and it came to be accorded very high priority in their workload. The components of the role were examined again and made explicit so that they could be communicated to other relevant people such as surgeons, nurses and new social workers and clearly understood by them.

This task, as it was defined, included several components. Initially the social workers helped the adults deal with the shock of the surgeon's news, often including carefully going over his communication again and ensuring that it had really been heard and understood. (Accusations that doctors have not given the appropriate information are not always justified; sometimes the patient's and relatives' anxiety and distress make them unable to absorb the most careful explanations.) This was intended to help towards some recovery from the shock and to free the parents' capacity to think and plan constructively. The social worker discussed the facilities the hospital offered to mothers and others present with children, such as visiting times, who might visit, living-in accommodation, the method of care in the Cot Unit, and so on. She solicited and answered questions as much as possible. She explored the home situation with the parents, the mother's other commitments, how she might free herself, who might be appropriate to take them over for at least some of the time, which of the child's other attachment figures might alternate with the mother in the hospital. She discussed financial matters concerning the quite high cost to a family of the child's stay in the hospital (estimated by one father as several thousand pounds in the course of his daughter's lengthy and repeated hospitalization) and what help might be available. The social worker concluded by giving her telephone number and emphasizing her availability in the interval between this interview and admission, to discuss problems or answer further questions.

The evidence from follow-up discussions suggests that this work by the social workers effectively began establishing the image of the hospital as a concerned and helpful place, not only for the children but for their families and their other concerns. It helped the mothers to feel genuinely wanted and needed and thus made a considerable contribution to optimizing maternal presence. We would emphasize that this was a service to all families in their normal reactions to hospitalization and did not single out only those families where there was reason to suppose that there was some special need for care.

(b) *After admission*

Once the child was admitted the burden of helping to sustain maternal presence fell on all hospital staff who were concerned with the child's care and treatment, but most notably and heavily on the staff of the Cot Unit: the nurses and nursery nurses, the nursery teacher and the social worker who spent a great deal of time there, available alike to children and people present with them and other staff. And we note again the importance of the social worker thus being available to all when all are under stress, and not only to such families as would be referred for specialized social work help.

The actual admission procedure was regarded as particularly important and we considered how it could best be done. In particular we wished to avoid a situation that too often happens in hospitals: patients and those who accompany them are not effectively in contact with staff except during medical and other interventions and may be left lost, lonely and anxious in strange and bewildering surroundings, unless helped by other patients and relatives. So an admission procedure of careful handover from one person to another was developed. Someone, frequently a hospital volunteer, accompanied the child and family from the admissions office to the ward and introduced them to the sister or, if she was not available, to the nurse in charge.[4] This was usually a fairly short contact and the sister then introduced them to the staff nurse in charge of the Cot Unit who, after a short initial contact again, introduced them to the nursery nurse to whom they were assigned (see pp. 173 ff. for a description of case-assignment). Although contact with the ward sister and staff nurse was important in establishing their authority, responsibility and concern for the child and the family and their availability if required, they, like the surgeon, have many other tasks that restrict the time and care they can give to any one patient and family. So the main burden of general care throughout the hospitalization, and especially at the point of admission, was to fall on the nursery nurse.

(c) *Role and function of the nursery nurse*

These were under constant review and consequently underwent continuous development as the study went on. The task on the day of admission was based on being present with or quickly available to the child and the family throughout the day. The nursery nurse had a number of functions in helping them to settle and feel as much at home as possible. She gave a lot of information about the Unit, Coxen Ward and the hospital, sometimes repetitively if people found it difficult to absorb and remember. She would solicit and answer questions, as far as she was able. (The boundary between general care questions and specialized orthopaedic questions had to be carefully defined and reference sometimes made to others for answers.) She sought information about the child and family with the objective of helping the hospital provide care as like home as possible – for example any particular likes or dislikes about food or dietary problems; sleeping habits, simple things like whether the child slept with a pillow or not; if the child was verbal, his familiar names for people and objects; ways of comforting the child. These were recorded so that they were available to other people in the absence of the assigned nurse.

A background to all these activities was the task of helping the family and the child with the stress and anxiety of actually coming into hospital. The nursery nurses helped both adults and verbal children to voice these anxieties and dealt with them as appropriate. Some could be dealt with fairly simply, for example by answering questions such as when the ward round would take place at which crucial decisions would be made about the child's treatment; sometimes by talking about other children in the Unit at various stages in their treatment, how the treatment was progressing, what the prognosis was. Fantasies about the child's condition and treatment (often worse than the reality) could be exposed and some relief provided by giving facts. Other, perhaps more nebulous, anxieties could be relieved by comfort and support and above all by respect for them and by conveying to mothers and other adults that they were not silly, hysterical or a nuisance because they were upset or sometimes cried, an attitude which is often too clearly expressed by hospital staff and adds to the burden of mothers.

An overriding anxiety in all mothers and other adults accompanying the children at this stage centred inevitably on what their role, functions and relationship with their child were to be while he was in hospital. This was dealt with extensively both by talk and by the nursery nurse's behaviour in relating to mother and child. Our review of this situation had impressed us all with the importance of keeping the mother, as far as hospital conditions and treatment permitted, in her normal mothering role and retaining her normal authority. This seemed to be crucial in sustaining the mother's view that she was actually wanted and needed, both by her child and by the staff. In too many hospitals where maternal visiting is unrestricted and even encouraged in principle, this can be defeated by subtle whittling away of the mother's role and relationship with her child; for example by nurses taking over ordinary child-care tasks so that the mothers begin to feel unnecessary, futile and inadequate –

a feeling only too easily engendered in mothers who may feel that anyway, for example, if they have borne a congenitally deformed child.

So, during that first pattern-setting day, the nursery nurse would explain the care system to the mother and other adults and show by her behaviour that she meant it. For example, the mother would give the child his meals, wash or bath him, put him to bed, play with him and comfort him, arrange his possessions, answer his questions if he was verbal. The nursery nurse was there to help if required but not, if it could be avoided, to take over. This was quite a difficult situation to handle, often with resistance on both sides. Mothers coming into hospital are often so impressed or even overawed by the 'experts' that they may be prone to hand over both the child and their authority for him. One has seen mothers literally try to put the child into the nurse's arms immediately on admission. Nursery nurses, for their part, may be only too ready to take on the child and the authority. They are in this job because they want to work with children rather than adults and, especially when they are fully trained, have considerable expertise and experience with the ill, injured or deformed child. So the nursery nurse is in a sense being asked to work against herself when she resists taking over the child. But it is vital that she does so, in the interests of both the child and the mother and of their relationship.

(d) *Helping mothers define and sustain their role*
Another inhibiting factor for mothers in behaving 'normally' is that they are in the strange and often disconcerting situation of having to carry out their usually rather private functions for their child in public, under the scrutiny of both other mothers and the 'expert' staff. The affectionate nonsense but meaningful sounds a mother enjoys making to her child in private may suddenly feel silly if overheard by other adults. Differences in child-care practices between mothers or between mothers and nurses may make a mother question whether hers are good enough and make her uncertain about how to behave or uneasy about behaving as she usually would. Since the child has something wrong with him anyway, mothers are particularly prone

to feel criticized. The author came on to the ward one day just as a mother smacked her child for doing something naughty. The mother, realizing she had been seen, turned to the author and said: 'I shouldn't have done that, should I?' A lot of work needed to be done, therefore, in helping the mothers overcome their inhibitions and behave spontaneously. Work also had to be done if a mother became really uneasy about her usual behaviour – especially in cases where it might really be inadequate – to help her modify her behaviour and her attitude. The line between unwarranted interference by the 'experts' and helpful intervention is by no means easy to draw.

Further, there were difficult judgements to be made by staff about what each mother would in fact be able to do. It is unrealistic to assume that all mothers are equally capable of sustaining their normal roles in the difficult situation of the hospital. The role had to develop differently for each mother, since it was patently of no help to push her beyond her capacity. Most mothers wanted to and could accompany their child when painful or frightening procedures were carried out, such as taking blood samples or taking off plaster casts. Some could not, and it would not have helped to insist. The assigned nurse could take over. Again there were times when a child could become too much for his mother. For example, it was an attentive, devoted mother who, after she had tried unsuccessfully for a very long time to calm a frightened, distressed, screaming child, said: 'Now I know why some mothers batter their children.' She was advised to go off the ward and rest while her assigned nursery nurse temporarily took over the care of her child, actually a not uncommon event at home, where someone else may take over the care of an ill or distressed child for a temporarily overstressed mother.

The sustaining of a normal maternal role and, through that, of maternal presence was, then, a continuous task throughout the child's hospitalization and one that made considerable demands on staff and mother alike. Staff had to surrender some of their direct contact with children and take on considerable responsibility for the support and at times the training of mothers: for example in how to handle children in orthopaedic appliances; in the supervision of children mobile in plaster casts; in the bodily care of children on traction.

(e) *Review of some concepts of care*

1. *The concept of maternal presence.* The development of these practices made us review the whole concept of mothers *visiting* their children in hospital and it began to appear that *visiting* was not an appropriate concept, since it has certain inappropriate implications. It seems to imply a certain distancing between mother and child. It may imply that the mother's presence is a concession and not a right; that it is not an accepted part of the child's treatment and prophylaxis; or that the hospital rather than the mother and family are now the authority over the child. So visiting as a concept was dropped. The mother and other family care-takers came to be seen as an essential part of the hospital care system. Finding a suitable term to describe the new concept did not prove easy; we came to use the term 'maternal presence' although that did not seem entirely satisfactory either, not giving enough credit to the vital role and high level of activity of the mother, or other relatives and friends, in the care of the hospitalized child.

2. *The unit of care.* Another concept that came under review was that of the 'unit of care'. It is usually assumed that the unit of care in a children's ward is the child. In view of the development in the care system in the Cot Unit and the amount of time and effort staff put in to support the role of the mother and family with the child, it began to seem appropriate to extend the boundaries of the 'unit of care'. This became the family and especially the mother with the child, not the child alone. The Cot Unit began to see itself as a family unit rather than as a children's unit.

3. *The implications of the liberal visiting policy.* The full implications of the previous visiting policy began to emerge as the study proceeded. It reflected, in fact, important aspects of attachment theory. It enabled the child to keep in contact with important attachment figures in addition to his mother, particu-

larly his father and siblings and his extended family, such as grandparents. This is particularly important for the long-stay child. Such people were also significant care-takers for the child when the mother herself could not be present (see also below, pp. 173 ff.). Further, it helped in many ways to sustain maternal presence. The mother was relieved of some of her conflict of responsibilities: notably, she could bring to hospital with her other young children for whom caring might have been difficult had she had to leave them behind. These other children were taken into the care system of the Cot Unit and looked after by the nursery teacher when appropriate or by nursing staff, if the mother herself was occupied in the care of the patient. Indeed, on a few occasions other children were also taken into general medical care when some symptom was noticed; for example a sibling was treated for obesity. Very importantly, the mother could be accompanied to the hospital by others who were significant to her, relatives and friends who were her normal support system and who could help her pass the often tedious hours in hospital when she had few of her normal activities with which to occupy herself – the ordinary running of the household, for example. Activities like reading, knitting, writing letters are limited and may seem rather meaningless to her in the hospital setting. Nor can she – nor is it desirable that she should – occupy herself continuously with her child. This would not be a mirror of the normal home situation, where mother and child may be occupied with their own concerns although available to each other when needed. The child may be asleep, or busy with toys or with other children, although his ability to do this with equanimity is dependent on the presence – though not the active intervention – of his mother. Mothers can *feel* not needed in such circumstances, although the disturbance of the child if they are not available contradicts those feelings; for example, the child actually checks out of the corner of his eye whether the mother is still there. The mother needs support, encouragement and meaningful relationships to help tide her over these periods of apparently meaningless presence.

4. *The extent of hospitalization.* Important judgements concern

how much of his treatment actually requires the child to be in hospital. This was brought to our notice by the treatment policy of the surgeon in charge of most of the Cot Unit children, who opted, whenever there was choice, for treatment which enabled the child to be cared for at home. Not only did this mean that the child could be treated for considerable periods in his normal family setting with normal relationships sustained, it also greatly facilitated maternal presence with the child when he did have to be in hospital. Periods in hospital were shorter and intermittent, so that the disruption of ordinary family life was reduced and the mother was subject to less conflict about other responsibilities and was more free to be with her child. It is difficult to exaggerate the contribution of this surgical policy to the sustaining of the child's normal relationships, particularly that with his mother, during treatment. This, however, is an area where we did not perhaps investigate the full possibilities during this study and where further exploration might prove valuable. For example, was there effective definition of the conditions of the children and the nature of the treatment that could be effectively handled at home? Children were sent home in plaster casts, for example, but not on traction. Was this inevitable? The extent of treatment at home would be greatly affected by the help available there; for example home support by nurses, health visitors or home helps so that the mother is supported in both home-nursing procedures and in her anxieties about her child. It would also be affected by the equipment that could be made available either by the hospital or by local services. Effective continued contact with the hospital is also important so that the mother can be sure of immediate advice and support and so that rapid readmission may be effected if necessary. Thus the hospital could become not only a place where children are treated, but the focus of an integrated care system which extends its services to its patients while they are being cared for at home – a widely extensive system of treatment and care (see also Dartington, 1979). The capacity of mothers and families to manage the treatment of a child at home varies, and a careful family assessment would need to be done before a decision could be made about the balance between home and hospital care. There was more than one occasion when a mother and child stayed a day or two longer in the hospital when the child was physically fit to go home because the mother and staff felt that the mother was not yet confident enough about the home management of her child at the current stage of his treatment.

CARING FOR A CHILD DURING HIS MOTHER'S ABSENCE

The effects of these changes gradually became apparent as what had been good maternal presence in the long-stay situation became really quite remarkable, and as the mothers and relatives moved even more strongly into being the focus of care for most children for a very great deal of the time. However, in spite of that, maternal presence could not be by any means continuous. For all children there were nights when mothers were not immediately available. Living-in accommodation for mothers and other relatives is in different buildings from the Cot Unit. Many mothers preferred to go home partly because of that and partly to sustain something of their normal life and relationships, care for their home and other people there and find relaxation from hospital life. Because so many mothers prefer to go home, there are sometimes considerable periods of the day when a child's mother may not be available.

We found, too, that mothers of long-stay children do not necessarily want to room in with their children. This is not the usual situation at home. They talked of something which we defined as 'dressing-gown' distance, in another room but easily available if the child needs them. Unfortunately, we were not able to test out this idea within the study.

Lastly there were a few children who had no mothers available for all or most of their time in hospital. These were of two kinds: children from overseas whose mothers could not travel with them and children from institutions or with previous hospitalization elsewhere whose parents had lost contact or concern for their children through separation. It was obviously important, therefore, to review the availability and appropriateness of other possible care-takers.

As noted above, a first resort in the absence of the mother

was another person from the child's natural attachment circle. Fathers, grandmothers, siblings, other relatives and friends helped greatly here. As the care system developed, it became part of the nursery nurses' responsibility to examine with the family what were the possibilities; to help the family mobilize such other care-takers effectively; and to make them welcome. But even these were not enough and more had to be provided from the hospital's own staff.

We considered how far the hospital could provide an approximation to a single other unique care-taker. Case-assignment seemed the obvious answer although it has clear limitations within the hospital setting, notably that full-time nursery nurses worked a forty-hour week, always during the day, while the child's daytime week (that is, the part of the week covered by day staff) was ninety-one hours. There was a separate night staff.

However, we judged that in spite of these limitations, case-assignment was the best step. The assigned nursery nurse's part in the admission procedure and subsequently in sustaining the maternal role has already been described. I will now describe briefly other significant aspects of the role as it developed. It was especially important for children whose mothers could never be present or were rarely present and here the nurse 'specialled' the child, took major responsibility for his general care, for maintaining liaison with his family as far as possible, for helping him through traumatic interventions, playing, comforting, being generally available: both a 'service' role and an 'attachment' role. In a less intensive way, she did the same thing for all children when no natural attachment figures were present. She also, whenever possible, accompanied the children to other parts of the hospital where mothers and other family adults were not permitted, notably to anaesthetics procedures and in the early stages of care in the post-operative recovery ward (see below, pp. 200 ff.).

In addition, the nursery nurse had a responsibility for working with the family to ensure the best continuous care for the child: for example, to help the family if its presence had to be limited, to be present at particularly difficult times for the child – such as admission, various treatment procedures including operations – and before discharge so that handover to the home could be optimized. She would also plan a box-and-cox system with mothers so that the child would maximally be cared for by one or other of them. So mothers would be kept informed about the nursery nurses' off-duty so that they could plan to be there if possible, or alternatively would plan their own absences so that the nursery nurse could be there.

The context for the case-assignment was also important, however, especially cover for the time the assigned nursery nurse was off-duty, even if the mother was there, bearing in mind that part of the nursery nurse's duty was to support and help the mother. One could not leave to chance the cover for families and children when nursery nurses were off-duty or temporarily absent on other duties, such as escort or post-operative recovery ward care. A careful programme of reassignment was therefore organized so that a nursery nurse on duty was always responsible for each family and child and both knew who it was. Occasionally the staff nurse took reassignments[5] and sometimes it was felt that another mother might be the most appropriate temporary care-taker for a child in the absence of his own mother or assigned nurse, but again it was not left to chance. The mother would be formally asked to take over, the limits of her responsibility defined and the nurse to whom she could turn if she needed additional help would be nominated. There was therefore nothing indiscriminate about the care of children and families.

The complexities of the situation are probably evident: for example, children's reactions to the temporary breaking of focal relationships when nurses went off-duty such as normal anger and resentment, particularly children who were 'specialled' because of total or almost total maternal absence. These children behaved in a way very like children separated from their mothers, often being withdrawn and rejecting when the assigned nursery nurse returned, clinging to the alternative care-taker and requiring hard and painful work from both nurses before the relationship could be re-established. Jealousies and rivalries could develop between nurses – for example about who was the child's favourite, the assigned or the temporarily assigned nurse. The temporary nurse, for example, might find it hard to co-operate in surrendering a child who had become attached to her and seemed to prefer her. These difficulties were not, however, regarded as contraindications to the system but as natural concomitants, problems to be worked out explicitly to help the system function and indeed from which staff, children and families could benefit if they were well handled. It was part of the general principle that maturation could take place through successful confrontation with such problems.

There is also a risk that despite care in reassignment the system may approximate to multiple indiscriminate care-taking, thus interfering with the child's opportunity to make and sustain attachments. Here the actual situation in the Cot Unit implemented an important principle: the Unit was small and only three nursery nurses – the minimum number who could span the ninety-one-hour daytime week – were required to staff it. Thus, the number of nursery nurses who would look after one family and child would be three – all of them, in the close and intimate situation of the Cot Unit, already familiar and usually trusted figures, experienced as being in close co-oper-ative relationships with the mothers and with each other. In other words, the system mirrored the normal family situation with the focal attachment figure, the assigned nursery nurse, and other subsidiary attachment figures, the other nursery nurses, taking over in her absence. The principle of smallness seems important so that the Unit can be staffed by the minimum number of nurses necessary to cover the timespan and care for all children. If the unit is larger it is better to break it down into smaller sub-units, each relatively independent in staffing and operation.

Finally, the case-assignment system had to be backed by a duty roster which took account of the needs of patients and families, and, at the same time, of the needs of nurses for adequate off-duty time. The basic roster was for three nursery nurses and a staff nurse and was on a regular three-week rotation. Staffing was heaviest at times of greatest need – for example admission, the main weekly ward round, the main operating day, with two or three nursery nurses on duty; and lightest at times of least need – for example weekends, when there were relatively few patients and family presence was at its peak, or at times of day when mothers were most likely to be present. The roster gave the nursery nurses two long breaks in the three weeks, one a weekend and the other midweek. The main difficulty was a continuous eight-day spell on duty without a major break which, however, the nurses accepted as the only way of getting two long spells off. An alternative two-nurse roster was prepared in case a nursery nurse should be away ill or on leave.

It appeared important that the staff of such a unit be permanent and not, as is more usual, student nurses or even a staff nurse who are transitory. The permanence is important to ensure continuity in the care of families and children through long and repeated stays in hospital and to avoid, as far as possible, too many broken relationships and the making of too many new ones. It is important also in view of the complex and difficult nature of the task of the nursery nurses operating the system. The task may be too much for student nurses engaged in learning the basics of their profession and perhaps they should not be expected to be able to do it. In fact, we found that even fully trained and experienced nursery nurses needed further training and support before they could get fully into this role. The demands of the task are such that a highly integrated group of staff is necessary to its effective performance – staff who have built up mutual trust and co-operation, know well each other's strengths and weaknesses and are deeply concerned for each other.

We are aware that this raises important issues about the training of student nurses. We feel that there is here perhaps another area that needs further review – that is, how student nurses can gain the experience necessary for their own development while providing optimum care for young child patients. The dilemma of providing proper care for patients as well as proper training for student nurses is not unfamiliar to senior nurses (Menzies, 1970; see above, pp. 43–85). The student nurses missed out on taking part in the care of small children but learned a good deal about the principles involved while working with older children in the rest of Coxen Ward and, on the whole, came to accept the situation.

THE HOSPITAL SETTING

Finally, in the initial process of review as well as at all times in the study, consideration was given to looking at ways in which the hospital setting differed both physically and psychosocially from the normal home setting, which of the differences were necessary and which were not and could therefore be changed.

(a) *Boundary control*

What emerged immediately as very different from the home and as potentially subject to change was the whole problem of what we called 'boundary control', which applied both to the Cot Unit as a whole and to the individual child patient with his family.

1. *The unit boundaries.* The normal home is a fairly bounded place. The outside doors form a barrier to people coming and going and they tend to be 'guarded' by members of the household who monitor which people actually cross the threshold. Comparatively few people other than the family, and those only intimates, have automatic right of entry. Not so the hospital ward. Although the sister has in theory control over the ward boundary, in practice not all sisters operate that control very stringently, especially as regards other members of the hospital staff who may come and go pretty much at will, sometimes even if they have no tasks to perform on the ward. Restrictions to entry may be minimal and, one sometimes feels, apply only to patients' visitors, whose numbers and times of entry may be restricted. There was, in fact, a very open situation indeed in the Cot Unit. It had a door opening directly to the hospital grounds which was not guarded; people came and went at will, both to the Unit and through it to the other part of the ward. There was a constant flow of traffic, causing considerable distraction and undue busy-ness. This door was closed to everyone except the current population of the Cot Unit. The

adults, staff and mothers particularly, guarded the door and it became almost entirely used by adults taking small children out and in to visit other hospital departments or to go on outings. This made a major contribution to making the hospital more like home. The Unit now felt like their own territory. The community inside could become more integrated and secure, relieved of constant intrusions and interruptions.

There was still, however, the other boundary, a wide gap between the end of the Cot Unit and the rest of the ward. This was also an open and relatively uncontrolled boundary broken many times a day by older children, their visitors, the staff there and other visiting staff. This boundary was at first more difficult to control. The Cot Unit hung an invisible notice on the then nonexistent door of the nonexistent partition saying 'No Admittance Except on Business' – that is to say, it was made known that casual visitors were not really welcome. This made some difference, but the main responsibility for operating boundary control fell on the Cot Unit staff, sometimes helped by the other adults inside the Unit. They did not find it easy to operate with enough authority. For example, the nursery nurses, very junior in the hospital hierarchy, found it difficult to be authoritative in relation to doctors or senior nurses. Later, a partition was built separating the Cot Unit from the rest of the ward. This was done in the face of considerable resistance, partly based on what seemed legitimate anxieties – for example about possible accidents through opening the door into children on the floor – partly based on quite hostile feelings about being deprived of access to the small children, with the implication that the visitors might disturb them. It could and did feel personal and hurtful to people who genuinely cared for the children and who now had to face the fact that their presence was not necessarily helpful. But the advantage of this partition to the Cot Unit was inestimable, and not only through boundary control. (I will discuss other advantages of the partition later, see pp. 181–3.)

The closing of the boundaries helped with another essential problem of space. The normal hospital ward is too big for a child, enormously bigger than any space likely to be found in a

normal home. It does not offer enough sense of being bounded and contained within something comprehensible. Small children need this holding together by space as well as by attached people, otherwise they may feel lost internally as well as possibly getting lost in fact. They literally feel all over the place. So the smallest unit possible is important in this respect as well as in respect to staffing (see above, pp. 176 and 177).

2. *The 'boundary' of the individual child.* The closing of the Unit, with more effective control of its boundaries, made a great contribution to protecting the boundaries of the individual child by effectively reducing the number of people with whom he had to make contact, now more or less those who actually had business with him and people he was likely to know well and, on the whole, trust – that is, the population of the Cot Unit. The numbers and nature of contacts then became more manageable for the child. This brought the situation nearer to the home setting, where the child's contacts are likely to be quite restricted in numbers and mainly with people he knows and with whom there is mutual attachment. His contacts with other people are usually mediated by an attached person, who often makes the first relationship with them and protects him from unwarranted intrusions, warding them off if necessary. The baby or small child has not yet developed the psychosocial equipment to do this for himself. He needs someone else to mediate on his behalf.

To parallel this situation in hospital is important but not always easy. Staff unknown to the child may arrive to do things for him: for example nurses under multiple indiscriminate care-taking, or visiting staff from outside the ward. Their concern for the child may make it hard for them to realize that they are not necessarily *persona grata*. The child may know them only as the woman who hurts him by sticking in needles, or the man who does something incomprehensible and frightening. The principle was established that no one from outside the Unit should approach a child on his own but always with one of the child's familiar care-takers – the mother if present, the case-assigned nurse, or possibly both (since the mother also often

needed help in dealing with these outsiders who sometimes did things that were strange and frightening to her too, and upset her if they distressed her child). Failing either of these, one of the other nursery nurses was there.

The same principle held almost everywhere else in the hospital, mothers and/or case-assigned nurses accompanying children to care for them and help mediate relationships. There was no doubt that this was of benefit to the children, and for that reason it was welcomed by other staff. In addition, staff came to realize that it made their work easier, reducing the child's distress and evoking readier co-operation.

(b) *Noise abatement*

A hospital tends to differ from a normal home in the greater amount of noise, often really too much for the children although they may apparently adapt, for example by withdrawal into themselves or learning to shout above the noise – this, of course, making the noise worse. Such adaptation may persist after discharge and is maladaptive to life outside the hospital. The closing of the Unit boundary and reduction of traffic contributed a great deal to noise reduction. Further, the partition cut off the noise coming from the rest of the ward; this was especially important at times like the midday rest and bedtime, when noisy television in the main ward and other noisy situations among the older children and their visitors sometimes made it difficult to get small children off to sleep.

Also, more subtly, there is the question of the population itself being less noisy. Hospital staff may, like some children, have adapted to the noise and fail to notice either it or its significance, so that they unwittingly contribute to it unnecessarily. So also may visitors, especially if their numbers are unrestricted and they include appreciable numbers of children. Work was therefore done to develop 'a culture of quiet' initiated and sustained by staff and transmitted to visitors, especially by example rather than by restriction. Lastly, we looked at the possibility of noise-absorbent furnishing, often missing in hospitals, such as curtains and carpeting. The Unit already had good curtaining. A carpet was laid and was an enormous help.

(c) *Privacy*

A closely linked problem is privacy and real aloneness – an opportunity to withdraw, to have a quiet think or read, perhaps to cry – a problem for both adults and children and not an easy one to solve in an open ward. Adults, of course, could leave the Unit and find a private space outside, but they would not always want to leave the child in order to do so. Providing a Wendy House helped, as did the arrangement of ward furniture to make relatively secluded spaces. The reduction of noise also helped, and again attention was given to developing appropriate attitudes: appreciation of and respect for the need for privacy and willingness to help provide it. Sometimes this involved making difficult judgements: for example about whether the child was happily and constructively 'private' or whether he was quietly bored and needed some company and stimulation. It is only too easy to go to one or other extreme – a ward of unhappy, quietly bored children or one where children rarely get any peace and quiet.

(d) *Supervision of the children*

The last point raises the question of supervision of children and the nature of adult–child interaction. In the normal home situation, supervision of even quite small children is often flexible and intermittent, the mother on demand. It is difficult to achieve such a situation in hospital. Mothers may initiate too much interaction because they may regard that as the reason why they are there and because they have little else meaningful to do. The mother's anxiety about the child's condition and treatment may make it difficult for her to leave him alone. She may brood over him and may need help to relax her watchfulness.

The conditions of a large open ward, with its open boundaries, may mean that mobile children can wander, get lost or endanger themselves as they could not so easily do at home, so that more supervision is actually necessary. Modification of conditions could and did help. The closing of the boundaries helped in a number of ways – notably, children could not easily wander out of the Unit. The space available became smaller

and felt safer. Mother and child felt closer together, and so mothers were more able to relax supervision. The carpet also helped by reducing the likelihood of minor injuries like bumps or splinters from the hard wooden floor. Both mothers and children felt more free to be separate and there was a closer approximation to the usual home situation. A tendency to too much interaction remained, however, and gave rise to anxiety in mothers – for example that the child might become too dependent and 'clingy' and that it might be difficult to re-establish the normal relationship at home.

CONSEQUENT EXPLORATIONS AND COUNTERBALANCING MODIFICATIONS

The three areas discussed above were those that immediately presented themselves in terms of the need for review of the existing situation and code of practice; we have examined some of the joint explorations of hospital staff, patients, mothers and families and the research team and how these led to modifications. The experience of all was, however, that out of the review of these initially defined areas there gradually emerged other important areas. A fresh look at them seemed necessary to take account of the changes that were happening and to sustain and support them. This was inevitable since important changes may create imbalance in an institution which may appear to invalidate the changes and lead to their being reversed, unless care is taken to introduce appropriate counterbalancing changes. Such review and counterbalancing changes are continuously necessary in any institution which has to respond to changing circumstances, if the response is to be effective and stable.

We will now describe three of the main areas in which the hospital staff, patients, relatives and the research team were together engaged in review and in initiating further changes felt as necessary to sustain the main areas of change. This is by no means a complete account of such changes. Staff on their own initiative also introduced counterbalancing changes in their own areas of operation, some of which we heard about, many of which probably never came to our notice. This is an important

bonus if one succeeds in developing a culture in which review and change are accepted. Individuals are freed to use their own judgement and initiative, ideas breed ideas and the process is cumulative. It is exciting and rewarding to both the professional workers and their clients.

STAFF ROLES, SKILLS AND ATTITUDES

The developments in the role and function of staff, particularly the nurses, made it necessary to review the appropriateness of existing skills and attitudes. I will deal in detail with three main topics here:

(a) Skills and attitudes in relation to child patients.
(b) Work with mothers and other adults.
(c) Staff support and training.

(a) *Skills and attitudes in relation to child patients*

A part of providing as normal a setting for the child as possible is to sustain his normal expressiveness, to facilitate his expressing his feelings appropriately and to provide appropriate response to them by others. Too often in institutional settings staff are out of touch with what is normal in a child and the response he needs. They understandably feel they are caring for the children well when the children are 'settled' – that is, cheerful, happy and accepting without too much protest whatever is done to them – and are apparently enjoying multiple indiscriminate care-taking. Children are cheered up, distracted, rewarded for being 'good' – cheerful and co-operative – and disregarded – if not actually punished by reprimand or neglect – if they are upset, frightened or angry. Attention is given to the docile child rather than the protester. Children may learn fast what gets them immediate rewards and attention and play along with it. The accepting behaviour which may interfere with healthy development is thus reinforced.

Together we questioned this view. The children are in highly abnormal circumstances, in a strange place, which often feels threatening and imposes real pain and discomfort. They might be expected at times to be lonely, bored, in pain, puzzled,

frightened. In such circumstances a normal child with appropriate attachment figures around him would be likely to cry, scream, seek attention, reassurance and comfort, and would get this response. This would help sustain him through his troubles and promote his continued normal development. Normal behaviour in a hospital setting would be likely to include a good deal of expression of distress and protest, a *normal* reaction to an *abnormal* setting.

It was important, therefore, for staff to have appropriate views about the normal and abnormal child, to develop ways of working with the children which facilitated normal expressiveness and to respond appropriately to it. For example, they learned not to concentrate too much attention on children who were for the moment content, playing happily or smilingly responsive – that is, immediately rewarding to the nurse – but to become sensitive to signs of distress and respond to them. For example, a quiet child might express distress only by a puckered face or an occasional quiet whimper. He could not fully express his distress if left alone. Attention to such a child often freed him to cry openly and to be comforted by cuddling and other appropriate ways. 'A good cry' is relieving and comforting, especially if in sympathetic company. Nurses sometimes had to 'unlearn' the view that they had done something awful to a child if, by giving him such attention, they had 'made him cry'. With children who could express their troubles in words, nurses learned to talk about problems with them. The nature of the talking was important: to respond sensitively and honestly without false reassurances or even downright lies. Appropriate play was also useful, to help in understanding and responding to the complexities of a small child's feelings.

A few examples may clarify this problem. A small child whose mother's arrival was delayed beyond the child's tolerance said: 'Mummy is my favourite person, but I'm angry with her', a moving, honest and normal comment. It was important not to dampen the anger by disrespecting it, denying it, treating it as naughty, but to accept it, sympathize with it and encourage the child to go on talking. Another child having an imaginary conversation with his mother on a toy telephone, said: 'I know

I've been a naughty boy, that's why you didn't come to see me.' The nursery nurse picked up the remark and worked with it.

The problems could at times go far beyond the limits of the hospital: for example, a small boy from overseas whose pregnant mother was unable to visit. The care given to this child by his assigned nurse included careful preparation for going home to find his mother occupied with a new baby. She used talking, doll play and getting to know real babies.

It was also important to prepare children in advance, if possible, for potentially traumatic events so that the shock, pain and distress of the actual event could be lessened. Children also sometimes needed help with the distress they suffered about what was happening to others. The developments were epitomized in the words of a staff nurse experienced with children who said: 'I've had to unlearn everything I thought I knew about children since I've been on this ward.' She did, as did others.

These developments had another result, which in turn needed review and attention. As the children's expressions of distress became more open and sometimes long-lasting, so the level of stress in staff went up. One cannot be really in touch with distressed children without feeling acute distress oneself. So, in addition to the development of new and more appropriate attitudes and behaviour, attention had to be given to helping the staff sustain and deal with their own distress, so that they were not tempted to revert to inappropriate behaviour and to erect inappropriate defences against full contact with the children. This area of exploration is discussed more fully below (see pp. 187–9).

(b) *Work with mothers and other adults*
It will be clear that the balance of the staff's work and responsibilities had changed. They were less occupied with the children and more involved in work with mothers, other relatives and friends. Some of them, notably the social workers, schoolteachers and senior nursing staff, were already skilled and experienced in such work. However, a great part of the burden of the task fell on the nursery nurses, who were the staff most constantly in touch with those adults in the ongoing life on the

ward and who, because of the case-assignment system, often developed relationships of great trust and intimacy with the mothers. Their initial training and experience had not usually prepared them for such work, nor had they chosen a profession in which they would ordinarily be expected to do it. It is much to their credit, therefore, that they were willing to undertake it and became very competent in carrying it out. This work involved, as did that with the children, being in close touch with and working with distress without denial, false reassurance or evasions but with respect, understanding and tolerance. It required a good deal of wisdom and understanding of the complexities of feelings.

Examples of the kinds of problems they confronted may again help to clarify the situation. A single mother with a history of several illegitimate pregnancies said to the nursery nurse that she would never have anything to do with men again. She immediately asked the nurse whether she should consult the Family Planning Association. This naturally puzzled the nurse, who felt she had to try and help with the problem. Nursing staff and the social worker had to intervene with a family where the father became so distressed by his child's treatment that he wanted to discontinue it, whereas the mother could bear it and wanted it to continue. We have already described a mother who was helped to leave her child temporarily when she was becoming overwrought. Training was required and support and care for the distress this work caused the nurses, if they were to work well and not revert to what were now felt to be inappropriate practices.

(c) Staff support and training

It is appropriate now to discuss how we explored measures that might be useful to provide the necessary training and to help with staff stress arising from new methods of working. In dealing with stress, we were aware of the danger that the stress would lead to defences being erected against experiencing it which would be detrimental to patient and family care. The use of such defences in the hospital setting has been extensively described elsewhere by the author (Menzies, 1970; see above,

pp. 43–85). It will suffice to say here that they include the denial of feelings, evasion of significant issues, multiple indiscriminate care-taking, some dehumanizing of the patient and sometimes the nurses, concentration on service and neglect of attachment functions, inappropriate delegation of responsibility. Such defences may be consistent with good service and competent care for physical needs, but are not consistent with good total patient care.

The activities of training and support were combined in an extensive system of individual discussions with the staff concerned and in seminars with as many staff as could be spared at a time. Both individual and seminar discussions were based on the ongoing experiences of staff in their work. Discussion of individual patients and families led to greater insight and understanding, improved work with them and facilitated the elucidation of general principles. The individual discussions also gave staff the opportunity to discuss more private and personal issues, generally to do with their experiences in their work but sometimes going beyond it. These more formal events were supported by continuous ongoing discussions as people met on the ward, in the canteen and elsewhere. In fact one could say that a *talking culture* developed in which important issues could be aired, confronted and sometimes, though not always, resolved. The provision for staff in many ways, therefore, matched what they in turn were expected to provide for patients and families. There was consistency.

In addition to the work with Cot Unit staff, similar work was done with student nurses who worked in the other part of Coxen Ward; in a monthly seminar which was initially for all ward sisters, charge nurses and nursing officers concerned with children and adolescents, and later included the social workers, schoolteachers and the consultant paediatrician; and sometimes in the Project Steering Committee. These groups helped to ensure consistency of care throughout the hospital and to facilitate transactions with other wards and departments (see also below, pp. 199 ff.).

Much of this work was at first done by members of the research team, but it was increasingly shared by the ward sister,

the social worker most involved with Cot Unit patients, the schoolteachers and by the consultant paediatrician appointed midway through the project. They gradually took the work over completely and after the study were joined by a consultant child psychiatrist. It was not seen as impossible, therefore, for such training and support to be provided by senior hospital staff when no outside resources are available.

THE MANAGEMENT OF THE COT UNIT

The Cot Unit had begun to function in a very different way; consequently it became necessary to review the way it was managed, to clarify and make explicit the details of the management system – such as the nature, extent and limits of authority and responsibility and the content of the different roles – and to consider whether changes were desirable. This was essential for the continued effective running of the Unit and for sustaining the positive new developments, minimizing friction and helping contain the inevitable anxiety consequent on change and its uncertainties. People needed to know as far as possible where they were and how they stood.

Further – and this is perhaps even less well understood and appreciated – the management system itself and the way people function within it can have positive or negative effects on those who manage and are managed, and not only on their immediate experiences. The management system can promote or interfere with maturation, promote growth and independence or foster immature dependency; can determine whether relationships are supportive and satisfying or are fraught with tension and disruptive feelings (Menzies, 1970; see above, pp. 43–85). This is of particular importance where the people for whose care the system exists are children, whose psyche is immature and plastic and whose normal development takes place partly through identification with people important to them. These people provide better models when they themselves behave in a way that is mature, independent, authoritative and consistent. The author has discussed elsewhere institutions in which adolescents are cared for and stressed the importance of the management system and the way people behave in it as a model for ego-

development in the adolescent clients (Menzies, 1979; see below, pp. 222–35). In other words, the management system itself is significant in contributing to the positive or negative effects of hospitalization as shown in the later psychosocial development of hospitalized children, a fact not commonly recognized.

In discussing the management of the Unit, we will be concerned not only with the more formal elements of the hospital management hierarchy, important as these are, but with the way in which every person in the Unit – staff, adults present with their children, and the children themselves – managed themselves and their own roles, functions and relationships.

(a) *Informal management*

I will discuss this self-management first, before returning to the more formal aspects of the hospital management system, and as an example I will discuss the mother's management of herself and her child, since mothers were by far the most commonly present and significant adults in the Unit, other than the nursing staff. Mothers were not, as has been said, visitors in the Unit but were highly important (although temporary) members of the care system for the child patients, undertaking when present most of the ordinary care of their own children and not infrequently of other children. Indeed, it would seem legitimate to regard them as supernumerary, temporary members of staff, their delegated task to care for their children. As such they had to be brought effectively into the general management system of the ward and accept its authority. This was not a disciplinary or authoritarian measure but one intended to help mothers know where they were, what were their responsibilities, duties and privileges, what they could appropriately do and what not. A particular aspect of this was to help mothers fit into features of the hospital system essential to good patient care and to respect the needs of treatment. It does not take much imagination to realize that the presence of large numbers of mothers without this guidance could be disruptive to effective care. Acting inadvertently or through ignorance, they could interfere

with treatment – for example by giving comforting food or drink to a hungry or thirsty pre-operative patient.

A great deal of staff effort went into defining these factors with mothers. This was not a simple problem, since it had to take into account both the availability of the mother and her personal capacity to care for her child in hospital. Mothers and staff worked at this together and both usually knew pretty clearly what the outcome was. As noted above, much attention was given to this immediately on admission and thereafter it was kept continuously under review. The mother's role and functions were not regarded as matters that could be left to chance, especially since mothers' anxiety and stress might make them less able than usual to think and plan effectively. Mothers were helped to mediate their relationships with others for their own and their child's benefit. For example, they might tend to withdraw diffidently during ward rounds, feeling they were not needed or might be thought a nuisance or, indeed, having been explicitly told in other hospitals that they should absent themselves during ward rounds. They often needed help and encouragement to sustain their maternal authority in relation to surgeons, and to give the highly desirable support and comfort to their children in this stressful situation. Likewise mothers had to be briefed and sometimes encouraged and supported to retain their authority and care for their children in other departments of the hospital where they could accompany them: in knowing where they could go and what they could do or, indeed, might be expected to do. We have mentioned mothers as possible reassignment personnel for children whose mothers and assigned nurses were both absent, and the care taken to define those functions. In other words, the mothers, as supernumerary members of the care system, had specific duties and authority delegated to them, as did the staff proper.

Mothers were also helped to accept and operate with both authority and self-discipline in relation to the general care system and to the needs of the Unit as a whole and of its child patients. Some major and minor situations come in here. For example, they had to accept that there were a few places in the hospital and a few times where, in the judgement of medical

and nursing staff, a mother's presence might interfere with the work of staff and be detrimental or even dangerous to the child – in general theatres or in plaster theatre when a general anaesthetic was administered or in the early stages of recovery in the post-operative care ward. Acceptance was not easy, since these were times of high maternal anxiety and concern and mothers found the separation, waiting and inactivity very difficult.

The Cot Unit put the children down to rest, hopefully to sleep, after their lunch so that the mothers could leave for a break and for their own lunch without the children being distressed at being left. Mothers who wished to remain had to accept the need for quiet and behave accordingly themselves and possibly help to keep visiting children quiet.

The number of families and friends who could be in the Unit might in itself lead to difficulties at times, especially at weekends and holidays, with so many people present as to threaten disruption to care and create a general sense of unmanageability. So there was a need for mothers and families to take authority and discipline themselves, bearing in mind that they were only one of a number of families, so that the total presence remained at manageable levels and their behaviour was appropriate.

This description may have made the handling of this situation sound more formal and formidable than it actually was. The burden of the work was in fact done in ongoing informal discussions between staff and mothers and sometimes between mothers and mothers, much of it being undertaken by the nursery nurses at appropriate moments as the child's treatment proceeded. The social workers also engaged in this work. Only occasionally was it necessary for a more senior member of the nursing staff to intervene and act authoritatively – to protect boundaries, prevent disruptive breaches of practice or very occasionally to deal with a situation when a mother actually had done this, for example when she could no longer bear to stay away from the post-operative recovery ward, and arrived there too early. The only formal event was a weekly meeting between mothers and the ward sister and social workers, initially attended by the research team. At this meeting such matters could be,

and frequently were, aired and critically reviewed. Sometimes this led to reinforcement of the existing situation, at other times to desirable modifications. For example, the repeated complaints by Cot Unit mothers about the difficulty in getting children to sleep when the other part of the ward was still active and noisy was an important stimulus to the building of the partition.

The mothers' group also played an important part in the management and containment of feelings, for example by giving information and sharing experiences. Staff gave information about such things as treatments and prognosis; mothers gave each other useful information about such things as high chairs, prams and car seats for children in plaster casts. They discussed such matters as hostile reactions from strangers when they were with a child in an appliance outside the hospital, epitomized by one mother: 'She [a woman in a shop] looked at me as if I was one of those battering mothers.'

As discussed above, it was important that feelings were regarded as something to be acknowledged and explored with hope of resolution. Here one may notice particularly the kinds of feelings that arise between people in such a situation: jealousy and rivalry between mother and nurse, mother and mother, nurse and nurse, possessiveness about children, the mother's fears about being thought hysterical or silly, criticisms of each other's methods of child care, and so on. If these feelings were not worked with and contained but were suppressed, they could rankle and fester, increasing stress for all and leading to behaviour inimical to the care of the children.

As these activities went on, there gradually grew up a culture or tradition in the Unit sustained both by staff and by generations of experienced hospital mothers. New members could increasingly easily be introduced into the culture and come to accept it. This culture once established, contributed greatly to the smooth running of the Unit and to the effective care of the child patients and their families.

(b) *The formal management system*

1. *The role and functions of the ward sister.* Of all the permanent staff on the ward, she in her role was perhaps the most consistently under review. Her authority and the validity of her previous experience were challenged by the new developments, although she was a most sincere and serious supporter of them. At times, too, her developing and changing authority and the validity of her new experiences were challenged, especially by close colleagues outside the Unit itself, by senior nursing staff, student nurses in the other part of the ward, other professions in the hospital. Her management practices, her teaching and support of staff, her relations with patients and relatives, had constantly to be examined and sometimes revised.

She eventually gave up some aspects of her work that were precious to her, and developed new ones that were strange and sometimes difficult. For example, as the new system of care developed, the nursery nurses came firmly into their new role and the risks of multiple indiscriminate care-taking were increasingly appreciated, the sister, like others, had to surrender a great deal of her direct contact with children and even parents. It is hardly possible to exaggerate what a sacrifice this was. She could no longer deploy her care and concern for the children so directly in contact with them, but instead had to sustain that care and concern and remain effectively in touch with children and families through others. Further, in her remaining contacts with children, the balance between social or general care and professional and orthopaedic nursing changed to emphasize the latter more. There was more of the work that distresses children and the nurse and less of pleasant interaction.

A corollary of this change was, of course, a change in the whole system of delegation in Coxen Ward. Responsibility for the running of the Cot Unit was now fully delegated by the sister to the staff nurse in charge who was responsible to her, and was in turn responsible for the nursery nurses to whom the general care of patients and families was delegated. Once again it was necessary to review and clarify the precise nature of the delegation, what each person was responsible for and to whom,

and work had to be done to help people learn and respect this. For example, the authority of the staff nurse over the boundaries of her Unit had to be firmly established since she, and not the ward sister, now had the overall view of the current situation there. At the same time, the sister had to keep in touch and continuously review how the people to whom she delegated were operating that delegation. She also had to trust them sufficiently to give them freedom to operate, even on occasion possibly to do something of which she disapproved or make a mistake for which she, the sister, still had ultimate responsibility.

At the same time, she could not be too distant. In addition to review she, as the most experienced nurse on the ward, could take, and had to take, an active part in the training and support of staff. So teaching and advisory functions operated alongside delegation and had to be so operated as to interfere minimally with this. She had to contain a good deal of the staff's uncertainty and anxiety about the changes as well as her own; she had to be available to them but not interfering. Much the same problems developed in her relations with mothers. She could not and did not cut herself off and establish undue distance. She was available always as a trusted figure and the ultimate authority, especially if something went wrong; for example if a child whom the surgeons had hoped to treat conservatively proved in fact to need surgery. Then again she had to be able to do this as far as possible without interfering with delegation in the Cot Unit or with case-assignment. The mothers' group was an essential factor in sustaining the sister's relationships with the mothers.

In effect, this meant that the sister's role, now more difficult and more challenging, was also more rewarding. The stress in the new role, and in the process of change into it, should not be underestimated. So the sister herself needed support and, in particular, effective confirmation of her role by a number of people. Very important were her nursing colleagues, the principal nursing officer, the nursing officer who was her direct superior, and the nurses in charge of other wards, departments and theatres with whom the Cot Unit was in constant interaction. It was needed also from medical and other professional

staff working on the ward. During the study, it was given very effectively by the Project Steering Committee. Sustaining this support was also a matter of continuous work for the sister herself.

2. *The staff nurse.* A similar review and restructuring of the staff nurse's role was necessary. Her role was in some ways a miniature of the sister's. She had to delegate effectively to the nursery nurses – notably the general care of child patients and families – but had to be available as an authoritative and experienced person without interfering in their work. She had to ensure attitudes and behaviour appropriate to the care system; to contain the anxiety of the nursery nurses, of patients and families; to be available to patients and families without diminishing the significance of the case-assigned nursery nurses and her work with them. She had also to carry relationships between the Cot Unit, the rest of the ward and the rest of the hospital. A difficult aspect of her role was sustaining herself and her staff through periods of relative inactivity, for example if many mothers were present and caring for their children themselves or if patient numbers fell. Boredom and a fall in morale constituted a risk to the maintenance of an appropriate standard of care.

None the less, some of the stresses of the sister's role were absent. The staff nurse, being present inside the Cot Unit, could more easily review the ongoing work and had to manage less uncertainty. Also she was available for temporary reassignment of child patients in the absence of more appropriate caretakers and had a different balance between professional and orthopaedic nursing and general child care. But the role was still a stressful one and the staff nurse in turn needed support, notably by close contact with the ward sister and from her trust, support and authority.

3. *The nursery nurses.* The ultimate nursing delegation was to the nursery nurses and the content of their role and functions was carefully reviewed, spelt out in detail and put in writing. It will be clear from the description above that this role had increased greatly in complexity and in stress content, so they

needed to know clearly where they stood – in particular how their role related to others. For example, the boundaries between orthopaedic and general care had to be tested and defined not in terms of procedures only but also in general – for example, as noted above, nursery nurses were not expected to discuss orthopaedic questions with the adults caring for the children. The boundary with the social worker was also tested and defined to establish by precedent what work nursery nurses could effectively do with mothers and other adults and when professional social work help was needed. The large amount of time the social worker spent on the ward working with the nurses and with mothers greatly facilitated this definition.

The nursery nurses, too, had a management responsibility, not only in managing their own role and functions but very importantly in the management of patients and families – for example as described above, helping them relate themselves effectively to illness and treatment and helping them conform to the general demands of the hospital situation. They might also have to help manage the intervention of other professional staff visiting the ward and their contacts with patients and families: to protect a child if an intervention was proposed at a bad time for him, if he was already very distressed or possibly asleep, and perhaps seek postponement if possible and with the backing, if necessary, of a more senior nurse such as the staff nurse or sister.

I will not discuss in detail the question of the management of other staff working on the ward, but simply put on record that a great deal of work was done by and with other staff to help them manage their visits and interventions in a way that was as consistent as possible with the general principles of child care being developed.

THE COT UNIT IN THE HOSPITAL AT LARGE

This section will be concerned with the Cot Unit as an open system taking part in the wider life of the hospital and highly dependent on other parts of the hospital for the care and treatment of its patients and families, particularly general and plaster theatres, the post-operative recovery ward, the Pathology, X-

ray and Physiotherapy departments, and social services such as the relatives' home, the hospital canteen and cafeteria. It could not, therefore, and did not behave as an encapsulated unit, secure within its own physical and psychosocial boundaries and with its own permanent staff not deployable in other parts of the hospital except in special circumstances, for example when a nursery nurse was seconded to the accident ward to begin her assignment with a child admitted there who would later probably come to the Cot Unit. The chances of the developments within the Unit becoming viable would have been greatly reduced if the Cot Unit had tried to sustain itself in isolation. The same would have been true if the Unit, along with other staff and the Project Steering Committee, had not taken responsibility for helping to build up relationships that furthered understanding and the development of procedures that both supported the work of the Unit and improved the care of the children. We have seen innovations elsewhere ultimately founder because of lack of understanding or active opposition from outside.

(a) *Potential misunderstandings of the position of the Cot Unit*
There was plenty of potential for such misunderstandings and for opposition in the environment of the Cot Unit. The Unit could be seen – indeed, was seen – as special and very demanding: requiring behaviour from staff that other patients and wards did not, or did not appear to demand, behaviour that other staff did not necessarily approve. An example of this was the closing of its boundaries to staff who had no function there. We have described above how this distressed kindly and well-intentioned visitors. A lot of hostility was felt and expressed about the ward sister's closing of the boundary.

Or again, the Cot Unit and the research team became objects of great suspicion and hostility when an older child died in the other part of Coxen Ward. A major difference of opinion arose between the Unit and some other hospital staff about how this should be handled. The Cot Unit, whose families and some of whose children were aware of the death, took it for granted by then that the subject would be openly discussed and worked with as a means of helping with distress for the dead child and

his family and the heightened anxiety of families about their own children. Nurses too – particularly the nursery nurses – opened up the subject among themselves and with the staff nurse and the sister, the social worker and the Tavistock team, as a preparation for and support in doing this work. Other staff outside the Cot Unit had a more traditional attitude: 'least said soonest mended'. They expressed quite legitimate anxieties about 'nurses crying or being hysterical in front of patients and families' and genuinely – although we thought mistakenly – believed that anxiety and distress would be increased if the topic was opened up. Their method of coping was business as usual, hoping to reduce stress by displaying competence and giving good ordinary care. Feelings ran very high indeed on this occasion and it would be fair to say that adequate resolution of the differences was not achieved.

Interestingly, too, the Cot Unit could be perceived to be special when it was not, sometimes because procedures there were more explicitly defined and more rigorously enforced. For example, the closing of the Unit's boundaries was seen as special, even unwarranted, although the fact is that any ward sister has the authority and responsibility to safeguard the boundaries of her ward and no competent and concerned ward sister is likely to allow unregulated movement in and out, if such movement is detrimental to patient care. It was again important to clarify these issues and much work was needed to help others understand and co-operate with the care system in the Cot Unit.

(b) *Liaison with other wards and departments*
Important also were the excursions which members of the Cot Unit made into other parts of the hospital for investigations, treatment or social activities. The nature of procedures needed to be reviewed, as did the relationship of staff there with the Cot Unit patients, families and staff. The conditions necessary for effective and safe treatment and care needed to be explored and their limits tested.

Appropriate behaviour for adults accompanying Cot Unit children elsewhere also needed to be examined and defined so

that they could manage their part in the procedures appropriately, acknowledging, if necessary, differences from what was permissible or desirable in the Unit itself. It was again regarded as important not to leave these matters to chance, with the way open for misunderstandings or ignorance which could lead to behaviour and relationships bad for treatment and general care and threatening to the new developments.

As an example of this, I will take the work done in regard to a mother accompanying her child in her role of focal care-taker, mediating his contacts and giving support and comfort. With most departments it was fairly simple; the mother's presence was accepted as appropriate, briefing was easy and effective, and in time mothers managed their part well on the whole, and staff found them helpful and welcomed them. This work also led to helpful innovations introduced by other staff members themselves. For example, the nursing officer in charge of the plaster theatre began to visit children and families in the Cot Unit to make their acquaintance in ordinary friendly circumstances before they went to plaster theatre, and she encouraged them to pay a social visit to the theatre before going there for treatment.

The situation was more complex and needed more work in two cases, where there was high risk and the need for special consideration for the medical and other treatment procedures: for theatre procedures which required a general anaesthetic and in the post-operative recovery ward.

Anaesthetists believed that it could be dangerous and make their work more difficult if the mother accompanied the child to theatre, since the child would probably become very upset when she left. It was accepted, albeit unwillingly, by the Cot Unit that the mother should not go with the child but that the child should be accompanied by a nursery nurse, usually his assigned nurse. In addition, once the subject had been opened up with them the anaesthetists themselves became innovative in a helpful way and reviewed their anaesthetics procedures. Premedication was altered so that the child was more likely to be already asleep or very drowsy when he left his mother on the ward.

Nor did the staff of the post-operative recovery ward consider it appropriate to have mothers present immediately the child came back from theatre. They had urgent and essential tasks to carry out and felt the mother's presence might interfere. Also they were anxious about the distress it might cause mothers to see their children immediately post-operatively and this was not without reason, for mothers did indeed become very distressed sometimes. The difficulty was perhaps increased by the staff feeling hurt or even insulted by the implication that their excellent professional care might not be all that was desirable for the child. It would be fair to say that some differences of opinion remained to the end. The Cot Unit and the research team believed, for example, that an apparently unconscious child might be more aware of his surroundings than the staff of the ward thought, and that the child, therefore, was more in need of the presence of his mother, her familiar sounds and touches. For example, an apparently unconscious child stirred and said: 'Mummy, that duck's hurting my back', a reference to an earlier incident in the X-ray department when the mother, to quieten a rather restless child, had said: 'Stand still, the lady's drawing a duck on your back and you're to keep it on to show Daddy.' But the ultimate authority of the sister for her ward was upheld and it was her responsibility to summon the mother when she regarded the mother's presence as appropriate. A nursery nurse from the Cot Unit could meantime be with the child if she could be spared from other duties.

It was important also to clarify the situation with mothers so that they could manage themselves and their child appropriately in the very different circumstances of the post-operative recovery ward. For example, restriction on the number and category of people present had to be accepted: not more than two adults and no children. They had to be very quiet in the interests of general patient care, and so on. Cot Unit staff were responsible for ensuring that mothers were properly briefed, and this was sometimes helpfully reinforced by the sister from the post-operative recovery ward visiting them in the Unit in advance. Again care was taken not to leave things to chance, with its risk of mishaps.

Work on this task was both formal and informal. The Steering Committee, for example, gave it a good deal of attention, its members including many of the significant people involved. Indeed, the work of the Steering Committee was invaluable in developing policy and principles and in integrating the work of the Cot Unit and its ramifications throughout the hospital. There was plenty of constructive criticism and difference of opinion while this went on, but these could usually be resolved and decisions reached when necessary, while Committee members carried the principles and decisions back into their own areas of work in the hospital.

The sisters' seminar was also a forum for such work and was particularly important in furthering consistency of attitudes and beliefs which could in turn further consistency in behaviour. Formal visits to and from other wards and departments also took place, with formal discussions and decisions about procedures and relationships. The coffee-time discussions after the ward round, attended by the surgical team mainly concerned with Cot Unit children and also by the ward sister, the social worker attached to the team and usually the research team, were also constructive. They allowed discussion of general care as well as medical issues and were particularly helpful in briefing new members and helping them accept the needs of the care system, since membership of the surgical teams changed fairly frequently so that continuity was in the long term held only by the consultant surgeon in charge.

The amount of work that went on informally was enormous and was done by all those closely involved in the work of the Cot Unit and committed to the changes, both with others on whom the changes impinged directly and with people who were not involved but interested. This could be – and often was – difficult and demanding work, for it was in those informal contacts that doubts and uncertainties about the changes in care and the hostility many people felt were most easily and clearly expressed. This work fell very heavily on the ward sister, much of whose free time while in the hospital – for example at lunch in the canteen – was taken up by it. Lunch was hardly off-duty for her. She had to explain, counter objections and defend from

criticism not only herself, her staff and her Unit but also what were sometimes regarded as the rather bizarre views of the Tavistock team about children and how they should be looked after. The social workers, the schoolteachers, the consultant paediatrician and the research team also spent a good deal of time and effort on this work.

It also fell very heavily on the nursery nurses, especially those resident in the hospital, who spent a good deal of their free time in the company of student nurses who often did not understand what was being done and why, might resent what seemed to be the very special position of the child patients and be angry that the Cot Unit's system of care largely deprived them of the opportunity of learning to care for small children. This was a difficult situation for the nursery nurses and greatly added to the stress of their job.

It was therefore extremely important in sustaining the developments in the Cot Unit that the staff concerned were prepared and able to undertake the responsiblity for and tolerate the stress of this work across the boundary of the Unit, to face the problems in the outside world and not to retreat too much into the more congenial and relatively peaceful situation within the Cot Unit while leaving its boundaries vulnerable.

CONCLUSION

I began this paper by describing the joint Royal National Orthopaedic Hospital and Tavistock study as 'an experience in the art of the possible'. I can conclude now by stating that a very great deal proved to be possible, and that it was possible and practicable within a real-life hospital situation. This resulted from the willingness of the people concerned to review the existing situation, to expose themselves to confrontation with the implications of existing practice – not always the most appropriate – to bear the doubts and uncertainties of change, and always with the good of patients and families as the overriding consideration. The care of the small children throughout the hospital improved enormously beyond what had actually been a more than averagely good care system at the beginning of the study. There was a follow-up study of children and families. I

will not go into detail but will simply state that the children were, for the most part, developing well and showed remarkably little of the classical signs of the institutionalized child. There were some difficulties, of course, but on the whole these were being adequately contained within the families.

Interestingly, much the same was true of the mothers. Although having a child in hospital, especially a long-stay hospital, cannot well be other than a terrible experience, there were rewards for them too, both in the care they were able to give their children and in the care and support they received themselves, in marked contrast to the experiences of many of them in other hospitals. Follow-up suggested that mothers who had been present a good deal had participated in the general opportunities for learning, that their mothering had often improved in quality, in sensitivity and attachment to their child, and that they felt more confident in it and more rewarded by it.

What is significant, too, is that the changes were brought about with very little increase in the resources devoted to the care of the children and families. The partition was the only capital cost; the carpet was a present. There is now the cost of three sessions for a consultant paediatrician, which were in any case needed to implement the Department of Health and Social Security's policy in relation to the care of children in hospitals (*Hospital Facilities for Children*, 1971). This expense is more than justified not only in sustaining the general care system and providing support for other staff concerned, but notably in improving the medical care of the children, for example improved diagnosis and treatment of conditions outside the province of an orthopaedic surgeon. More recently a consultant child psychiatrist has been appointed for three sessions; her role includes supporting the general care system and giving teaching and support to staff and students as well as caring for individual patients and families. In this particular study there was also the cost of the service as distinct from the research aspect of the Tavistock team's work.

We make this point in order to emphasize that financial cost does not seem a valid argument against reviewing and changing

the method of care for small children in hospitals, or against continuing to run an improved system. It is especially cheap if one takes into account the prophylactic effects on the children's subsequent development.

The personal cost of the project is another matter and also deserves mention. No one deeply involved could avoid increased stress and turmoil as attitudes and beliefs were questioned, differences of opinion confronted, past inadequacies reviewed, and awareness of suffering and possible damage to children increased. Uncertainties and doubts were inevitably rife. It was not easy. Anyone seriously contemplating similar changes must be prepared for that. The cost may, however, be balanced by the rewards, and this was so for many of the staff engaged on the study. There is little doubt that the roles of the staff mainly concerned were upgraded in terms of content, responsibilities, authority and the exercise of discretion. They required a fuller deployment of the capacities of staff – indeed, a deployment of the whole of the person in a deep, sometimes difficult, often very rewarding relationship with others: staff, patients and families. For those who remained in post – and that was almost everyone – the rewards both in increased job satisfaction and in personal growth were great. It felt exciting and worthwhile. This, we may note in passing, is in marked contrast to the effect of traditional nursing organization on qualified nurses, students and patients (Menzies, 1970; see above, pp. 43–85).

It follows also from our general framework that the review process is not a once-and-for-all thing; it must be continuous, a part of the orientation to the work situation, although perhaps being intensified at certain times especially in relation to other important changes, so that balance is maintained. It is one of the important results of this study that this does seem to have become part of the philosophy around the Cot Unit and more widely in the hospital. Not only has the work in the Unit continued to develop, but other developments have taken place too. For example, the ward sister has worked out a different sort of modified case-assignment system for the older children in her ward, which not only allows for the different needs of

these children but is appropriate to the use of transitory student nurses.

Lest the hospital and the research team appear to be smug and self-satisfied, however, we should remember, in concluding, areas of possible review, some of which we have already mentioned – for example home versus hospital treatment – to which we gave little or no attention, partly because our resources did not make it possible; partly because we realized too late that these areas needed attention.

We were aware of, but did not review, the implications of operating this type of care system for basic staff training. It was our impression, for example, that training for work with children only too often leads to serious misconceptions about their true nature: their basic needs, the features of normal development, the significance of their behaviour and expressiveness. It also tends to diminish awareness of the need not to interfere with, but indeed to help sustain, the focal mother–child bond. There seems to be some scope, then, for reviewing training in child development and child care. Further, the need to care for families – and especially to support mothers – emphasizes the necessity for training in work with adults, especially adults under stress. Little training in this work seems to be given within the present courses.

Another area where training seems desirable is in management skills for those who are to carry out the complicated management tasks involved in such a system, particularly with so many non-staff adults taking part in care. New tasks emerge requiring new skills and new attitudes, especially as management includes the effective containment of stress.

Last, but still very important, are the physical conditions of the hospital. These were accepted more or less as they were and only minor modifications were made. It was part of our remit to do this. The achievements, despite the not very appropriate physical conditions, suggest that much could be done in other hospitals where the physical conditions are also not very appropriate. However, we did become doubtful about the suitability of a traditional hospital setting for long-stay children, especially for those who are not in the ordinary sense ill most

of the time and for whom, in consequence, the quality of general child care may be the crucial consideration for a great part of their time in hospital. It would be most important, therefore, in contemplating new units for such children or major modification in existing units, to review the situation carefully, to survey the conditions required for proper medical, nursing and other care critically, to align them with the needs of children for conditions as like a normal home as possible, and so to ensure the most effective compromise. This would surely be very different from a traditional hospital setting.

NOTES

1. 'We' always implies the hospital staff and the research team together.

2. A detailed discussion of the work towards these objectives is given below in 'Initial areas of exploration', pp. 161–2.

3. See p. 186 below for further discussion of this point.

4. This practice has been discontinued, volunteers not now being available.

5. The size of the Cot Unit has now fallen in consequence of the fall in the number of under-fives in the population at large and the treatment-at-home policy, and the Unit's size does not now merit a staff nurse. The ward sister now takes some reassignments.

6 Thoughts on the maternal role in contemporary society (1975)

THIS PAPER focuses attention on society's relationship with death and considers how this affects the role and functions of the mother, particularly in the care of the baby and very young child.

SOCIETY'S RELATIONSHIP WITH DEATH

Freud's agony and disillusion arising from the First World War led to his perspicacious comments in 'Thoughts for the times on war and death' (1915) – perspicacious and also, unfortunately, predictive for the future. He comments on our defensiveness against realizing the inevitability of our own death or that of people close to us, and adds that this defensive attitude to death 'has a powerful effect on our lives. Life is impoverished, it loses in interest, when the highest stake in the game of living, life itself, may not be risked.' The paper returns many times to this point: that an inadequate relationship with death diminishes the quality of life.

Matters have become no better since, with the Second World War and the development of destructive weapons that beggar the imagination. Many psychoanalysts and other writers have commented on society's difficulty in confronting the meaning of death. In *Death, Grief and Mourning* (1965), Gorer describes death as a taboo subject, having largely replaced sexuality as such. Mention of death is sometimes treated as an obscenity. Such attitudes inhibit the process of mourning as describe, for example, by Freud (1917), Abraham (1924) and Melanie Klein (1940), as do the relative lack in contemporary society of public mourning rituals and private support from friends and relatives.

Gorer, like Freud, comments on the danger of inadequate mourning, stating that it prolongs the symptomatology of mourning, may prevent ultimate recovery and impoverishes the life of the survivors. This impoverishment is increased by the practice of institutionalizing the dying, institutionalization being one of society's defences against confrontation with intolerable problems. Thus, dying is often not an experience that the dying person shares with close relatives and friends, which makes effective mourning more difficult for them.

Miller and Gwynne, in *A Life Apart* (1972), made similar comments: 'To die or to be bereaved is to commit a social gaffe and, as with social gaffes of other kinds, the recommended procedure is "least said, soonest mended".' Their work with the young chronic sick led them to add: 'the cripple, especially the victim of an incurable and progressive disease, is an ugly reminder of mortality.' Society is liable to put them into 'limbo institutions' where the prolongation of life, regardless of the quality of that life, may become an end in itself.

DEFENCES IN SOCIETY AGAINST THE SIGNIFICANCE OF DEATH

Defences against the significance of death are not only personal and private. Society, and institutions within it, also have characteristic defences which are operated in common by their members. Jaques (1955) has called these socially structured defence mechanisms.

There are a number of society-based defences relevant to our theme. I have already mentioned society's proneness to institutionalize problems felt as too difficult to confront. Society thus splits off the problem, locates it in a small, split-off part of itself and partially disowns it. The unfortunate result of this is that the institutional care-takers are not well supported, and the quality of care tends to be low. The person with the problem and his natural care-takers are alike impoverished by separation.

Secondly, it does not seem accidental that death has tended to replace sex as a taboo subject. Rather it suggests the use of sexuality as a defence against the fear of death and of the futurelessness of society and oneself in it, a caricatured

representation of the power of the life instinct over the death instinct. Such a defensive manoeuvre and failed confrontation also lead to impoverishment and triviality of relationships, sex being increasingly divorced from meaningful personal relationships, especially those centred on conceiving, bearing and rearing children.

Thirdly there is the acquisitive society, reflecting a *'carpe diem'* attitude, not only in the urge to nonpersonalized sexuality but in amassing often relatively meaningless possessions *now* and not waiting to acquire them in the too-uncertain future. This seems an attempt to compensate for the low quality of emotional life as already described. It could also be called the 'I want' philosophy of society, the 'I want' being little related to the realistic possibility of getting what one wants or to consideration of the sacrifices the 'I' may require of others to get what he wants. This can be carried so far that people behave almost as though society's resources were unlimited. Political statements increasingly imply that all we need is more money: the resources it represents will somehow then magically become available. Money is treated almost as a thing in itself not as a symbol. This reflects a potentially psychotic and destructive social process, reflected in the rapidly diminishing real value of money (Bion, 1961).

This acquisitiveness seems linked to the fact that society is becoming increasingly dependent, especially – but not only – in the developed welfare states. By dependency is meant here not reality-based dependency needs – for example in the young or sick – but more primitive, even psychotic, phenomena such as those described by Bion (1961) under the formulation of basic assumption dependency. These phenomena are particularly liable to arise when a group or larger institution is in difficulty about confronting the reality of its situation or feels that there is no real solution. Characteristic of such a group is the flight from reality and its opportunities and limitations and a belief in magical solutions of problems. Bion describes the group in basic assumption dependency as 'met in order to be sustained by a leader on whom it depends for nourishment, material or spiritual, and protection'. There was a time when God himself might

have fulfilled that role, providing everything in the next world if not in this. Now, the all-sustaining leader tends to be the state and its lesser agencies, which are expected to meet needs to an increasingly unrealistic extent. For example, the basic-assumption-dependency society tends to institutionalize people in trouble, demanding more and more institutions while the authorities tend to stretch resources almost to the bounds of possibility to provide them. The need to believe in the hoped-for magical solution prompts denial of the inadequacy of the solution achieved, notably again the poor quality of the life provided by institutions. The belief in institutionalization also discourages, or even prevents, mobilization of natural care-takers. The help and support which could enable them to care for people in need themselves – to the psychosocial benefit of both parties, sustaining love and concern, avoiding the pain of separation, rejection and guilt – are not available to them.

THE MATERNAL ROLE AND DEATH

Society's relationship with death and mourning is significant for the maternal role, because it seems that a sizeable component of that role concerns death and mourning. The mother has to deal with death and mourning both in her own feelings and reactions to her baby and in his feelings and reactions. Such aspects of the role seem at least as significant as the more culturally acceptable and emphasized views so often used to deny them: the idealization of motherhood, its joys, excitements and hopes.

The baby may perhaps be regarded as the reminder of mortality, even if not an ugly one. Birth is a reminder of death if only because, in a sense, it is the opposite, the final establishment of a new life. Birth is frequently experienced as a moment of great danger for both mother and child, for which strenuous survival preparations are made. In the ensuing period the realistic fragility of the baby, its vulnerability, its lack of capacity for unassisted survival, add to the feeling of hazard. Nor is it only a matter of physical survival. The situation is equally fraught on the psychological side. The baby has no more capacity for unassisted survival and effective development psychologically than physically. Threats, or actual experience of psychotic phenomena, are as real as threats or fears about physical death and are often experienced as much the same thing.

Mothers and babies, separately and together, must deal with these fears about the physical and mental survival of the self and the other. In both, these experiences are at times on a primitive and psychotic level. The whole experience of pregnancy, birth and the care of the baby makes the mother re-experience primitive feelings and archaic object relationships as described, for example, by Pines (1972) and Winnicott (1956). Winnicott has also described as 'primary maternal preoccupation' the strange psychological state of the mother at the beginning of the infant's life, saying significantly that but for the pregnancy and birth this would be regarded as an illness. Freud (1917) makes a similar point about mourning following significant loss: 'it is only because we know so well how to explain it that his [the mourner's] attitude does not seem to us pathological.' The mother's success in working through these reactions is crucial, both for her own development and for that of her baby. Her capacity to cope with her own anxiety for her baby's life intimately affects her capacity to help him work through his anxiety about his death, and hers, which in turn is crucial for his psychological survival and the quality of his future life.

Following Freud and Melanie Klein, one may stress the importance of the death instinct and its impact on the early psychological experiences of the baby, notably acute fears for the survival of himself and the other, particularly his mother, as the derivative aggression is deflected outwards. The complex and intense anxiety situations provoked in the baby by the interplay of his life and death instincts, his positive and negative feelings and impulses, associated with omnipotence and a defective capacity to distinguish reality and phantasy, give rise to experiences of psychotic intensity as a part of normal development, as described for example by Melanie Klein (1948a) as the paranoid-schizoid and depressive positions. If normal development is to proceed, rapid and effective help must be available to the baby in dealing with these states, ensuring that they are temporary and are replaced by more tolerable states of mind.

Very important in these interactions is the mother's capacity to feel what the baby feels and respond appropriately. This implies that she should have enough capacity to take in the baby's massive projections of intense feelings and phantasies, to accept them without undue diminishment through denials or other defences, and not to be physically overwhelmed by them as the baby fears he will be. The 'good enough' mother values and respects the reality of his feelings while making a more reality-based assessment of their phantasy content. By her reactions she conveys back to him an appropriately modified version of what he has projected.

I find Bion's (1963) formulations of these processes useful: the mother seen as a 'container' who can contain what the baby projects and work with it, her capacity for reverie being crucial. Bion (1962, 1967) also discusses the role of the mother in helping the baby develop his own capacity for thinking and so become more able to deal himself with these situations. He states that the prior experience is of having thoughts particularly provoked by maternal absence and frustration and that thinking is a development forced on the psyche by the necessity for dealing with thoughts. Thus the baby has primitive thoughts or phantasies but at first no thinking apparatus; this must be supplied by his mother. If the mother–child interactions go well, the baby takes in not only helpfully modified versions of his projections but also the maternal thinking apparatus that thought them for him. Through repetition of this process and consequent identifications, he in time establishes his own thinking apparatus. If this process does not take place effectively, however, the baby tends to introject not a comforting, progressive experience but what Bion has called a nameless dread, severe contentless anxiety which intensifies psychotic experiences and defensive manoeuvres, ominous for the baby's future development.

These processes also help to build an effective identity, itself a reassurance against fears of death or madness. The baby comes to be and to know himself as he is known and reflected back to himself by others, both the quality of the other's response and its consistency being important. The mother needs to reflect a more realistic version of the baby and convey her love and concern for him and his for her, and she must be able to do this without too many inconsistencies due to factors lying outside her immediate relationship with the baby, either from inside herself or from outside the relationship.

The normal baby's experience includes repeated losses and the need to carry out adequate mourning. One may easily under-estimate the frequency and intensity of these experiences, even among babies cared for in good, ordinary circumstances. Not only major, but also many repeated minor experiences of loss and how they are handled are of the greatest developmental significance.

Internally based experiences of loss stem from the baby's aggressive feelings, his death wishes against loved people and his omnipotence. The loved and loving mother may be experi-enced as lost even while realistically present, the situation being yet more poignant, however, if she is actually absent. The loss is easily connected with the loss of good aspects of the baby himself related to and identified with her. A more protracted absence of the mother – and it need be for only a very short time – may act as a dreadful confirmation of the phantasy of permanent loss and lead to obvious states of depression and despair even in quite small babies. The child's rudimentary time sense and the connection of the mother's absence with his own aggression make it only too easy for him to believe that she has gone for good. Other forms of loss include those which stem from progress itself, the most notable of which is probably weaning. Development of motility may mean loss of familiar positions or places; temporary loss of a familiar self-image is another problem – for example, if a child is reflected back to himself by an unfamiliar care-taker: a great hazard for institu-tionalized babies.

Learning to deal with inevitable experiences of loss, to assess them realistically, to tolerate and work with the complex feelings associated with them, is a crucial aspect of development. The baby needs much help if he is to develop his capacity for mature mourning and so achieve a high quality of life and a capacity for deep and meaningful relationships. The baby needs such help at all stages, from the early paranoid-schizoid position, where psychotic fears are at their height and mainly concerned with his own survival; through the depressive position, where his care and concern, guilt and responsibility for others with whom he is identified come more to the fore; until he has more or less successfully worked through the depressive position and no longer has an excessive need to defend himself against such experiences.

The baby or very young child, then, needs a containing person who respects and values his anxiety and depression, assesses appropriately their content and conveys understanding, security and the tolerability of such experience; who can mourn with the baby for his losses, which may indeed coincide with her own – for example, at weaning – and set a pattern of normality for such experiences. The relationships and processes I have described are difficult and painful for both mother and baby, although rewarding when they are seen to be resolvable by the pair and set in context of the directly gratifying aspects of the relationship.

In what I have said up to now I have largely taken for granted that the person caring for the baby is his mother, an assumption that may seem reasonable enough but which one should perhaps consider further, especially in view of societal pressures to make this less likely. The developmental processes with which the baby needs continuous help seem to require also that the help comes for the most part from one person, especially in the early stages, if his development is to be successful. For example, consistency in modes of communication and response are important if the baby is to learn to interpret responses meaningfully and benefit from them. He needs a consistent picture of himself as reflected by the other if he is to build an integrated identity. Bowlby in *Attachment and Loss* (1969, 1973), followed by many others, has described the idiosyncratic patterns of behaviour that develop between these nursing couples, learned by both and reciprocally used, if things are going well, with increasing assurance and security. There is much evidence about the importance for the baby's development of his being cared for in the early stages within the context of such familiar patterns.

The baby's own mother, in normal circumstances, seems the most appropriate person to be the almost unique care-taker. She approaches her task with a predisposition for devotion to that baby which no other woman is so likely to have – a devotion supported by her love for the baby's father. For its full realization, the maternal predisposition to devotion and its behavioural concomitants need close and continuous contact with the baby. The mother needs his joys and sorrows, his fears and his relief, rewards when she manages him well and he responds positively, temporary despairs when she fails, if she is to find the relationship deeply meaningful in both its good and bad aspects and to make it meaningful to her baby.

Such views appear to have been incontrovertibly established by a mass of research – that the overriding need of the baby, and indeed of the mother, is that the two should have close and continuous availability during the early months and years of the child's life. The research has been both clinical and field-based, carried out by workers too numerous to mention, who start from very different theoretical and practical bases. Their results have often been formulated in very different ways, but are remarkably consistent. Bowlby is a rich source of relevant references. To deprive the baby of the continuing close relationship with a single care-taker, usually the mother, is to put his development seriously at risk.

THE CONTEXT FOR MATERNITY PROVIDED BY CONTEMPORARY SOCIETY

To be a mother is extremely demanding and it would be difficult to overestimate her need for support and comfort. The context in which she performs her role has a crucial influence on the balance between positive successful interchanges and negative disturbing ones; those which contribute to growth of both mother and baby and those which are potentially pathological. Unfortunately, the context which contemporary society provides for the support of the mother tends to be defective in certain ways and may add to rather than diminish stress.

It seems unlikely that any mother could function really effectively if she had a relationship only with her baby and with no one else. She needs someone who can let her behave rather in the way she must let her baby behave: someone into whom she can put her excessive, unrealistic – although *normal* – anxieties, and who will give her appropriate and tolerable versions of them. Someone, too, who can take the baby from her temporarily if a situation becomes too fraught – a person devoted both to her and the baby. In the normal family situation the husband and father is probably the most appropriate person, on whose patience and sensitivity great calls will be made. A problem in Western societies is, of course, that the husband may not be sufficiently available to his wife and child – absent for the whole of long days at work, for example. The situation is often exacerbated by the unavailability of other appropriate relatives. The effectiveness of such help, if available, may be limited by taboos on talking about certain things, especially about anxiety to do with the baby's survival or modified versions of this, for example anxieties about his physical and mental development. Too often the mother herself, imbued with these attitudes, feels her anxieties and phantasies to be silly and may deny them, or at least keep them secret and not effectively seek help.

The situation is often worsened when the mother's main source of help is one of the institutions the state provides in competition with, or as a substitute for, natural care-takers, the husband or extended family. For example, at what is for most mothers and babies a crucial period in their relationship – immediately before, during and immediately after birth – mothers and babies are increasingly institutionalized, and too often in the same hospitals which are so inadequate in the care of the dying. Although these institutions may relieve the mother's anxiety by providing good physical care, they often activate anxieties in other ways. They give her little spiritual nourishment. On the contrary, they often diminish her and her maternity. Too little sanction is given for the expression of distressed feelings; they are treated as '*only*' the disordered phantasies of women in a so-called abnormal psychological state, to be discouraged and disregarded. This view is very much opposed to that of Winnicott, described above. Only too often the same kind of process goes on in institutions that supervise well babies, emphasis being on physical and material progress rather than on psychosocial support.

The acquisitive society is, on the whole, antipathetic to the full operation of the maternal role. Each nuclear family is under social pressure to sustain a high material standard, difficult without the second income provided by the wife. Material sacrifices must be made if the mother is to care for her baby and even if they are made willingly some resentment is likely, leading to pressure inside the family for the mother to contribute a second income. The constant pressure from society for women to be at work may be even more difficult to resist. For example, the frequently understaffed 'women's professions' like nursing, social work and teaching constantly put pressure on women to return to work. It is implied or explicitly stated that women who 'only look after their family and home' are lazy and irresponsible. A version of this view is put forward, for example, by Myrdal and Klein (1956) in *Women's Two Roles*. They stress the woman's obligation to contribute to society's wealth, although writing about twenty years ago they did exempt the mothers of young children from that obligation and stressed the importance of the mother's presence for the healthy development of the child. The mothers of today's young children are not, unfortunately, exempt from these pressures. Their relationship with their baby is too often infiltrated by conflict, guilt and a sense of persecution about not using their marketable skills.

Another aspect of acquisitiveness is the attempt to sustain a full career for its own sake while having children. The very real loss to the mother of giving up her career even temporarily is stressed while the sacrifices and risk to the children of not having adequate maternal care are denied or rationalized in various suspect ways. There is an implication that no choice ought to be necessary between career and children, and no sacrifice.

This reflects society's tendency to denigrate motherhood as

a highly complex and demanding occupation in its own right. This is a composite of many attitudes, including envy of women, both by men and by women who have difficulty in accepting full femininity. Important in it seems, however, a reflection of the taboo on death and mourning, dealing with which, I have suggested, is such an important aspect of mothering. If the existence of a crucial and difficult aspect of the role is even partially denied, the role itself is diminished and loses dignity.

It seems, then, that contemporary society is less supportive to mothers and babies than it might be: exerting pressures, placing obstacles, and surrounding the mother with attitudes that are antipathetic to her role. Obviously this is only one side of the question and one would not want to deny the positive support and understanding that also exist, although these are less vociferous and appear, perhaps, more in actions than in words.

Society in a sense expresses its ambivalence by a split in views and behaviour. One side is encouraging – that is, the large number of families, the majority, where mothers give their babies close, continuous care and are well supported in spite of antipathetic pressures. By contrast, negative attitudes to motherhood are acted out on behalf of society by a smaller number of mothers who put their babies into the care of institutions from a very early age, at least in the daytime, this being done with the collusion and support of society. The coexistence of these two groups seems to imply that they perform a useful function for each other and society and are in a complicated interaction. For example, each satisfies by proxy some of the desires of the other; each is envied and attacked by the other. Thus, 'the career woman', perhaps openly contemptuous of the woman who devotes herself to her children, still expresses through her split-off wishes to do the same, and vice versa. The need to sustain this situation as a defensive acting-out manoeuvre in society may indeed partly explain why society tolerates, or even encourages, the placing of growing numbers of young children in institutions in spite of the evidence about how damaging they are.

Different types of women are notable among those who use

children's institutions. For example, there is the mother who has herself been a deprived child, is not capable of deep, stable and meaningful relationships and cannot tolerate the stress of caring for her baby. She repeats her own experiences in reverse and tends to become a depriving institution-using mother. She is often rather inarticulate. The other is very different: feminists and career women with strong views about women's rights and vociferous about them – a vociferousness not, unfortunately, shared by their babies. They are acquisitive, too, and disregard the sacrifices they impose on their babies, and indeed on themselves, by such behaviour. Intellectual knowledge of research findings on the mother–baby relationship is met by emotional blocking about its implications for themselves and their babies. They may consciously regard social care for children as quite adequate and may also regard the family as outmoded (see, for example, Juliet Mitchell, *Psychoanalysis and Feminism*, 1974).

The children's institutions, like other institutions for society's problem people, are not adequate substitutes for the natural care-takers they replace. They also are too often limbo institutions, the children having little contact with the world outside. Inside the institution the child is deprived of normal family activities and relationships through which he develops his knowledge of the real world. The system of multiple indiscriminate care-taking, on which institutions are almost inevitably organized, denies the child the necessary single care-taker, one mother-substitute, to whom he can become appropriately attached. Perhaps the most serious problem of the institutionalized child is, however, the extent to which the institution *per se*, and its staff, develop personal and socially based defences that prevent them making effective contact with the reality of their client population.[1] This too often means that they discourage normal attitudes and behaviour and reinforce abnormal ones. In particular, they tend to be impervious to grief and mourning in a situation where the children have much to grieve for: in the loss of their mothers and homes. One should not lightly blame the institutions for developing defensive attitudes and behaviour. They have a well-nigh impossible task in fostering normal development under such circumstances, often with totally inadequate staff/child ratios and a client population which may include many already disturbed children. The institutionalized child care seems to act out a split-off denial of the crucial importance of the mother–child relationship which if effectively recognized would, in fact, define a different unit as requiring help – that is, the mother–child unit, preferably in the family context.

In conclusion, I would reiterate that the forces against the effective deployment of the maternal role in our society are quite powerful, subtle and subversive and reach their epitome in split-off form in the institutionalization of large and growing numbers of children.

NOTE
1. For a description of such socially based defences, see Menzies, 1961b (see above, pp. 43–85).

Staff support systems: task and anti-task in adolescent institutions (1979)

M OST OF US, as we achieve some seniority in our professions, have to assume managerial responsibilities in institutions. This shift is not always easy, since there are inconsistencies between the two roles, but it must be made effectively for many reasons, not least being the contribution of good management to staff support. Rice (1963) has said that the effective performance of a primary task is a major source of satisfaction and that in so far as behaviour is adult and reality-based, people are loath to surrender such satisfaction.

The responsibility of management for effective task-performance is a contribution to staff support, both through positive job satisfaction and through protecting staff from the anxiety, guilt and depression that arise from inadequate task-performance. My concern is not so much with positive activities of management as with the difficulties that beset good management, particularly in institutions that care for people.

PRIMARY TASK

The primary task can in theory be defined simply as the task which the enterprise must perform in order to survive, but from the viewpoint of efficient institutional performance it must also be clearly defined in practice. Quite simply, unless the members of the institution know what it is they are supposed to be doing, there is little hope of their doing it effectively and getting adequate psychosocial satisfactions from this. Lack of such definition is likely to lead to personal confusion in members of the institution, to interpersonal and intergroup conflict and to other undesirable institutional phenomena to which I will return later, all of which reduce the satisfactions of membership.

In some institutions task-definition is quite simple; for example, in commercial institutions it is to make a profit, since without making a profit they will not survive, although the precise methods adopted to make a profit may be more open to debate and subject to change in changing circumstances.

Many professional workers, however, have to function in institutions where they do not have the luxury of such an easily definable primary task and where attempts to achieve adequate definition are often countered by pressures from outside. Clearly such factors also make effective task-performance and related task-satisfactions harder to achieve. Such institutions may be referred to collectively as the humane institutions. They have also been described as 'people-changing institutions' (Street *et al.*, 1966). They have a number of problems which we can now consider.

MULTIPLE TASKS

Frequently there is no single task which has overall primacy, but any one of two or more may take priority at a given time in given circumstances. A very good example of this is a teaching hospital, which has many tasks. The care of patients may feel like the primary task but, in fact, it has to yield primacy on occasion to the training of medical students. Large formal ward rounds may be good for students but are rarely regarded as good for patients. Further, since teaching hospitals are also nurse-training schools, there may be conflict between patient care and the needs of nurse training, and conflict between medical and nurse-training needs. Mediating the variable primacy of tasks in such institutions is no easy responsibility and calls for frequent decisions about moment-to-moment primacy at all levels in the organization, often without adequately defined managerial policy. It also makes it more difficult to sustain adequately the feeling that the total organization is effective and to provide adequate support through job satisfaction for its members, since the level of performance of each task tends to be reduced by the legitimate demands of the others.

CONFUSION IN TASK-DEFINITION

The humane institutions, dealing as they do with human beings as their throughput, are also unusually subject to influence from the wider community in terms of task-definition. This can also lead to confusion and doubt. Various penal institutions provide a good example of such confusion. Public pressure orientates them in at least three relatively incompatible directions: punitive, custodial and therapeutic. These incompatible objectives are often reflected internally in the attitudes and personal objectives of both staff and clients. They result in inadequate task-definition, sometimes explicit and always implicit. At present institutions, both for criminals and delinquents and for psychiatric patients, are tending explicitly to adopt definitions orientated to the therapeutic and rehabilitative, but this by no means prevents the implicit infiltration of custodial and punitive objectives. This overt and covert conflict between the task-definitions makes effective performance of the explicitly stated tasks difficult and often leads to staff feeling unsupported in their roles, to low job satisfaction and to high stress. Such institutions show up badly in morale indicators such as staff turnover, student wastage, sickness and absenteeism, not to mention system-provoked bad behaviour by clients.

INADEQUATE RESOURCES FOR TASK

Professional workers are often ambitious in what they would like to do for their clients and so tend to define the tasks of institutions in fairly ambitious terms. Unlike the profit-making institutions, which just go bankrupt and die if they set objectives beyond their means, humane institutions can often survive in this state, even if they are not functioning well. Adequate therapy for the total population of clients jointly served is an overambitious objective in terms of the total resources the community can devote to such clients. However, in the separate institutions staff tend to pursue such objectives as ends in themselves. They do not relate the defined task or objective to possible means, or may not be in a good position to do so. The result is chronic overwork, chronic disappointment in results, painful and fruitless struggles with resource-dispensing authorities, low satisfaction and high stress. Yet the alternative, a more realistic definition of task in relation to likely resources with less beneficial results with clients, is also painful, or even intolerable. It is possible that confrontation would lead ultimately to a greater sense of support and job satisfaction through performing a less ambitious task more effectively.

Society as a whole throws this problem back on the humane institutions. It fails to define objectives realistically in relation to means or to face the problem of allocating resources differentially to different needs. The dominant societal attitude is that everyone should have what help they need or even want, an attitude reflecting Aneurin Bevan's basic orientation to the National Health Service (Ministry of Health, 1944): every patient has the basic right to all the treatment he needs. One can sympathize with the objective, but if one is realistic one must admit that it cannot be achieved because resources will not allow it. The failure of society at large to face this problem confronts the humane institutions with the need to do it for themselves; and in so doing often having to meet the disapproval and excessive demands of society.

Scarcity of resources may make desirable the devotion of more to the best 'bets' and only limited objectives, such as good custodial care, for the others. Such discrimination is hard to face in the institutions concerned without society's support. The result is more ambitious objectives everywhere and the chronic inadequacy of resources to achieve them, unless management is very tough.

DIFFICULTY IN PRECISE DEFINITION

For the humane institution it is indeed difficult to define its task precisely and in other than the most general terms. Take, for example, the therapeutic communities. Their objective is therapy. What exactly does that mean? How clear is the typical therapeutic community about the precise change it hopes to achieve in its client population? The problem is clearly stated by Street and others (1966), where all the institutions described are orientated to producing more effective members of society, but what they mean by that differs considerably.

Or take schools. The objective can be described as education, but what does that mean? Every pupil, parent and teacher is likely to have his own personal definition of this objective, often not easily subject to verbal formulation. Even on the more academic side, the struggle with curricular reform suggests a possible multiplicity of objectives. How much more difficult to define the wider task of schools in educating pupils for life in general, or even in a particular society! How precisely is the educational system, or even a particular school, to define that task? The solution of this particular problem is not aided by the fact that society in general is confused. Moral and value systems, life objectives and career prospects are all in a state of flux. Developments in schools seem to reflect uncertainties in the situation. Education for effective community participation seems now to be hived off in schools under the concept of pastoral care, care for the human needs of all pupils or special care for disturbed pupils. To me this represents an opting out by the school system from an important aspect of its primary task because of the difficulty of relating education to a confused society and also because that society itself is perhaps over-dominated by an unrealistic caring philosophy, regardless of resources. It would be a terrible criticism of an educational system to say that it is educating its pupils for dependency.

REDEFINITION OF TASK INTO ANTI-TASK

There is thus a danger of primary task being implicitly redefined when the task as originally and perhaps more realistically defined becomes too difficult, or when societal pressures against realistic task-definition are too great. In other words, task may implicitly slip over into anti-task; for example, the education system not being realistically orientated to maturation and preparedness for life in society but to providing for dependency needs which may be anti-maturational. In an institution for deprived boys to which the author was consultant, real educational difficulties and the related difficulties for staff in achieving educational progress had encouraged an implicit redefinition of the educational task in terms of therapy. The real therapeutic effect of being able to read, write and do simple arithmetic and of making a contribution to life in the community was in danger of being ignored.

Such difficulties do not relieve managers of the responsibility of achieving adequate task-definition. They only demand more toughness. It remains crucial that staff should know what they are expected to achieve and should have adequate management support in doing so, which may also imply support in not doing things which may be desirable in themselves but are realistically impossible or too expensive.

SOCIOTECHNICAL SYSTEMS

The performance of the primary task of an enterprise requires an appropriate organization. Such an organization has two aspects: (1) the choice and application of an appropriate technology; (2) the choice and application of an appropriate social system – what Trist and others (1963) have called a sociotechnical system. The most appropriate sociotechnical system is that which gives the best fit to primary task-performance. The basic model is an open system where the organization imports material from the environment, converts the material into something different and re-exports it to the environment. In the case of humane institutions the most significant import is, of course, the human import of clients who must be 'converted' – changed, and sent back to the outside environment more able, it is hoped, to sustain life there effectively.

Problems in establishing sociotechnical systems, although not peculiar to humane institutions, are usually more intense there. For example, a system appropriate to custodial care is likely to be inappropriate to carrying out therapy, and vice versa.

THE TECHNOLOGY

Further, the humane institutions often have to function in conditions where the available technologies are themselves hard to define and depend on the actual qualities and behaviour of the people who operate them. We are ourselves the instruments of technology. It is usually more difficult to define what a person does than a machine. Clear and realistic choice between technologies may, therefore, be difficult or impossible. For example, the precise effects of different therapeutic techniques are hard to establish by follow-up study, and one often has to function without clear guidance as to the success of different techniques or technologies. The choice of technology is, therefore, much subject to the personal idiosyncrasies of the people concerned, to their beliefs and hunches and their own models of human interaction.

There is the risk, then, that the choice and detailed application of technology may be inappropriately influenced by the human needs of the permanent members of the institutions and be less than appropriately related to effective primary task-performance. One can be aware of this problem in theory, but it is difficult to guard against its effects in practice.

THE SOCIAL SYSTEM

Primary task-performance requires a social system that relates technology to task and relates the people and groups who carry out different parts of the task to each other. Task and technology together do not wholly prescribe the nature of the social system, although they put significant constraints on it and may rule out certain types of social system. The chosen social system is likely to reflect strongly the psychological and social satisfactions that members of an institution seek in their membership and work in the institution. These needs are of different kinds and are both positively task-orientated and potentially anti-task. In so far as they are task-orientated, they include the satisfactions arising from being able to deploy oneself positively and fully in relation to task, co-operating effectively with others and experiencing both personal and institutional success in task-performance. People require such satisfactions and their realization is an essential aspect of staff support. Such co-operation by the members contributes towards a social system orientated to the effective use of technology in task-performance.

Unfortunately for task-performance, members of institutions are also likely to seek satisfaction of personal needs that are anti-task; very often they need to mitigate the stresses and strains of the task itself and of confrontation with the human material on which the task is focused. In other words, members try to establish a social system that also acts as a defence against anxiety, both personal anxiety and that evoked by institutional membership. Jaques (1955) has referred to 'a socially structured defence system'. This will appear in all aspects of the institution both formal and informal, in attitudes and interpersonal relations, in customs and conventions and also, very importantly, in the actual formal social structure of the organization and its management system.

The social system is a mixture of elements, some orientated to primary task-performance and some to other implicit objectives, which we can summarize under the term 'primary anti-task'. Good management must obviously be orientated to sustaining task-orientated elements and discouraging anti-task; but management in the humane institutions is in more trouble than in the institutions that process things.

There are a number of reasons:

1. The distinction between social system and technology is not clear. The social system is itself part of technology, and as part of the experience the institution provides for its clients it has a therapeutic or anti-therapeutic effect. It is important, therefore, that the social system provide a genuinely therapeutic model for clients, orientated to helping them develop and cope more effectively with the world outside.

The management system is a significant part of the model, as I realized when working as management consultant to an approved school. A main preoccupation there was the need to develop better ego-functioning in boys with primitive, unintegrated egos and, among other things, to provide effective models for identification. We tended to see both the management system in itself and the functioning of individual managers within it as such ego-models, with therapeutic or anti-therapeutic potential; and much work has been done in trying to realize the former. For example, we have worked at clarifying the boundaries of subsystems and the authority within and across their boundaries, and ensuring that managers were really responsible for the staff within their own subsystems and did not have to operate with staff over whom someone in another system had authority. This is a confusing situation only too frequent in humane institutions; for example, the confusion between the medical and nursing hierarchies in hospitals and the exact location of authority between them. We also aimed at maximum delegation down the hierarchy to increase the opportunity for staff in direct confrontation with boys to act with management authority, a model of good management-cum-ego functioning.

2. A danger may arise in the interlocking of the social and technological systems in humane institutions when the social system, and particularly the managerial structure, become excessively infiltrated by attitudes and behaviour derived from professional attitudes to therapy. The institution may become too permissive, too nondirective, and lacking in firmness and boundary control. The staff may, in fact, both lack for themselves and fail to give to clients the firm, authoritative management which is a necessary feature of both staff support and client therapy. Very frequently, it seems, the explicit or implicit model for operating units is some version of the family, which may be inappropriate. It denies the reality that this is a work situation which needs management with clarification of roles, responsibilities and relationships. Further, the so-called family model often denies the reality of the family. A well-functioning ordinary family is likely to have a complicated and effective management system even though it would not be described in those terms and is often not noticed because it is implicit and stable over long periods. In institutions the same effect can be achieved only by making explicit the managerial functions and relationships.

3. The effects on staff of the human 'material' they work with are especially great in institutions whose clients are people in trouble. The clients are likely to evoke powerful and primitive feelings and fantasies in staff who suffer painful though not always acknowledged identifications with clients, intense reactions both positive and negative to them, pity for their plight, fear, possibly exaggerated, about their violence, or harsh, primitive, moral reactions to their delinquency. The acknowledge-

ment and working through of such feelings is not easy, although it is an important part of staff support and primary task-performance to do so. In so far as feelings cannot be worked with personally or institutionally, they are likely to be dealt with by the development of defences against them; and in so far as they relate to institutional phenomena they will tend, as I suggested above, to become institutionalized through collusive, implicit interaction between members. They come to be built into the structure, culture and mode of functioning of the institution and thereby impair task-performance.

The danger is that since the anxieties defended against are primitive and violent, defences will also be primitive. The author has described this elsewhere in a study of the defensive system in the nursing service of a general teaching hospital (Menzies, 1970; see above, pp. 43–85). Such social defences are inevitably anti-task. They relate the institution to its members, clients and task in a way which is not fully realistic. They may deny the full implications of the client's problems, often preventing the full deployment of staff capacities. Anti-therapeutic systems of interpersonal relationships between staff and between staff and clients are built up. They are also resistant to the change and development in institutional functioning which is essential in a changing society to ensure effective task-performance.

Such problems are illustrated in an organizational model which is only too common in humane institutions, and which the approved school where the author worked struggled to change. It is common for resources directly used by or on behalf of clients to be controlled centrally and dispensed in kind by someone like the matron. Several consequences tend to follow. Such resources are often rather scanty in relation to need: this is likely to lead to complaints against the person-in-role who dispenses them, who may well become notorious for her meanness and lack of understanding of need. Staff more directly involved with clients may well go into collusion with them in developing a paranoid system defensive against the pain and difficulty of confronting the problem of scarce resources with clients, and opt out of their own responsibility for the situation. Such a situation is anti-therapeutic in that it stabilizes a paranoid defence system in clients who are prone to that anyway and militates against the opportunity to develop more ego-based confrontation with the reality of scarce resources, surely a problem in real life in the community at large. The author was invited by the matron to help her in dealing with a situation she was coming to find intolerable: the image projected on to her or, more correctly, her role. Effective dispensing of food resources was very difficult and she felt she was not carrying out her task effectively. What we gradually evolved was that the control of food resources was delegated downwards and across subsystem boundaries into the residential units, who were given the money for food to be dispensed as they saw fit. The matron no longer controlled the resources but took up an advisory and service function to the house mothers. The central store became a shop which house mothers could use or not as they saw fit and which had to compete with other shops. The central kitchen provided ready-cooked food at the house mother's request, for which she paid. Very interesting and, it is hoped, positive developments resulted. The paranoid defence system was greatly weakened. House mothers were now in a position to confront scarcity with boys. Their previously underused capacities were more fully deployed, their authority and professionalism increased. Staff satisfaction increased from doing a realistic job well, with subsequent strengthening of staff support. And, incidentally, food was no longer seen as being in such short supply.

Defence systems are in the end likely to be anti-supportive to staff. This is not only because they reduce their level of performance and their satisfaction from it, but also because they tend to their personal diminution. Comments about such personal diminution were common among the nurses in the teaching hospital; they were grieved by it and felt unsupported in their efforts to discharge their responsibilities efficiently.

4. Clients may intervene in the development and maintenance of the sociotechnical system in a way that is powerful and anti-task and provokes related powerful, anti-task, reactions from staff. One formulation of this is the concept of the anti-task

subculture. It can develop quickly and powerfully and can also be sustained over long periods, if staff do not intervene in a task-orientated way. Too often, indeed, staff collude with it because of the difficulties of confrontation or because they get satisfaction from it themselves. They do this minimally by denying the existence of the subculture or, if aware of it, by trying to keep it as a separate encapsulated entity. At worst they may be drawn into it: for example, meeting violence or threats of violence by harsh punishment, or themselves being drawn into homosexual acting out.

More subtly they can react by establishing or trying to establish another subculture to counter the first, which is, however, equally anti-task. Rice (1963), following Bion (1961), has described this feature of group and institutional life. Interesting developments took place in the approved school when it had had an unusually large intake of boys reputed to be potentially violent and where there had also been several unusually severe outbreaks of violence. Staff felt threatened, not only by the boys' violence but also by the temptation to counterviolence they experienced in themselves. They were working at the problem in a task-orientated way but also subtly developing a subculture to counter violence – that is, a move to provide unusually, and probably unrealistically, for dependency needs: dependency to counter violence. This succeeded in concentrating the problems to an unrealistic extent in those staff whose job it was to meet real dependency needs in domestic provision; they in turn became distressed because they could not meet the unrealistic demands on them by other staff, perhaps more than the demands made by boys, to provide for dependency. Needless to say, this was not contributing much to a solution which could be found only by staff and boys confronting the violence together. It was, of course, also anti-staff-support because it was defensive rather than task-orientated.

5. The real task of humane institutions can in a sense be described as relating to dependency needs; for example, in adolescent institutions dealing with young people in trouble or meeting educational needs. Neither task can, of course, be

effectively accomplished only by gratifying dependency needs, but these needs are there and the institutions must relate to them somehow. These institutions have, therefore, as their work task a function that is close to an anti-task phenomenon. This puts them at risk. Their efforts to function on a realistic work level will be unduly infiltrated by phenomena that derive from anti-task group dynamics. The effectiveness of task-performance will thereby be reduced, for example, by gratifying dependency needs rather than by struggling for maturity, towards independence and realistic functioning. Both staff and client are diminished by such situations and will feel unsupported in their performance of their common task, with likely negative reactions. Elizabeth Richardson (1973) quotes a staff member at Nailsea School who thought the behaviour problems of upper-school pupils might be related to the lack of appropriate courses rather than simply the problems of the pupils as people. This is an interesting comment which suggests that behaviour difficulties in any school may be linked with the relative failure to carry out the primary task of education effectively. If so, neither pastoral care nor school counselling for individual pupils is likely to improve matters much. Work orientated to better task-performance might.

It seems, therefore, that the management of humane institutions has an unusually difficult task in ensuring the best fit between sociotechnical systems and primary task. This calls for an unusual degree of management skill from people who do not easily see themselves as managers.

CONCLUSION

This chapter has stressed the importance of effective institutional management as a major factor in staff support. We have concentrated mainly on one particular aspect of management: its responsibility for effective task-performance. Incidental mention only has been made of other aspects of good management that support staff: for example, clarification of roles, task and responsibility and the relationships involved in them, and the support arising from being given fully challenging tasks with the authority to carry them out.

In discussing the importance of primary task-performance, attention has been mainly concentrated on the difficulties that hinder effectiveness rather than the positive means that achieve it. This choice was made deliberately, since it appears that there is less understanding of interference to task than of positive activities in management, not least because the negative features are indeed hard to cope with and we are tempted to deny them ourselves.

A very important characteristic of good management seems, therefore, to be a developed capacity to keep oneself and others out of the kinds of difficulties discussed: to struggle with task-definition, to get it as precise and realistic as possible and to sustain the values that go with it, to protect the institution and its staff from undue pressures across the boundaries, to mitigate anti-task phenomena such as in socially structured defence systems or subcultures, to effect such institutional changes as are desirable for task-effectiveness, and to reconcile the needs of task and the psychosocial needs of the members of the institution, both staff and clients.

This may perhaps seem to advocate a somewhat ruthless preoccupation with task. The management of an institution requires some measure of that ruthlessness, but this concern for task need not and should not necessarily be linked with lack of concern for people. In the main, it is likely to prove the contrary. Much of the task-orientated activity, is, in fact, directly good for people. For example, striving for adaptive and mature defences rather than primitive and counteracting the development of destructive subcultures are rewarding. Above all, such task-orientated activities facilitate the support given to staff through belonging to an institution that functions well and gives both the rewards for work well done and the rewarding relationships that go with them.

8 The development of the self in children in institutions (1985)

HE THEORETICAL BASIS for thinking in this paper* centres on a particular aspect of the development of the self, development that takes place through introjective identification. Healthy development depends greatly on the availability of appropriate models of individuals, relationships and situations for such identification. These models may be found in the adults who care for the children, their relationship with the children and with each other, and the setting for care. Healthy development may also require the management of the child's identification with inappropriate models, for example with other children in institutions for delinquent or maladjusted children.

Institutionalized children are likely to find the most significant models for identification within the institution itself, both in the institution as a whole and its subsystems and in individual staff members and children. This leads to the concept of the institution as a therapeutic milieu whose primary task may be defined as providing conditions for healthy development and/or providing therapy for damaged children. Thus all the child's experiences in the institution contribute positively or negatively to his development, not only those more narrowly defined as education, individual or group therapy or child care. Indeed, it has been the author's experience that the benefits of such

* Reprinted from *J. Child Psychotherapy* (1985) 11: 49–64. The reader will notice some repetition of passages in Chapters 5 and 7. Unavoidably the same case material had to be used, although the theoretical perspective has somewhat evolved in this paper.

provision may well be counteracted by more general features of the institution.

This formulation would then lead one to take a very wide view of the institution in considering its effectiveness in carrying out its primary task. One would include its whole way of functioning; its management structure, including its division into subsystems and how those relate to each other; the nature of authority and how that is operated; the social defence system built into the institution; its culture and traditions. In line with the theme of this paper, one would consider these in the context of how far they facilitate the provision of healthy models for identification, or alternatively inhibit the provision of such models.

Although one regards the whole institution as the model, in practice, of course, the impact of the institution on its child clients is mediated to a considerable extent through its staff members, who are the individual models for identification. While it is true that they will have their own individual personalities with strengths and weaknesses as models, it is also true that the way they deploy their personalities within the institution will depend on features inherent in the institution, the opportunities it gives staff for mature functioning or the limits it puts on this. The author has discussed elsewhere the severe limits that a traditionally organized nursing service imposes on the mature functioning of both trained and student nurses (Menzies, 1970; see above, pp. 43–85).

Thus, in considering the adults as models, one would give attention to maximizing the opportunity for them to deploy their capacities effectively and to be seen by the children to do so. Indeed, one may go further: experience has shown that in a well-managed institution for children, the adults as well as the children actually gain in ego-strength and mature in other ways. The adults thus provide better models.

The author's interest in the importance of the whole institution as a therapeutic milieu has developed over many years of working in two institutions for disturbed children where her formal role was that of management consultant and her task was to work with staff in keeping under continuous review the way the institution as a whole was functioning in relation to the primary task. The role involved both a considerable understanding of the way institutions function and a psychoanalytically based understanding of child development. Similarly, in a collaborative study with the Royal National Orthopaedic Hospital designed to improve the care of young children making long stays and to mitigate the long-term effects of hospitalization, it was found necessary to pay considerable attention to the way the Cot Unit for young children was managed and related itself to the management of the hospital as a factor affecting the quality of child care.

Against this background, it would appear possible that views about the development of children in institutions have been unduly pessimistic. So many of the early investigations were done in institutions whose whole organization was inappropriate for healthy child development. For example, the bad effects of hospitalization on young children were demonstrated first in hospitals with inadequate maternal visiting and multiple indiscriminate care-taking by a large number of nurses which effectively prevented attachment between a child and his care-takers. The same has been true, on the whole, for children in day and residential nurseries. In fact, these institutions deviated much more from a good model of care than is realistically necessary, as also from the kind of setting a good ordinary family provides for a child to grow up in. More recent work provides some grounds for a more optimistic view of the developmental potential of children's institutions. They can be operated very differently from, for example, the old-fashioned hospital and can come much closer to the good ordinary family.

The section that follows discusses in some detail ways in which institutions can be organized or reorganized so as to provide improved models for the child's identification and for his development, and gives examples of work in institutions. I will comment on various aspects of this: ego-development, superego-development, the development of a firm sense of identity and of authority and responsibility for the self, attachment possibilities, the growth of a capacity for insight and confrontation with problems.

THE POTENTIAL OF THE INSTITUTION AS A MODEL FOR IDENTIFICATION

DELEGATION AND ITS RELATION TO STAFF'S ATTITUDES AND BEHAVIOUR

It is in general good management practice to delegate tasks and responsibilities to the lowest level at which they can be competently carried and to the point at which decision-making is most effective. This is of particular importance in children's institutions, since such delegation downwards increases the opportunity for staff to behave in an effective and authoritative way, to demonstrate capacity for carrying responsibility for themselves and their tasks and to make realistic decisions, all of which are aspects of a good model.

But this has not traditionally been the practice in many children's institutions; the functions, responsibilities and decision-making are centralized at a high management level, with a consequent diminution of the responsibility, authority and effectiveness of the staff more directly in contact with the children. In my consultancy with an approved school (a residential school for delinquent boys) I became involved in working with staff to change the management structure and functioning in one such area. The setting was traditional, with a matron who dispensed food in kind to the house mothers who provided meals for the staff and boys in the houses where the boys lived. There were all sorts of deficiencies and inefficiencies in the system, both practically in its effects on food provision and psychosocially in its effect on the behaviour of staff providing food and the models they presented to boys. The food allowance was not very generous and there were constant complaints about its inadequacy; indeed, boys were not very well fed. But the effect of the reality of the food allowance was compounded by the fact that, since the responsibility for food provision and decision-making lay with the matron, there was a notable tendency for the house mothers to disclaim their responsibility and authority; for example, to blame the matron if things went wrong, rather than feel an obligation to cope with them themselves.

A small example illustrates this point. Two boys went for a

239

walk one evening and came back hungry. The house mother gave them two of the eggs she had been given for the breakfast next morning, thus leaving herself two short. She was disconcerted and angry when the matron would not – could not – give her more. Matron was blamed instead of the house mother's taking responsibility for her own actions. The model presented to the children was one of irresponsibility and of blaming the other.

The system gradually changed. Ultimately the house mothers were given the money to buy the food themselves. With it they were explicitly given the responsibility and authority for the efficient use of the money. The matron gave up her authority and responsibility for direct food provision and instead became an adviser and supporter of the house mothers if they wished to use her in that way. The former central foodstore became a shop where the house mothers could spend their money if they wished, but they had no obligations to do so if they preferred to shop elsewhere.

In time there were a number of very positive effects of this change. The house mothers visibly grew in authority and stature as they faced and accepted the new challenge and, for the most part, very effectively took over the task of food provision. The task itself was more realistically and effectively performed. One heard less and less about scarcity, and the boys were actually better fed. Most importantly, the confrontation with scarcity and complaints about ineffective provision now became a face-to-face matter between the house mother, her colleagues in the house and the boys. The boys were thus given an important learning experience for life in the world outside: in learning to deal with scarce resources themselves, not just to complain about them. Initiative and ingenuity were freed. The resources of the estate itself, such as fruit, were better used and gardening by staff and boys developed on a considerable scale to augment food supplies. The therapeutic effects of the change in the staff models presented and in the participation of the boys in the new system can hardly be exaggerated.

There was another important consequence in the matter of ego-development and defences. As the author has described elsewhere (Menzies, 1970; see above, pp. 43–85), members of an institution must incorporate and operate to a considerable extent the defences developed in the institution's social system. Here a thoroughly paranoid defence system had developed around the provision of food. The matron was regarded as a 'mean bitch'; if only she were more generous, everything would be all right. Responsibility on the part of the house mothers was converted into blame against the matron and the boys were collusively drawn into the system. This defence was primitive and anti-maturational, but gradually disappeared as the new system developed to be replaced by a more adaptive system of acknowledged responsibility and confrontation with reality.

The implications for staff as superego models may also be evident in the carrying of more mature authority for oneself and one's own behaviour and the replacement of blame of the other by more realistic assessment of oneself and one's own performance.

This is but one example of a series of similar changes that gradually changed the provision by staff of ego, superego and defensive models, the importance of which can hardly be over-stressed for children whose personality development is immature or already damaged or both. The ego and superego strength of staff was both fostered by the changes and given more opportunity to be effectively demonstrated to the children. They in turn were also involved more effectively in control over their own circumstances and given less opportunity to regard themselves as helpless and nonresponsible victims of uncontrollable circumstances. It was seen as essential to carry out these other changes so as to achieve consistency and avoid presenting the children with conflicting and confusing models.

Effective delegation implies more than taking responsibility and authority for oneself, however; it implies also that the individual can accept and respect the authority of superiors and be effectively accountable to them, and that he can take authority effectively for his subordinates and hold them in turn accountable for their performance. This is again important in the provision of models for children whose relationship with authority is immature and possibly already disturbed. Thus authority channels must be clear; staff must know to whom they are responsible and for what, and for whom they are responsible and for what.

It seems a fault in many children's institutions that they do not handle authority effectively. There may be too much permissiveness, people being allowed or encouraged to follow their own bent with insufficient accountability, guidance or discipline. If this does not work (and it frequently does not, leading to excessive acting out by both staff and children) it may be replaced in time by an excessively rigid and punitive regime. Both are detrimental to child development. The 'superego' of the institution needs to be authoritative and responsible, though not authoritarian; firm and kindly, but not sloppily permissive.

INSTITUTIONAL BOUNDARIES AND THE DEVELOPMENT OF IDENTITY

An aspect of healthy development in the individual is the establishment of a firm boundary for the self and others across which realistic and effective relationships and transactions can take place and within which a sense of one's own identity can be established. Young children and the damaged children in many institutions have not developed effective boundary control or a firm identity within it, and need help from the institution in doing this. How then can the institution provide models of effective boundary control? The institution as a whole must control its external boundaries and regulate transactions across them so as to protect and facilitate the maintenance of the therapeutic milieu. This function will not be considered in detail, since it is less likely to impinge directly on the children than the management of boundaries within the institution. Any institution is divided into subsystems some of which perform different tasks, as with the education and living subsystems in a residential school. Some of them do the same tasks for different clients, for example a number of houses in the living area. The way these subsystems control their boundaries and conduct transactions across them is of great importance for the development of the children's personal boundaries.

A danger in children's institutions seems to be that the boundaries are too laxly controlled and too permeable and that there is too much intrusion into the subsystem from outside and into the individuals within it. There seems to be something about living in an institution that predisposes people to feel that it is all right to have everything open and public and to claim right of entry to almost everywhere at almost any time. Nothing could be more different from the ordinary family home which tends jealously to guard its boundaries, regulating entry and exit and, particularly, protecting its children both from unwarranted intrusions and from excessive freedom to go out across the boundaries. And nothing could be less helpful to the development of children in institutions.

Problems appear particularly in the children's living space, their homes effectively while they are in the institution. It seems important therefore that these present a model of effective boundary control, with realistically regulated entry and exit by permission of the people in the subsystem, notably the staff, not an open front door through which people wander in and out at will. To put it differently, the members of the subsystem need to take authority for movement in and out.

This was an important aspect of the work in the Cot Unit in the Royal National Orthopaedic Hospital where, at first, the boundaries were much too open. The Unit opened directly into the hospital grounds and people walking there seemed to feel free to drop in and visit children *en passant*, often with very kindly intentions of entertaining and encouraging them. Further, the Cot Unit provided the most convenient means of access to the unit for latency children and people *en route* for that often stopped to spend time with the young children. The physical boundary between the Cot Unit and that for latency children was open and there was a good deal of visiting by older children and their families. Altogether the situation seemed highly inappropriate for the healthy development of the children. Individual children were too often 'intruded into' by strange, even if kindly, adults. Relationships between children, mothers and Unit staff could be disrupted by the visitors, as could the ongoing work of the Unit. So the external door was closed to all except members of the Unit. Unit staff and visiting families had the authority and responsibility to control or prevent unauthorized entry. At first an invisible notice saying 'No Admittance Except on Business' was hung in the space between the two units, and again staff and visiting adults helped to control the boundary. Later, a partition was built that effectively separated the two units and made boundary control much easier. The benefits of this boundary control to the ongoing life of the Unit and to the child patients were inestimable.

But there remained the problem of the large number of people from outside the Unit who had legitimate business there: surgeons, the paediatrician, pathology staff, physiotherapists, and so on. Their crossing of the boundary also needed to be monitored to mitigate possible detrimental effects to the children's boundaries. Small children have not developed effective control of such contacts with people who may be strangers and who may do unpleasant, frightening or painful things to them, such as taking blood samples or putting them on traction. The normal way that such contacts are mediated for the child is through a loving and familiar adult who can comfort the child and negotiate on his behalf. It became the rule that such visitors approach the child through his mother if present, or through his assigned nurse, or both. Sometimes the visitor would be asked not to approach the child for the moment if the intervention could be postponed and if the adult care-taker judged the moment inappropriate, for instance if a child was already upset or asleep. The adults both protected the child's boundaries and presented models of boundary control.

Similarly, the transactions across the boundaries outwards which involved children were carefully monitored. Work was done with other hospital wards and departments to ensure consistency in the principles of care between their work and that of the Cot Unit. There was explicit agreement about where mothers or other family adults could accompany children, and so on.

Effective control over boundaries can have another positive effect on the development of identity. It gives a stronger sense of belonging to what is inside, of there being something comprehensible to identify with, of there being 'my place', or 'our place', where 'I' belong and where 'we' belong together. Children cannot get identity from or identify with a whole large institution. They get their identity through secure containment in a small part of it first, and only through that with the whole.

This raises the related issue of the desirable size of what is contained within the boundary if it is to be comprehensible to the child. Too often, it seems, the basic unit is too big. For example, a hospital ward of, say, twenty beds is too big for the small child, both physically and psychosocially. He cannot 'comprehend' it and risks getting lost and confused. The physical space does not contain him securely within its boundaries and the number of staff is such as to risk multiple indiscriminate care-taking, a care system which is inimical to the establishment of a secure identity since it makes it difficult for the child to become familiar with the identity of the other and to have his own identity consistently reflected back to him by the other (Menzies, 1975). The Cot Unit was fortunate in being a twelve-bedded unit, usually less than full which could be staffed by a staff nurse, three nursery nurses and a nursery teacher during school hours. It was physically quite small and secluded once the partition was built.

An effectively bounded small unit is likely to facilitate the development of an easily identifiable and relatively integrated group within the unit, with the staff as its permanent core. This was important in providing support to children and families in the distressing circumstances of long stay in an orthopaedic hospital and in helping to keep anxiety at tolerable levels. This in turn helped prevent the development of inappropriate and anti-maturational defences. In institutions for disturbed children it may also be important in facilitating therapeutic work with the children within the unit through using the dynamics of the group. In a sense it makes escape from appropriate confrontation with realities inside the unit more difficult and facilitates the process of learning from them.

There are boundaries of a more subtle kind that are also significant in providing models for children, notably the boundaries of authority and responsibility. For example, the authority for running the unit needs to be firmly located in its head and his authority should not be undermined by people from outside, such as his superior, directly intervening inside it. The authority and responsibility for managing the Cot Unit was delegated firmly to the staff nurse, and the ward sister did not cross that boundary although she still held ultimate responsibility and kept in close touch with the work there. The ward sister sustained this, although she found it personally depriving and frustrating to be thus distanced from the young children. Similarly, when the head delegates some tasks to his staff the authority needs to be clear and he should not transgress the boundary by direct intervention.

Problems can arise in institutions if the same people work at different times in different subsystems when their authority and the authority under which they operate can become unclear. For example, teachers in an approved school sometimes work in the living area outside school hours. If they continue to think of themselves as 'teachers' under the authority of the headmaster they are confusing an authority boundary, as the headmaster has no management responsibility for the living system. The headmaster in an approved school much concerned for the welfare of his teachers had to learn – painfully – not to think and talk of 'my staff' when they were working in the living area: similarly the heads of the houses had to learn to think of the 'teachers' as 'their staff' and take authority over them effectively. These may again seem strange preoccupations for people concerned with the care of children in institutions, but they do seem appropriate since confusion or inadequate definition of authority boundaries can confuse staff about who or what they are and threaten their own sense of identity and what they identify with. This confusion will subtly convey itself through their attitudes and behaviour to the children, with detrimental effects on their sense of identity and their development.

The final point on this topic concerns the protection of the boundaries of the self and the management of transactions across them, with particular reference to the processes of projection and introjection and their effect on the sense of self. Excessive projection can and does change in a major way the apparent identities of both the projector and the recipient if he cannot control what he takes in. Both can feel unreal and strange to themselves and both can act strangely and inappropriately. Similarly, inappropriate introjections can create a false identity and an unstable sense of self. It seems to be a crucial responsibility of the staff in children's institutions to control their own boundaries so as to manage the effects of both projection and introjection and hold them within realistic and therapeutic limits. In so doing they will help the children to control their projections and introjections and strengthen the development of a true and stable identity. Young children and disturbed children are likely to project massively into care-takers. Indeed, it is to some extent a normal method of communication, telling the other what the child is feeling or what for the moment he cannot tolerate in himself. For example, the apparent 'consciencelessness' of a delinquent child can result from the splitting off and projection of a harsh and primitive superego which is unbearable to the child. The deprived, inadequately mothered child may violently project into the care-takers an idealized mother figure with the demand that the care-taker be that mother and compensate for all his deprivations. The danger for the care-taker, and so for the child, is that the projections may be so compelling that the care-taker acts on them instead of taking them as communications. His personal boundaries are breached, his identity temporarily changed and the transaction ineffectively controlled.

The staff of approved schools, for example, may act on the projected primitive superego and treat the children in a rigid and punitive way which is anti-therapeutic. This represents an acting out by staff with children instead of a therapeutic confrontation with the problem. Or staff can respond to the demands for compensation for early deprivation by an overgratifying regime which is equally anti-therapeutic, since it evades confrontation and real work with the problem.

Similarly staff must be alert to the introjections and false identifications which children use in their desperate search for a self and a sense of identity. These may lead, for example, to false career ambitions in pseudo-identification with idols, identification with delinquent gangs, or apparent and sudden but false improvement based on pseudo-identification with the staff or the principles of the institution.

Inappropriate projections and introjections between children and staff are by no means the only problems. One must also take note of projections and introjections between staff and staff, between children and children and between subsystems. For example, it is fairly common to find in institutions a situation where all subsystems but one are said to be in a good state, but one is in a mess. Frequently this is less a reality than the results of intergroup projections, subsystems projecting their 'bad' into the one and encapsulating the 'good' in themselves. All such phenomena are, of course, anti-developmental and anti-therapeutic and real progress can be made only in so far as people and subsystems can take back what belongs to them, discard what does not and work with the external and internal reality of their situations.

This has always seemed to me one of the most difficult tasks confronting the staff of children's institutions and one for which they need much help and support. This emphasizes the need for the staff to be a close and supportive group able to confront together the projection and introjection systems and to help rescue each other when one or more of them are caught. It requires a culture of honesty and mutual confrontation which is by no means easy to achieve. It requires also a certain permanency and long-standing relationship between the staff which is notoriously difficult to sustain in children's institutions, which tend to have a high labour turnover.

A consultant from outside the group who can view the situation with a 'semi-detached' eye may be a great help here in understanding with staff the nature of the projections and introjections and helping to re-establish the basic identity of both the staff group and the individuals with it.

INSTITUTIONAL PROVISION FOR THE DEVELOPMENT OF THE CAPACITY FOR RELATIONSHIPS

The theoretical basis for the discussion here lies in the work of John Bowlby (1969) and many co-workers. Briefly, the capacity to develop lasting and meaningful relationships develops in accordance with the opportunity the child, especially the very young child, has to form secure attachments. The good ordinary family gives an excellent opportunity where the young child is likely to form a focal intense attachment, usually (though not always) with his mother. He forms other important although less intense attachments with others including his father, siblings, other relatives and friends, his attachment circle extending as he grows older. Moreover, the people in his circle of attachment also have attachments to each other which are important to him for identification. He not only loves his mother as he experiences her but identifies with his father loving his mother and extends his 'concept' of the male loving the female. For the most part, although not always, institutions have dismally failed to replicate that pattern. The multiple indiscriminate care-taking system in which all staff indiscriminately care for all children effectively prevents child–adult attachment. This has been traditional in hospitals and can also be seen in day and residential institutions for physically healthy children. The Robertsons' film *John* (Robertson, James, 1969a,b) shows how multiple indiscriminate care-taking effectively defeats John's efforts to attach himself to one nurse. Further, it has been my experience that multiple indiscriminate care-taking also tends to inhibit attachments between staff so that there is a dearth of attachment models for the children. The situation is of course often compounded by staff turnover, hospital wards being staffed largely by transitory student nurses and day and residential nurseries tending to have high labour turnover.

I am indebted to my colleague Alastair Bain (Bain and Barnett,1980) for a dramatic observation of the child's identification with an inadequate model of relationships in a day nursery and its perpetuation in his later relationships. The observation concerns what he calls 'the discontinuity of care provided even by a single care-taker which occurs when a nursery has to care for a number of children'. He writes:

> Their [the children's] intense needs for individual attention tend to mean that they do not allow the nurse to pay attention

to any one child for any length of time; other children will pull at her skirt, want to sit up on her lap, push the child who is receiving attention away.

One can see this very clearly in *John*. Bain goes on:

during the periods between moments of attention, the young child experiences his fellows as also receiving moments of attention . . . He will also experience as the predominant pattern of relationships between adult and child, a series of discontinuities of attention, a nurse momentarily directing her attention from one child to another . . . He and his moment are just part of a series of disconnected episodes.

The follow-up of these children showed them to have identified with and to be operating on that model, the model of episodic and discontinuous attention, forming in turn a series of episodic and discontinuous relationships with their world shown through fleeting superficial attachments and also in episodic discontinuous play activities and later in difficulty in sustaining continuous attention at school. I have come to call this the 'butterfly phenomenon': the child flitting rather aimlessly from person to person or activity to activity.

Fortunately, institutions do not have to be like that. It is possible to eliminate multiple indiscriminate care-taking and get closer to the family model. Dividing the institution into small units with firm boundaries as described above provides something more like a family setting, even if it is still somewhat larger. Within that setting attachments between staff and children form more easily. Even further, with an institutional setting it is possible to provide something nearer to a focal care-taker by assigning children to a single staff member for special care and attention. What this would include varies according to circumstances and needs. In the hospital the assigned nurse took special care of the child and his family, helping the mother care for the child when she was present, doing most of the general care herself if the mother was absent. She escorted him to theatre or to post-operative care if the mother was not allowed to be present. She comforted him in distress, talking to him if he was verbal and especially talking through problems. For example, a child was overheard having an imaginary conversation with his absent mother on a toy telephone and saying: 'Mummy, I know I've been a naughty boy and that's why you don't come to see me.' The nurse picked that up and worked with the child about it. In residential settings there may be the importance of bedtime for deprived children, of outings like dental or medical visits, playing together, working with distress and problems, having a special relationship with the child and his family together if he is still in contact with his family.

Workers can never equal the mother's almost total availability to the young child since staff have limited working hours, but experience has shown that deep and meaningful attachments can be formed between the child and the assigned care-taker. For example, in the Royal National Orthopaedic Hospital, a small boy came from overseas: his pregnant mother, with a large family of other children, could not accompany him and his father could rarely visit. The assigned nurse developed a closely attached relationship with him (her other assigned children having mothers present). She not only did general care but talked to him about his family, of which the boy had photographs, thus establishing some continuity. She also helped prepare him for going home to find a new baby by talking, by doll play and by relating to babies, of whom there were always some in the Unit. It was very moving to watch them together. Parting when it came was very painful for both, but for both the rewards were enormous. In particular, the child's capacity for attachment was sustained.

The gaps in the availability of the focal care-taker are difficult for the child, but not impossible to handle. In small, firmly bounded units children do form subsidiary attachments to other adults, and indeed to each other, and the care-taking need not become indiscriminate. The Cot Unit had explicit reassignment plans when the assigned nurse was off-duty. Further, with older children in residential settings, adults can and indeed must also relate in an attached way to groups of children engaging in enjoyable activities with the group or handling the group in a state of distress or crisis.

251

In addition, the small bounded group gives a good setting for the adults to form meaningful relationships with each other. This not only again provides good models of attachment behaviour but also facilitates reassignment when necessary. The child tends to accept the second adult more easily and to use him better if he has seen him in a good relationship with the first. In the hospital, for instance, when a child was admitted and accompanied by his mother, the nurse would frequently have relatively little to do with the child at first, but concentrated on building her relationships with the mother. The good relationship they established undoubtedly helped the child accept the nurse if and when the mother had to leave, and begin to form an attachment to her.

My references to transitory staff and high labour turnover may seem to suggest that attachments are always under threat from adults leaving. But in fact we found that in units operated as described there would be a dramatic fall in staff turnover. The Royal National Orthopaedic Hospital was fortunate that the Cot Unit was staffed by nursery nurses who were permanent staff and not by transitory student nurses. But in a profession, nursery nursing, that notoriously has an enormously high labour turnover, there was almost no labour turnover during the study and as the care method developed all three nursery nurses stayed over three years, an inestimable benefit for long-stay and repeat-stay children. The work had in fact become more challenging and rewarding and the attachment to the children increased the nurses' wish and sense of responsibility to stay with the children.

The work is not only more rewarding, however, it is also more stressful. Multiple indiscriminate care-taking can in fact be seen as a defence for staff against making meaningful and deep contact with any one child and his family, a contact which frees the child's expressiveness and makes the care-taker more fully in touch with his distress and problems as well as his joys. It can be quite shattering temporarily for staff to move from multiple indiscriminate care-taking to case-assignment, a move which may include the disruption of concepts about what a child is like. One staff nurse said: 'I have had to unlearn everything

I thought I knew about children since you [the author] have been here.' Too often staff think of the healthy normal child as one who is 'settled', calm, accepting of everyone who approaches him, relatively unprotesting about what is done to him. They need to learn that in the abnormal circumstances of the hospital, the 'normal' child is likely to be frightened or miserable quite a lot of the time, to protest at interventions, to object to the presence of strangers and to be apparently more difficult – certainly a more distressing child for adults to work with.

Again the staff may need help with this – help that can come from a strong attached staff group who support and care for each other, from senior staff, or from an outside consultant. In a sense one may say that the staff need to experience the same concern and support for their stresses as they are expected to provide for children and families, a consistency in the method of care.

I will conclude this section by trying to draw together some of the points I have made within a rather different theoretical framework. Bion (1967) has described the importance for the infant's development of his mother's capacity for reverie – that is, how she takes in his communications, contains and ponders over them intuitively but not necessarily consciously, and responds to them in a meaningful way. It is particularly important, in relation to fear and distress, that the mother can take in his projections and return them to the infant in a more realistic and tolerable version. The function of reverie is important also for staff in children's institutions. It can be reverie in the individual staff member or it can be something analogous to reverie in group situations, staff talking things through in an intuitive way together. The communications on which staff must work are often massive and very disturbing and staff in turn need support of the kind I have mentioned. Like the ordinary devoted mother (Winnicott, 1958) they need themselves to be contained in a system of meaningful attachments if they are to contain the children effectively. They need firmly bounded situations in which to work and they need the support of being able to talk things through in quieter circumstances away from the core of the children's distress and problems.

THE DEVELOPMENTAL EFFECT OF THE INSTITUTION'S SOCIAL DEFENCE SYSTEM

The author has described elsewhere the development and operation of the social defence system in institutions (Menzies, 1970; see above, pp. 43–85). The institution develops, by collusive interaction among its members, a system of defences which appear in the structure, the mode of functioning and the culture of the institution. Continued membership tends to involve acceptance and operation of the accepted social defence system, at least while present in the institution. However, the social defence system is sustained and operated by individuals, notably staff members, and this plays a part in their effectiveness as models for identification. There appears to be a need for constant vigilance if the defence system operated in the institution is to be sustained at a mature level and indeed to be adaptive rather than defensive, for it will be under constant threat. It will be under threat because the stress and disturbance present in the children will predispose staff to use massive defences against confronting the disturbance in a painful although potentially therapeutic way. I have referred to multiple indiscriminate care-taking as one such defence. It can be associated with massive denial of the meaning of the children's communications, with a manic defence that denies its seriousness, with rigid punitive regimes which try to control disturbance rather than working it through. I also described above a paranoid defence system connected with the evasion of a difficult responsibility.

The children may be a threat in another way in that they in turn tend to operate massive and primitive defences against their distress which are in turn not only individual but also tend to become socialized as they relate to each other in various group situations. This may have a powerful effect on staff, who are usually outnumbered by children as the children try to force staff to enter into collusion with their social defence system. Hard work, courage and suffering are often needed if staff are to resist these pressures and sustain more mature defences as a model and as a facilitation of confronting and working through problems.

In the world of approved schools and institutions for delinquents such phenomena are known as subcultures in which problems such as homosexuality or violence are acted out away from staff or, sadly, sometimes with them, and are recognized to be inimical to the therapeutic culture of the institution.

Work done on a consultancy visit to an approved school may illustrate this. I was told first by professional staff that there was great discontent among the domestic staff in the living units. They felt they could not achieve a high enough standard of work and were not getting job satisfaction. I was at first unclear what I was supposed to do about this, but gradually I felt I was beginning to understand. I heard a lot about violence among boys, of which there had recently been more than usual – some of it very destructive. More than usually violent boys were said to have been admitted recently or were about to be admitted to the school. The professional staff were not only afraid of the boys' violence, but were anxious also about the impulses to counterviolence they felt in themselves. Up to that point, they had not felt able to confront the violence adequately as a problem to be worked at. Instead they had developed an antitherapeutic and subcultural method of trying to prevent it, by gratification and appeasement. They hoped, not necessarily consciously, that if they provided a very high standard of care in living units, they could in effect keep the boys quiet. Professional staff then put subtle pressures on domestic workers to provide a quite unrealistic living standard, a pressure which the domestic workers in turn accepted and tried to put into operation. In reality they could not and consequently suffered painful feelings of inadequacy and failure. We disentangled this in the course of a long day's discussion during which professional staff faced their fears of violence more openly, realized that developing a subculture of dependency to counter a subculture of violence was not likely in fact to deal with the violence or to be therapeutic, and so became more able to work with the violence directly. The domestic workers were relieved of the projections into and pressures on them and could once again apply themselves to a realistically defined task from which they got satisfaction.[1]

Such subcultures are perhaps less likely to appear in institutions which have the features I have suggested as more appropriate for the development of the healthy self in the children – for example authoritative, responsible staff, well-defined delegation, small, fairly bounded units, effective opportunities for reverie. But no institution is likely to avoid them fully; hence my comment about the need for constant vigilance, possibly again with the help of a consultant.

CONCLUSION

I hope I have succeeded in justifying my optimistic view that institutions for children can be developed in such a way as to provide more effectively for the development of a healthy self than has too often been the case in the past and, unfortunately, is still too often the case in the present. Changes in the desired direction can and have been achieved in institutions, although often at the cost of considerable turmoil, doubt and uncertainty among staff while they are being made.

The effect of such developments on children has been encouraging. At the Royal National Orthopaedic Hospital, no children who had been hospitalized under the new care system showed the typical signs of institutionalization or of any serious damage to their development. There were problems but none serious, nor of a kind that could not be contained in the families and worked with there. Some of the children, indeed, seemed to have gained rather than lost ground. We acknowledge with respect and gratitude the major contribution many mothers made to this result, but it was also evident in unmothered children. I have already mentioned one small boy from overseas who actually developed well, but perhaps the most dramatic example was another small boy with foreign parents who were in this country but who very rarely visited. When the mother did come, she could not really make a relationship with him but only carried out a few simple tasks usually designed to make him look more like a boy from his own country. This was almost meaningless. On admission at nearly four years old he had no language, neither his own nor English, and had most violent temper tantrums so that, for example, due notice had to be given of interventions, so that he could be given tranquillizers in advance. Everyone except the author diagnosed him as mentally defective. The author diagnosed him as psychotic, not only on the direct evidence he presented but also from his history.

He had been driven from pillar to post, from foster home to residential nursery, day nursery and round and round again. He had passed much time in inadequate children's institutions with no attachment, no containment, no good models. During his thirteen months in hospital (the longest continuous stay of any child) he was devotedly cared for by his assigned nurse and the nursery teacher especially, but also by other staff in the small, close attachment circle of the Unit. When he left he had an age-appropriate English vocabulary, had completely lost his temper tantrums, and had begun to use toys and other methods to work over in a constructive way his hospital experience. A fortunate coincidence for him was that the staff nurse had to resign her post for family reasons and decided to foster children as a means of working at home. She took the boy home with her, thus sustaining an important attachment. He then continued to develop well and settled well into a normal school.

The results in the desperately damaged boys in the approved school do not usually match up to that level, but it is notable that there is in general much less acting out in the school, fewer abscondings, less violence and much more constructive activity than one usually finds in such institutions. The results are also above average in terms of life performance in general and, in particular, in fewer of the repeated delinquencies that take so many such boys later into other institutions like Borstals, prisons or mental hospitals.

Much remains to be done, however, to convert other children's institutions into places more suitable for children to grow up in a healthy way. Since powerful pressures are now evident in our society to put children into institutions, there appears to be an urgent and serious need to improve these institutions if children are to be given the best opportunities for development and the 'vicious circle' effect of early institutionalization prevented, such as delinquency, mental illness, or repeated institutionalization.

NOTE

1. What I have described as subcultures of violence and dependency are closely linked with Bion's formulation of basic assumptions of fight/flight and dependency as observed in small groups (Bion, 1961). The point Bion makes about the basic assumptions is that they are characterized by psychotic phenomena, are evasive of reality instead of confronting it, and do not evidence a belief in work as a means of carrying out tasks or in the time and suffering needed to do so. So they are anti-therapeutic.

Bibliography

All works are published in London unless otherwise indicated.

Abraham, K. (1924) 'A short study of the development of the libido', *Selected Papers on Psycho-Analysis*. Hogarth, pp. 418–501.

Bain, A. (1982) *The Baric Experiment: The Design of Jobs and Organization for the Expression and Growth of Human Capacity*. Tavistock Institute of Human Relations Occasional Paper no. 4.

Bain, A. and Barnett, L. (1980) *The Design of a Day Care System in a Nursery Setting for Children under Five*. Unpublished report to the Department of Health and Social Security.

Baritz, L. (1965) *The Servants of Power: A History of the Use of Social Science in American Industry*. New York: Wiley.

Barnett, L. (1987) Video: *Buddle Lane: A Day Nursery Becomes a Family Centre*. VHS: 40 mins. Obtainable from Lynn Barnett, Iddesleigh House Clinic, 97 Heavitree Road, Exeter, Devon.

Bergman, T. (1965) *Children in the Hospital*. New York: International Universities Press.

Bion, W. R. (1955) 'Group dynamics: a re-view', in Klein, Heimann and Money-Kyrle, eds (1955), pp. 440–77.

— (1961) *Experiences in Groups, and Other Papers*. Tavistock and New York: Basic.

— (1962) 'A theory of thinking', *Int. J. Psycho-Anal.* 43: 306–10, also in Bion, W. R. (1967).

— (1963) *Elements of Psycho-Analysis*. Heinemann.

— (1967) *Second Thoughts*. Heinemann.

Bott, E. (1957) *Family and Social Network*, 2nd edn. Tavistock, 1971.

Bowlby, J. (1951) *Maternal Care and Mental Health*. Geneva: World Health Organization Monograph Series, no. 2 (HMSO and New York: Columbia University Press).

— (1969) *Attachment and Loss*, vol. 1, *Attachment*. Hogarth.

— (1973) *Attachment and Loss*, vol. 2, *Separation: Anxiety and Anger*. Hogarth.

Bowlby, John, Figlio, Karl and Young, Robert M. (1986) 'An interview with John Bowlby on the origins and reception of his work', *Free Assns* 6: 36–64.

Brain, D. J. and Maclay, I. (1968) 'Controlled study of mothers and children in hospital', *Br. Med. J.* 2: 278–80.

Brown, E. R. (1979) *Rockefeller Medicine Men: Medicine and Capitalism in America*. Berkeley, CA/London: University of California Press.

Burlingham, D. and Freud, A. (1942) *Young Children in Wartime: Report of a Residential War Nursery*. Allen & Unwin.

Carey, A. (1967) 'The Hawthorne studies: a radical critique', *American Sociological Review* 32:403–16.

Court, S. Donald M. [Chairman] (1976) *Fit for the Future. Report of the Committee on Child Health Services*. HMSO.

Curtis Committee (1946) *Care of Children Committee Report*. HMSO.

Dartington, T. (1979) 'Fragmentation and integration in health care', *Sociology of Health and Illness* 1: 12–39.

Department of Health and Social Security and The Welsh Office (1971) *Hospital Facilities for Children*. Pink Paper, HM [71] 22.

Dicks, H. V. (1970) *Fifty Years of the Tavistock Clinic*. Routledge & Kegan Paul.

Emery, F. E. and Trist, E. L. (1962) 'Socio-technical systems', in C. Churchman and M. Verhulst, eds *Management Systems: Models and Techniques*, vol. 2, Pergamon, pp. 83–97.

Fenichel, O. (1946) *The Psychoanalytic Theory of the Neuroses*. New York: Norton.

Fisher, D. (1978) 'The Rockefeller Foundation and the development of scientific medicine in Britain', *Minerva* 16: 20–41.

Fitzgerald, D. (1986) 'Exporting American agriculture: the Rockefeller Foundation in Mexico, 1943–53', *Social Studies of Science* 16: 457–83.

Fosdick, R. B. (1952) *The Story of the Rockefeller Foundation*. New York: Harper & Brothers.

Freud, A. (1952) Film review: *A Two-Year-Old Goes to Hospital*, *Psychoanal. Study Child* 7: 82–94.

— (1965) *Normality and Pathology in Childhood*. Hogarth.

Freud, S. (1893–5) *Studies on Hysteria*, in James Strachey, ed. *The Standard Edition of the Complete Psychological Works of Sigmund Freud*, 24 vols. Hogarth, 1953–73. vol. 2, pp. 1–305.

— (1914) 'On narcissism: an introduction'. *S.E.* 14, pp. 67–102.

— (1915) 'Thoughts for the times on war and death'. *S.E.* 14, pp. 273–302.

— (1917) 'Mourning and melancholia'. *S.E.* 14, pp. 237–60.

— (1926) *Inhibitions, Symptoms and Anxiety*. *S.E.* 20, pp. 77–178.

Gorer, G. (1965) *Death, Grief and Mourning in Contemporary Britain*. Cresset.

Heimann, P. (1952) 'Certain functions of introjection and projection in earliest infancy', in Isaacs, Klein and Riviere, eds (1952), pp. 122–68.

Heinicke, C. M. and Westheimer, I. J. (1965) *Brief Separation*. Longman.

Hill, J. M. M. and Trist, E. L. (1953) 'A consideration of industrial accidents as a means of withdrawal from the work situation', *Human Relations* 6: 357–80.

Hinshelwood, R. D. and Manning, N. P., eds (1979) *Therapeutic Communities*. Routledge & Kegan Paul.

Isaacs, S., Klein, M. and Riviere J., eds (1952) *Developments in Psycho-Analysis*. Hogarth and The Institute of Psycho-Analysis.

Janis, I. L. (1958) *Psychological Stress: Psychoanalytic and Behavioural Studies of Surgical Patients*. Chapman & Hall.

Jaques, E. (1953) 'On the dynamics of social structure', *Human Relations* 6: 3–24.

— (1955) 'Social systems as a defence against persecutory and depressive anxiety', in Klein, Heimann and Money-Kyrle, eds (1955), pp. 478–98.

— (1956) *Measurement of Responsibility: A Study of Work, Payment and Individual Capacity*. Tavistock and Cambridge, MA: Harvard University Press.

Klein, M. (1921) 'The development of a child', *Contributions to Psycho-Analysis, 1921–1945*. Hogarth and The Institute of Psycho-Analysis, 1948, pp. 13–67.

— (1932) *The Psycho-Analysis of Children*. Hogarth.

— (1940) 'Mourning and its relationship to manic-depressive states', *Contributions to Psycho-Analysis, 1921–1945*. Hogarth and The Institute of Psycho-Analysis, 1948, pp. 311–38.

— (1948a) 'A contribution to the psychogenesis of manic-depressive states', in *Contributions to Psycho-Analysis, 1921–1945*. Hogarth and The Institute of Psycho-Analysis, 1948, pp. 282–310.

— (1948b) 'The importance of symbol formation in the development of the ego', in *Contributions to Psycho-Analysis, 1921–1945*. Hogarth and The Institute of Psycho-Analysis, 1948, pp. 236–50.

— (1952a) 'Notes on some schizoid mechanisms', in Isaacs, Klein and Riviere, eds (1952), pp. 292–320.

— (1952b) 'Some theoretical conclusions regarding the emotional life of the infant', in Isaacs, Klein and Riviere, eds (1952), pp. 198–236.

— (1952c) 'On observing the behaviour of young infants', in Isaacs, Klein and Riviere, eds (1952), pp. 237–70.

— (1959) 'Our adult world and its roots in infancy', *Human Relations* 12: 291–303. Also reprinted as Tavistock Pamphlet no. 2, Tavistock, 1960.

Klein, M., Heimann, P. and Money-Kyrle, R. E., eds (1955) *New Directions in Psycho-Analysis*. Tavistock and New York: Basic.

Kohler, Robert E. (1976) 'The management of science: the experience of Warren Weaver and the Rockefeller programme in molecular biology', *Minerva* 14: 279–306.

— (1987) 'Science, foundations and American universities in the 1920s', *Osiris* (2nd series) 3: 135–64.

Martin, Helen (1970) 'Antecedents of burns and scalds in children', *Br. J. Med. Psychol.* 43:39.

Mayo, E. (1933) *The Human Problems of an Industrial Civilization*. New York: Viking, 1960.

Menzies, I. E. P. (1951) *Technical Report on a Working Conference for Public Health Nurses, Noordwijk, The Netherlands, 1950*. World Health Organization.

— (1959) 'The functioning of social systems as a defence against anxiety: a report on a study of the nursing service of a general hospital', *Human Relations* 13: 95–121.

— (1961a) 'Nurses under stress', *International Nursing Review* 7 (no. 6): 9–16. *Nursing Times* (1961) 57: 141–2, 173–4, 206–7. This volume.

— (1961b) 'The functioning of social systems as a defence against anxiety' (reprint of article published in *Human Relations* 13: 95–121). Tavistock. This volume.

— (1965) 'Some mutual interactions between organizations and their members'. Paper read at the Sixth International Congress of Psychotherapy, 1964, London. *Psychother. Psychosom.* 13: 194–200.

— (1970) *The Functioning of Social Systems as a Defence Against Anxiety*. Tavistock Institute of Human Relations Pamphlet, no. 3.

— (1971) 'An action research study of the day care of children under five: preliminary notes'. Centre for Applied Social Research (Child Development Research Unit), Tavistock Institute of Human Relations.

— (1975) 'Thoughts on the maternal role in contemporary society', *J. Child Psychother.* 4: 5–14. This volume.

— (1979) 'Staff support systems: task and anti-task in adolescent institutions', in Hinshelwood and Manning, eds (1979), pp. 197–207. This volume.

— (1986) 'A psychoanalytic perspective on social institutions'. Paper given at University College London in the Freud Memorial Lectures series.

— (1987) 'The aftermath of disaster: survival and loss'. Paper given at the Tavistock Clinic conference, 'The Aftermath of Disaster: Survival and Loss'.

Miller, E. and Gwynne, G. (1972) *A Life Apart*. Tavistock.

Ministry of Health (1944) *A National Health Service*. HMSO, Cmnd 6502.

Mitchell, Juliet (1974) *Psychoanalysis and Feminism*. Allen Lane.

Money-Kyrle, R. E. (1961) *Man's Picture of His World*. Duckworth.

Morowski, J. G. (1986) 'Organizing knowledge and behaviour of Yale's Institute of Human Relations', *Isis* 77: 219–42.

Myrdal, F. A. and Klein, V. (1956) *Women's Two Roles*. Routledge.

Oswin, M. (1971) *The Empty Hours*. Allen Lane.

Pines, Dinora (1972) 'Pregnancy and motherhood: interaction between fantasy and reality', *Br. J. Med. Psychol.* 45: 333–43.

Revans, R. W. (1959) 'The hospital as an organism: a study in communications and morale'. Preprint no. 7 of a paper presented at the Sixth International Meeting of the Institute of Management Sciences, September 1959, Paris. Pergamon.

Rice, A. K. (1958) *Productivity and Social Organization: The Ahmedabad Experiment*. Tavistock.

— (1963) *The Enterprise and its Environment*. Tavistock.

Richardson, E. (1973) *The Teacher, the School and the Task of Management*. Heinemann Educational.

Robertson, James (1953) Film: *A Two-Year-Old Goes to Hospital*. Tavistock Clinic and New York: New York University Film Library.

— (1958a) *Young Children in Hospital*. 2nd edn. Tavistock, 1970.

— (1958b) Film: *Going to Hospital with Mother*. Tavistock Institute of Human Relations and New York: New York University Film Library.

— (1969a) Film: *John, 17 Months: For Nine Days in a Residential Nursery*. 16 mm: sound: 45 mins. Concord Films Council and New York: New York University Film Library.

— (1969b) Guide to the film *John*. Concord Films Council.

Robertson, James and Robertson, Joyce (1967–71) Film series: *Young Children in Brief Separation*. Tavistock Institute of Human Relations and New York: New York University Film Library.

Segal, H. (1957) 'Notes on symbol formation', *Int. J. Psycho-Anal.* 38: 391–7.

Skellern, E. (1953) *Report on the Practical Application to Ward Administration of Modern Methods in the Instruction and Handling of Staff and Student Nurses*. Royal College of Nursing.

Sofer, C. (1955) 'Reactions to administrative change: a study of staff relations in three British hospitals', *Human Relations* 8: 291–316.

Spence, J. C. (1947) 'Care of children in hospital', *Br. Med. J.* 1: 125–30.

Street, D., Vinter, R. D. and Perrow, C. (1966) *Organization for Treatment*. Collier-Macmillan.

Taylor, F. W. (1947) *Scientific Management*. 3 vols. in 1. New York: Harper.

Trist, E. L. (1973) 'A socio-technical critique of scientific management', in D. Edge and J. Wolfe, eds *Meaning and Control: Essays in Social Aspects of Science and Technology*. Tavistock, pp. 95–119.

Trist, E. L. and Bamforth, K. W. (1951) 'Some social and psychological consequences of the longwall method of coal-getting', *Human Relations* 4: 3–38.

Trist, E. L., Higgin, G. W., Murray, H. and Pollock, A. B. (1963) *Organizational Choice: Capabilities of Groups at the Coal Face under Changing Technologies*. Tavistock.

Voices (1987) Television series: six discussions about psychoanalysis chaired by Michael Ignatieff. Brook Productions for Channel Four. Also published in book form as Bill Bourne, Udi Eichler and David Herman, eds (1987) *Voices: Psychoanalysis*. Nottingham: Spokesman/Atlantic Highlands, NJ: The Hobo Press.

Wilson, A. T. M. (1950) 'Hospital nursing auxiliaries', *Human Relations* 3: 1–32.

Winnicott, D. W. (1956) 'Primary maternal preoccupation', in Winnicott (1958), pp. 300–5.

— (1958) *Collected Papers: Through Paediatrics to Psychoanalysis*. Tavistock.

— (1965a) *The Family and Individual Development*. Tavistock.

— (1965b) *The Maturational Processes and the Facilitating Environment*. Hogarth.

Young, R. M. (1972) 'Darwinism and the division of labour', *The Listener* 88 (17 August 1972): 202–5.

— (1981) 'The naturalization of values in the human sciences', in *Problems in the Biological Sciences*. Milton Keynes: Open University Press, pp. 63–110.

Index

WHAT HAPPENS IN GROUPS

Psychoanalysis, the Individual
and the Community

R. D. HINSHELWOOD

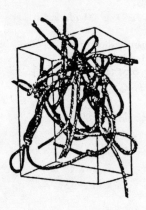

People are often utterly taken aback by
the odd and alarming things that happen
in groups, all sorts of groups – study
groups, offices, clubs, political
organizations, teams.

This is a book about the ways in which
individuals collectively and individually
seek to protect themselves from the worst
aspects of group life. They develop, mostly
unwittingly, specific group cultures, effects
and problems. The numerous illustrations
are taken from the wealth of small groups,
large groups and multi-group systems that
appear in a therapeutic community. The
book is designed to be accessible to
anyone working within groups,
committees or institutions.

The author draws on the writings of
other observers of group dynamics, in
particular Bion, Jaques and Menzies Lyth.
His unique contribution is to apply the
insights of Kleinian psychoanalysis to the
meetings of the groups. He develops a
way of categorizing group cultures – rigid,
fragile and flexible, which is intended to
point to a basis for the development of a
method of intervention into group and
institutional life. Aside from the author's
clarity and clinical acumen, he has written
a truly useful book.

R. D. Hinshelwood is a psychoanalyst and
consultant psychotherapist in the National
Health Service, with twenty years'
experience of working with groups and
therapeutic communities. He is co-editor
of *Therapeutic Communities: Reflections
and Progress*. In 1980 he founded, for the
Association of Therapeutic Communities,
the *International Journal of Therapeutic
Communities*, and is the founder and
editor of the *British Journal of
Psychotherapy*.

288 pages
Paperback   0 946960 89 5   £9.95
Hardback   0 946960 88 7   £27.50

FAB **Free Association Books**
26 Freegrove Road
London N7 9RQ

Please include £1 to cover p. & p.
Telephone credit card orders to (01) 609 5646
Send for free catalogue

A DICTIONARY OF KLEINIAN THOUGHT

By R.D. HINSHELWOOD

The ideas of Melanie Klein and the post-Kleinians have a growing influence among psychoanalysts and psychoanalytic psychotherapists. Yet they are not always easy to grasp — partly because of how Klein wrote, partly because they refer to very primitive processes and partly because they are best communicated by clinical experience, discussion and supervision.

R.D. Hinshelwood has identified the main concepts in Kleinian psychoanalysis along with the subsidiary ones in the work of such Kleinians as Bion, Segal, Rosenfeld and Meltzer. The dictionary defines all these, gives the main places where they appear in Kleinian writings and provides a bibliography of the literature and an exposition of the ideas of the main figures in this tradition.

The book is both an intellectual tool and a practical guide to a framework of ideas which has hitherto been somewhat inaccessible.

R.D. Hinshelwood studied medicine at University College Hospital, London and trained as a psychoanalyst at the London Institute of Psycho-Analysis. He is a consultant psychotherapist at St Bernard's Hospital, Southall, has taught on various training programmes and is in private practice in London. He is the author of *What Happens in Groups* (FAB) and the editor of the *British Journal of Psychotherapy*.

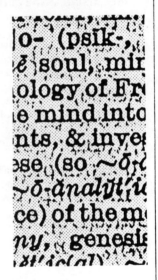

800 pages
Hardback   0 946960 82 8   £35.00

Free Association Books
26 Freegrove Road
London N7 9RQ

Please include £1 to cover p. & p.
Telephone credit card orders to (01) 609 5646
Send for free catalogue

This first edition of
CONTAINING ANXIETY IN INSTITUTIONS
was finished in August 1988.

It was typeset in 10½/14½pt Ehrhardt
on a Linotron 202 and printed on
80 g/m² vol. 18 paper with a
Crabtree Sovereign MP56.

This book was commissioned by
Robert M. Young, edited by Ann Scott,
copy-edited by Gillian Beaumont,
indexed by Peter Rea,
designed by Carlos Sapochnik and
produced by Selina O'Grady and
Martin Klopstock for Free Association Books.

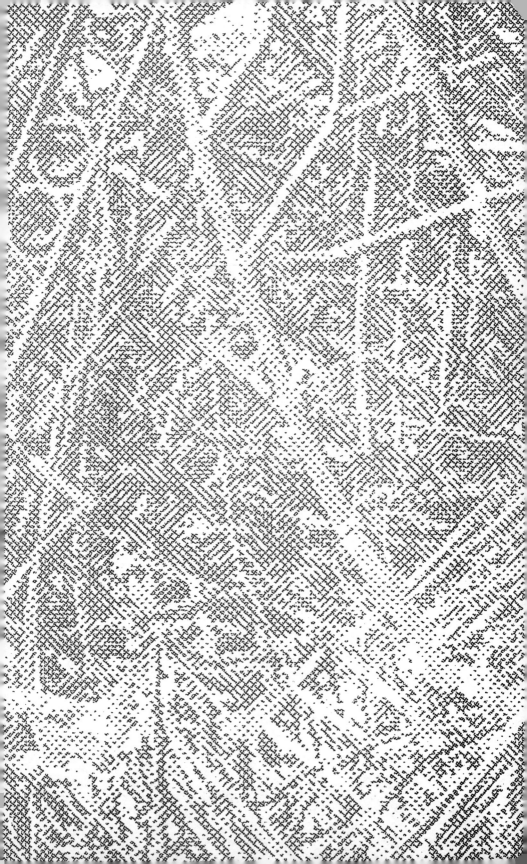

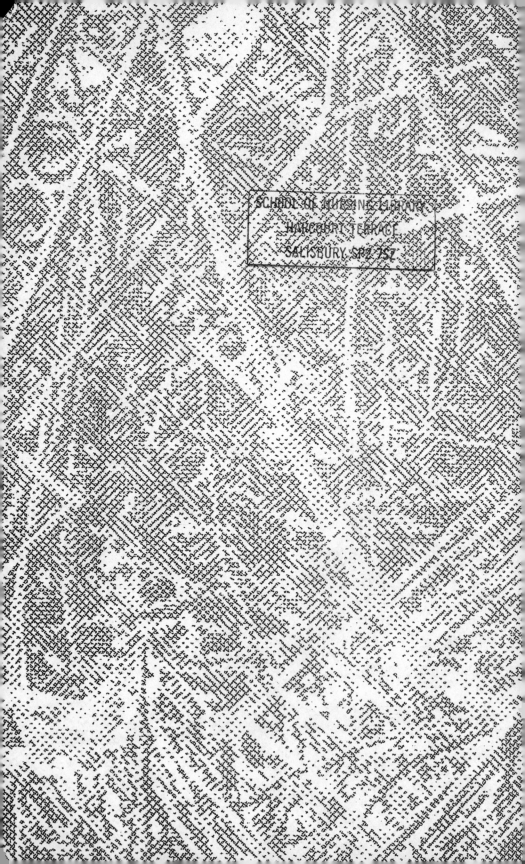

an ordinary hospital setting is appropriate for long-stay children as against a children's home with the relevant medical, nursing and auxiliary services visiting or seeing the child elsewhere. Having said that, however, one has to acknowledge that the majority of children's homes do not themselves provide adequately for what the separated and distressed children in them really need, in spite of the Curtis recommendations. Seeing the film *John* would cure one of any idea that such homes provide adequate care for children out of their families. Children's homes, like hospitals, may need considerable modification before they become an adequate substitute for a normal home and ensure the healthy development of the children. What is needed is a children's home as like a normal home as possible. Relevant considerations would include: size – it needs to be small, say six to eight children with the minimum number of staff to look after them, so as to minimize the danger of multiple indiscriminate care-taking as in *John*, and to promote closeness and intimacy; case-assignment, so that there is a possibility of real attachment; staff who can understand children and promote natural expressiveness, especially when the child is distressed; well-managed boundaries to protect against intrusion as in a good home, and so on. In addition, the hospital/children's home must help to maximize the participation of mothers and other family care-takers in the care of the child. To establish such a home would be quite a daunting proposition, as indeed is discussed in the second RNOH paper.

J. C. Spence adumbrated this idea when he said it would be better if the children lived in small groups under a house mother and from there went to their lessons in a school, to their treatment in a sick bay, and their entertainment in a central hall (Spence, 1947). He added: that 'there would be no *dis*advantage in the house mother's having nursing training, but that in itself is not a qualification for the work she would have to do; her duty is to live with her group of children and attempt to provide those things of which they have been deprived.'

James Robertson also has many times put forward the idea that what is needed is a children's home. The striking thing is that the views of such people have had so little effect on the care of these children.

I also accept this recommendation. Such a change could make a crucial difference to the future mental health of these children. It would provide the basic things children need in the absence or insufficient presence of their mother and their ordinary family environment. Nursing qualifications do not seem strictly necessary for the head of this kind of unit, although they are certainly not a disadvantage provided the person concerned is highly skilled in coping with the emotional needs of children and also of her staff, since the work would be very stressful. This person, and the house staff, would then mediate the relationship between the child and other hospital staff as an ordinary mother does with the family doctor, child welfare clinic, schools, and so on.

A consultant paediatrician to the children's home is also important. The Department of Health and Social Security, in giving advice on hospital facilities for children in general, said that the general responsibility for the management and oversight of a children's department should rest with a children's physician (DHSS and Welsh Office, 1971). Individual responsibilities for the treatment of individual children would rest with consultants in various specialities.

That it is possible to change a children's institution providing conventional group care into one run on family-group systems has been demonstrated by Anna Freud and her co-workers at the Hampstead Nurseries (Burlingham and Freud, 1948). The transition resulted in an upsurge of demanding and other normal family-type behaviour, usually suppressed in institutional children, and also in an improvement in the state of the children. In this case the child had a second foster-mother, always the same one, when his own foster-mother was off-duty, rather like a home-based child cared for by a well-known aunt or close friend when his mother is 'off-duty'. The nurse/foster-mothers felt enormous strain in their restructured roles and needed great support, a point to which I will return later.

An important difference between the hospital situation and the ordinary children's home is in fact the much greater avail-